CPE
Practice
Tests ▶ Plus

Vanessa Jakeman
Nick Kenny

Certificate of Proficiency in English: Top 20 Questions

1 How many marks are needed to pass the exam?

➤ To pass the exam with a grade C, you need around 60% of the total marks.

2 Do I have to pass each paper in order to pass the exam?

➤ No. Each paper doesn't have a pass or fail mark. The final grade A, B, C, D or E is arrived at by adding the weighted marks from all the papers together.

3 Are marks deducted for wrong answers?

➤ No. If you're not sure, make a guess, you may be right.

4 Am I allowed to use a dictionary?

➤ No.

5 In Paper 1 (Reading), Part 1 has more questions, so is it more important?

➤ No. The four parts are equally weighted. In Parts 2, 3 and 4, each question has 2 marks, whereas in Part 1, each question has 1 mark.

6 In Paper 1 (Reading), how long should I take on each question?

➤ This is up to you. You can do the tasks in any order and knowing how to use your time well is a part of the test.

7 In Paper 2 (Writing), what happens if I don't use all the given information in Part 1?

➤ You will lose marks. The examiners are looking for both the correct information and good language. So read the question and the input text(s) very carefully.

8 In Paper 2 (Writing), what happens if I write too many or too few words?

➤ The word count is given as a guide only. Don't waste time counting; the examiners don't, they are more interested in your English! It is unlikely that very short answers will contain enough information or ideas to fulfil the task. Over-long answers are more likely to be rushed and to contain mistakes. Plan your time so that you write about the right amount and have time to check what you have written.

9 In Paper 3 (Use of English), Part 1, if I'm not sure, can I give two alternative answers?

➤ No. If there are two answers, and one of them is wrong, no marks are given. So, it's better to decide which of your answers is better!

10 In Paper 3 (Use of English), Parts 1 and 4, do contractions count as one word or two?

➤ Two, e.g. *don't* = two words, *do* + *not*.

11 What happens if I misspell a word in Paper 3 (Use of English)?

➤ You will not get the mark. All spelling must be correct in Paper 3.

12 What happens if I misspell a word in Paper 4 (Listening), Part 2?

➤ You will not get the mark. Check your spelling carefully and don't write more than is necessary. The more you write, the more likely you are to misspell something. The answers will be familiar words that you should be able to spell correctly.

13 How many times will I hear each recording in Paper 4 (Listening)?

➤ Each text is played twice.

14 In Paper 4 (Listening), do the questions always follow the order of the text?

➤ Yes, they do. However, some questions will test your understanding of the whole text.

15 In Paper 4 (Listening), Part 2, do I have to use the words in the recording or other words?

➤ The word(s) you need to write are the ones you hear on the tape. However, you do have to make sure that they fit into the gap, both grammatically and for the meaning.

16 In Paper 4 (Listening), Part 2, what happens if my answer is too long to fit on the Answer Sheet?

➤ Most answers are single words, groups of 2–3 words or numbers. If you think the answer is longer, then it is probably the wrong answer. Don't write more than is needed to complete the gap.

17 In Paper 4 (Listening), do I have to complete the Answer Sheet as I listen?

➤ No. You can write the answers on the question paper. You have five minutes at the end to copy them on to the separate Answer Sheet. Copy carefully; follow the numbering of the questions, write clearly and check your spelling.

18 In Paper 5 (Speaking), do I have to go with another student? Can I choose my partner?

➤ You cannot be examined alone as the ability to discuss with another student is being tested in Part 2 and also Part 3. In some centres you can choose your partner, in others not. You should ask the local organiser.

19 Is it a good idea to prepare what you are going to say in Paper 5 (Speaking), Part 1?

➤ It's a good idea to practise, but don't forget that the examiners give marks for natural communication in English. If you give a prepared speech which doesn't answer the examiner's questions, you will lose marks.

20 What if my partner makes lots of mistakes, or doesn't talk in Paper 5 (Speaking), Parts 2 & 3?

➤ Don't worry. The examiner will help if necessary. Don't forget, you are not in competition with your partner. If you can help them, this will impress the examiners. Remember that Part 2 and the second phase of Part 3 are about interaction, so you have to ask and answer questions as well as saying what you think.

Contents

Introduction

Exam Overview

The **Certificate of Proficiency in English (CPE)** is an examination offered by the University of Cambridge Local Examinations Syndicate (UCLES). It is administered twice a year, in June and December. The CPE offers a high level qualification to people wanting to use English for professional or study purposes, including high level academic work. There are five papers in the exam and **each paper receives an equal weighting of 20 per cent of the marks**. In order to pass the examination, candidates usually need **a minimum of about 60 per cent of the total marks**. Candidates who pass are awarded one of three grades: Grade A, Grade B or Grade C. Grades D and E are failing grades.

Paper	Time	Content	Number of questions	Number of marks
Paper 1 Reading	1 hour 30 mins	**Part 1**: Three unrelated short texts with six multiple choice cloze questions each. **Part 2**: Four short texts on a theme with two multiple choice questions each. **Part 3**: One gapped text with seven questions. **Part 4**: One long text with seven multiple choice comprehension questions.	40	62
Paper 2 Writing	2 hours	**Part 1**: One compulsory question, contextualised through instructions and short input text(s). **Part 2**: Candidates answer one question from a choice of four, including the set book option.	2	Band score: see page 8
Paper 3 Use of English	1 hour 30 mins	**Part 1**: One open cloze text with fifteen questions. **Part 2**: One short text with ten word formation questions. **Part 3**: Six sets of three gapped sentences. **Part 4**: Eight key word transformations. **Part 5**: Two texts with four questions and a summary writing task.	44	75
Paper 4 Listening	Approx. 40 mins	**Part 1**: Four short extracts with two three-option multiple choice questions each. **Part 2**: One monologue with nine sentence completion questions. **Part 3**: One text with five four-option multiple choice questions. **Part 4**: One dialogue with six three-way matching questions.	28	28
Paper 5 Speaking	19 mins	**Part 1**: Interview based on examiner's questions. **Part 2**: Collaborative task based on visual prompts. **Part 3**: Individual long turn based on a written prompt followed by further discussion.	(Not applicable)	Mark based on Global Achievement

How to Use this Book

This book is designed to help you prepare for the Certificate of Proficiency in English (CPE) examination. There are six complete tests, which are all at the same level as the exam. For **Paper 4 Listening**, there are **three cassettes** with all the instructions, pauses and repeats, just like in the real exam. In **Tests 1 and 2**, you should concentrate on familiarising yourself with the tasks. Don't worry about the timing in these tests; you can practise doing the tasks within a time limit later on. In **Tests 3–6** you should concentrate on doing the papers within the time limit and monitoring your progress.

Before you begin

Before you begin doing the tests, you should read this section carefully and study the guides for each paper (pages 6–17). For each paper, make sure you understand:

- how much time you have.
- how many parts there are.
- what each task looks like.
- what you have to do in each task.

Test 1–Test 2

In Test 1 and Test 2, there are **Tip Strips** which will give you advice about how to do each type of task. They also give you clues to help you find the answers to some of the questions. It is a good idea to attempt each part of each paper separately.

- Read the instructions and check that you understand what you have to do.
- Read the Tip Strip for advice on how to do the questions.
- Read the text or other information on the page and think about your answers.
- Answer the questions.
- Look at the advice on individual questions in the Tip Strip.
- Check your answers.

For **Paper 5 Speaking**, you can practise some parts of the test on your own, but for other parts you will need to practise with a partner. To help you with Paper 5, you can listen to **a recording of some students doing the tasks in Test 1 on the cassette**. The recording will give you an idea of how to approach the different tasks. You are not allowed to use a dictionary or other books in the exam, so try and do the tests without any help. We suggest that you use your dictionary and other reference books when you check your answers. This will help you to see why you have made mistakes, and will give you a chance to make a note of new words or other things you have learnt by doing the tests.

Test 3–Test 6

You should now try to do whole papers in the given time if possible. This will help you to think about how you need to organise your time on the day of the exam. For **Paper 1 Reading**, where there is a lot to read, *CPE Practice Tests Plus* gives you **guidelines on how long you should spend on each part**. Look for the Tip with the clock symbol in Test 3, Test 4 and Test 5. In Test 6, there is no help; you must organise your time as in the real exam. As you progress through the tests in the book, keep a record of how many questions you get right so that you can monitor your performance in each task. You should also keep a record of how long each task takes you. This will help you to plan your use of time on the day of the exam. Furthermore, it is a good idea to keep a note of new vocabulary and language you have learnt.

When checking your scores, remember that each paper is worth 20 per cent of the whole exam. Although each paper has a different number of marks, they are equally important. In order to pass the exam, you need to get around **60 per cent of the total marks**, but you **do not need to get a particular mark in any one paper**.

Guide to Paper 1 Reading

General information

- Paper 1 tests candidates' **ability to understand the meaning of written English at word, phrase, sentence, paragraph and whole text level**.

- The texts in Paper 1 may include extracts from **newspapers, magazines, novels and various types of non fiction material**. All are taken from **authentic sources**. There is a range of styles of writing, register and purpose amongst the texts chosen, but the target audience is always the **educated non-specialist reader**.

- Candidates have **1 hour 30 minutes** to complete Paper 1.

- Candidates **mark their answers directly on to the Answer Sheet in pencil.** There is an example Answer Sheet on page 173.

- Paper 1 accounts for **20 per cent of the total marks** in the exam.

Part	Task type and focus	Task format	Number of words	Number of questions	Number of marks
1	Four-option multiple choice cloze Idioms, collocations, fixed phrases, complementation, phrasal verbs, semantic precision	Three unrelated texts. Each text has six gaps and is followed by six multiple choice questions.	375–500	18	18
2	Four-option multiple choice questions Content, detail, opinion, attitude, tone, purpose, main idea, implication, text organisation features (exemplification, comparison, reference)	Four texts from different sources, but linked by a theme. There are two multiple choice questions for each text.	600–900	8	16
3	Gapped text Cohesion, coherence, text structure, global meaning	One text from which seven paragraphs have been removed and placed in jumbled order after the text. Candidates must decide from where in the text the paragraphs have been removed.	800–1100	7	14
4	Four-option multiple choice questions Content, detail, opinion, attitude, tone, purpose, main idea, implication, text organisation features (exemplification, comparison, reference)	One text with seven multiple choice questions.	700–850	7	14
			Total: Approx. 3000	**Total:** 40	**Total:** 62

How to approach the tasks

Part 1

This part of the paper tests your knowledge of vocabulary.

- Read the text for general understanding before you do the task. The option you choose must fit the meaning of the passage as a whole.

- If you're not sure of the answer, try reading the sentence with each of the options in the gap. Which sounds best?

- Check the words before and after the gap carefully.

- Think about why the other options are wrong.

- When you've finished, read through the whole text again to check your answers.

- If you don't know the answer, guess. No marks are deducted for wrong answers.

Part 2

This part of the paper tests your reading comprehension.

- Read each text carefully. Don't worry if you don't understand every word.

- Try to answer the question, or complete the question stem, before you look at the options.

- Underline key words in the question or question stem, then find the part of the text where the answer is located.

- Underline the key words in the text as well.

- Find the option which best matches the text. Highlight those parts of the text which confirm the answer.

- Think about why the other options are wrong. If you don't understand the text completely, you may still reach the right answer by a process of elimination.

- If you don't know the answer, guess. No marks are deducted for wrong answers.

Part 3

This part of the paper tests your understanding of text structure, that is, how pieces of writing are organised into paragraphs and how the ideas are linked through cohesion and coherence.

- Read the main text first, ignoring the gaps, to get a general understanding of its subject matter and organisation.

- Read the text around each gap carefully. Look at the whole paragraph before and after the gap.

- Read paragraphs A–H. Check for topic and language links with the paragraphs in the main text.

- Highlight words that refer to people and places.

- Highlight time references — this will help you to follow the development of the argument.

- If you're not sure of your answer, try reading the section of text with each of the options in the gap.

- When you've finished, read the completed text again to be sure it all makes sense.

- Remember, you can only use each letter once, and one letter will not be used.

- If you don't know the answer, guess. No marks are deducted for wrong answers.

Part 4

This part of the paper tests your reading comprehension.

- Read the text carefully. Don't worry if you don't understand every word.

- Try to answer the question, or complete the question stem, before you look at the options.

- Underline key words in the question or question stem, then find the part of the text where the answer is located.

- Underline the key words in the text as well.

- Find the option which best matches the text. Highlight those parts of the text which confirm the answer.

- Think about why the other options are wrong. If you don't understand the text completely, you may still reach the right answer by a process of elimination.

- If you don't know the answer, guess. No marks are deducted for wrong answers.

Guide to Paper 2 Writing

General information

- Paper 2 tests candidates' **ability to write specified text types with a range of functions**.
- Candidates have **2 hours** to complete Paper 2.
- Candidates **write their answers in a question booklet in pen**.
- Paper 2 accounts for **20 per cent of the total marks** in the exam.

Part	Task type and focus	Task format	Length of answer
1	One compulsory task Candidates will be required to write one of the following text types: • an article • an essay • a letter • a proposal The function is discursive: presenting and developing arguments, expressing and supporting opinions, evaluating ideas, etc.	A contextualised writing task. Guidance to the context and content from both instructions and one or more short texts. There may be a visual prompt as well.	300–350 words
2	One task from a choice of four. One of the choices is a question on each of the three set book options. The following text types may be required: • an article • an essay • a letter • a proposal • a report • a review The function may be to describe, persuade, narrate, evaluate, make recommendations, give information, summarise, etc.	A contextualised writing task. Guidance to the context and content through instructions of not more than 70 words.	300–350 words

Band scores

Each piece of writing is assigned to a 'band' between 0–5. Within each band there are three performance levels. For example, in the highest band, Band 5, levels of performance in descending order are as follows:
- Band 5.3
- Band 5.2
- Band 5.1

Band 3 indicates an 'acceptable' performance at CPE level.

How to approach the tasks

Part 1

You must read the instructions and input text(s) carefully and use them as the basis for your writing. One of the skills tested here is your ability to absorb the information provided and respond to it in a different form.

Part 2

You must follow the instructions given in the question you choose to do. You have more freedom to introduce your own ideas into the task as in this part, unlike Part 1, information about content is not provided.

Question 5 in Part 2 is related to the set books (works of literature) which some candidates may have studied and prepared. Don't choose this option if you haven't studied one of the set works in detail!

Here is some advice on how to tackle the writing tasks in both parts of Paper 2.

- Underline the main points in the instructions (and input material in Part 1).
- Plan your piece of writing.
- Decide how many paragraphs you will write and what the topic of each paragraph will be.
- Remember that you need to address all the points in the instructions (and input material in Part 1).
- Think about your target reader and the style of writing that is appropriate for the task.
- Think about what you need to include in your introduction.
- Remember to give both sides of an argument.
- Remember to give examples of points you make.
- Remember to write a good conclusion.
- When you've finished, check against the instructions (and input material in Part 1). Have you done everything you need to do?
- Read through your answer and check it carefully. Is your spelling, punctuation and grammar correct? Is your style of writing consistent?

Marking

Parts 1 and 2 of Paper 2 (Writing) carry equal marks. Each piece of writing is double marked by fully-trained examiners using detailed criteria. In both parts, task achievement is a key feature in assessment. Your answer must:

- address the points outlined in the instructions (and input text(s) in Part 1).
- include all the relevant information.

The criteria used by the examiners in awarding marks are:
- content
- task achievement
- organisation and linking of ideas
- accuracy of language
- range of vocabulary and grammatical structures
- appropriate register
- effect on the target reader

Note:

If your answer is much shorter than the 300–350 words required, you are penalised. Poor spelling and punctuation are penalised. Handwriting that interferes with communication, but does not prevent it, is penalised. If your answer is totally illegible, you receive 0.

General information

- Paper 3 tests candidates' **ability to demonstrate their knowledge and control of the language system by completing various tasks at text and sentence level.**

- Candidates have **1 hour 30 minutes** to complete Paper 3.

- Candidates **mark their answers on two Answer Sheets in pencil.** There are example Answer Sheets on pages 174–175.

- Paper 3 accounts for **20 per cent of the total marks** in the exam.

Part	Task type and focus	Task format	Number of words	Number of questions	Number of marks
1	Open cloze Grammatical/ lexico-grammatical	One text with fifteen gaps.	Approx. 200	15	15*
2	Word formation cloze Lexical	One text with ten gaps.	Approx. 200	10	10*
3	Gapped sentences Lexical (e.g. collocation, phrasal verbs, idioms, patterns in which lexical items occur)	Six sets of three sentences. Each sentence has one gap. The gapped word is common to the three sentences in a set. Candidates must write one word which is appropriate in all three sentences.		6	12*
4	Key word transformations Lexical/lexico-grammatical	Eight items. For each item, a sentence is followed by a gapped sentence and a given word. Candidates must complete the gapped sentence using the given word so that its meaning is as similar as possible to the first sentence.		8	16*
5	Comprehension questions and summary writing task Question focus: awareness of language (recognising and understanding the force of lexical items, rhetorical and stylistic devices and referencing) The summary tests information selection, linking, sentence construction	Two texts with two questions on each text. The summary task requires candidates to select relevant information from both texts.	Approx. 500	5	22**
				Total: 44	Total: 75

*   Answers must be correctly spelled.
**   The four questions on the texts carry two marks each (4 x 2 = 8 marks).
     The summary writing task carries four marks for content and ten marks for summary
     writing skills (4 + 10 = 14 marks).

How to approach the tasks

Part 1

This part of the paper tests your **knowledge of grammar**. You will read a text with fifteen gaps. Only one word fits into each gap. The words are mostly structure words rather than vocabulary items, e.g. prepositions, pronouns, linkers, etc. Some words may form part of phrasal verbs or fixed expressions.

- Read the text for general understanding before you do the task. The word you write must fit the meaning of the passage as a whole.

- Check the words before and after the gap carefully.

- Read the whole sentence to be sure it makes complete sense with your word in the gap.

- When you've finished, read through the whole text again to check your answers.

- Make sure you have spelled the words correctly.

- If you don't know the answer, guess. No marks are deducted for wrong answers.

Part 2

This part of the paper tests your **knowledge of all kinds of affixation**, particularly the formation of nouns, and the use of prefixes or suffixes to modify the meaning of words.

You will read a text with ten gaps, each of which must be filled with one word. This word must be formed using the word in capitals at the end of the line. For example you may need to:

- add a prefix to a word to make it negative.

- add a suffix to a verb or adjective to form a noun or adverb.

- add another word to form a compound noun etc.

The word you form must make sense, both in the sentence and in the context of the text as a whole.

- Read the text for general understanding before you try to do the task.

- Decide which part of speech is needed for each gap (e.g. noun, verb, adjective, adverb).

- Look at the whole sentence, not just at the line including the gap.

- You may need to:
  - add a prefix (e.g. re-, over-, under-, mis-).
  - add a suffix (e.g. -ful, -able, -ness, -ly) to the base word given.
  - change the form of the word (e.g. receive ⟶ receipt) or create a compound word (e.g. wild + life ⟶ wildlife).

- Be careful: some words may need a negative prefix (e.g. un-, in-, dis-) or suffix (e.g. -less) to make sense in context.

- Be careful: often more than one change must be made to the base word. You may need to add both a prefix and a suffix to form a word that makes complete sense in context.

- Check whether the plural or singular form of a word is needed.

- If the gapped word is a verb, check which form of the verb is needed.

- Most answers will be longer than the base word given.

- Check that you have spelled the words correctly.

Part 3

This part of the paper tests your **knowledge of vocabulary**, especially those words which have different meanings when used in different contexts. Areas of language such as the use of collocation and phrasal verbs are tested directly in this section.

There are six questions in this part. Each question is made up of three sentences from which one word has been removed. The same word, in the same form, can be used to complete the gap in each of the three sentences.

- Read all three sentences before thinking about what the missing word might be.

- The same word, in the same form, must fit all three gaps.

- In each gap, the word will have a different meaning or will be used in a different context.

- In some gaps, the word will form part of a phrasal verb or longer expression.

- Look carefully at the words before and after the gaps.

- Check that your answer fits all three gaps.

- Check that you have spelled the word correctly.

- If you don't know the answer, guess. No marks are deducted for wrong answers.

Part 4

This part of the paper tests your **knowledge of vocabulary and grammar.** There are eight questions in this part. Each question contains a sentence followed by a second sentence from which certain words have been removed. Only the words at the beginning and end of the second sentence are given. One of the missing words, the key word, is given in bold type above the second sentence. You must complete the second sentence by writing in the missing (3–8) words, including the key word in the form given.

- Read both sentences carefully before you write your answer.

- Your answer must include all the information in the first sentence. The information will be expressed in a different way in the second sentence.

- Your answer must follow on from the words at the beginning of the second sentence, and be completed by the words after the gap.

- You must use the key word in your answer. You must not change the form of the key word.

- You will, however, often need to change the form (e.g. verb → noun) and order (e.g. active → passive) of words from the first sentence and use these in your answer.

- Sometimes your answer will include words and expressions not used in the first sentence, but which express the same idea.

- Make sure your answer has no more than eight words. Be careful: contractions (e.g. don't, isn't, I'll) count as two words.

- Check to make sure that the second sentence is as similar as possible in meaning to the first sentence.

- Check that your spelling is correct.

Note:
Each of the questions in Part 4 is worth two marks. To get both marks, your answer must be perfect. Answers which are only partially correct, or which contain errors may receive one mark.

Part 5

This part of the paper has a two-fold purpose. It tests your **comprehension of a text through your awareness of the language** (recognising and understanding the force of lexical items, rhetorical and stylistic devices and referencing). It also tests your **ability to select appropriate information and to organise this into a coherent paragraph**.

The texts in this part come from different sources. After each text there are two comprehension questions. You should answer these questions with short answers.

- Read through both texts before you begin to answer the questions.

- Your answers to questions 40–43 do not need to be full sentences, but they must be clear to the examiner.

- Some questions will ask you to find and write down words or phrases from the text.

- Some questions will ask you to explain the meaning of a part of the text. Use your own words for these answers, don't copy from the text. Explain yourself clearly, but do not write too much.

In the final question, question 44, you have to write a summary of 50–70 words. This summary will include information from both the texts you have read. In your answer you must address the points outlined in the instructions. You must use your own words in the summary.

- Read the instructions carefully. Underline the key words in the instructions.

- Find and underline the relevant parts of the texts before you begin your summary.

- Remember you get marks for both content and language.

- Make sure you answer the question exactly. Do not include irrelevant information.

- Make sure you include at least one content point from each text.

- You may use content words from the texts, but use your own words to express the ideas. Don't copy phrases and sentences from the texts.

- Make sure your answer is within the word length.

- Express the ideas simply and clearly. Don't repeat yourself.

- Use linking expressions to connect your ideas.

- Check your answer for spelling, grammar and punctuation.

Note:
In the summary writing task, examiners are looking for relevance, coherence, conciseness, the use of linking devices and the ability to re-express ideas in achieving the task. Accuracy of spelling, grammar and punctuation is also important.

Guide to Paper 4   Listening

General information

- Paper 4 tests candidates' **ability to understand spoken English in different contexts.**

- The texts in Paper 4 may include **interviews, discussions, conversations, radio plays, talks, speeches, lectures, commentaries, documentaries and instructions.** All are taken from **authentic sources**.

- The recording will have **a variety of English native speaker accents.** Background noises may be included to provide information about context, but will stop before the speaking begins.

- Candidates **will hear each part twice.**

- Paper 4 is approximately **40 minutes** long.

- Candidates **mark their answers on the question paper.** At the end of the test, they have five minutes to transfer their answers to the **separate Answer Sheet in pencil.** There is an example Answer Sheet on page 176.

- Paper 4 accounts for **20 per cent of the total marks** in the exam.

Part	Task type and focus	Task format	Length	Number of questions	Number of marks
1	Three-option multiple choice cloze Gist, detail, main idea, function, purpose, topic, feeling, attitude, opinion	Four short unrelated extracts from monologues or texts involving interacting speakers. There are two questions for each extract.	Approx. 4 mins (Approx.1 min per extract)	8	8
2	Sentence completion Specific information, stated opinion	Candidates complete gaps in sentences with information from a monologue or prompted monologue.	Approx. 4 mins	9	9*
3	Four-option multiple choice Opinion, gist, detail, inference	A text involving interacting speakers with multiple choice questions.	Approx. 4 mins	5	5
4	Three-way matching Stated and non-stated opinion, agreement and disagreement	Candidates match statements on a text to either of two speakers or to both when they express agreement.	Approx. 3 mins	6	6
			Total: Approx. 40 mins	**Total:** 28	**Total:** 28

* Answers must be correctly spelled.

How to approach the tasks

Part 1

In this part you will hear four unrelated extracts.

- Before you listen to each extract, look at the instructions. Who will you hear? What will they be talking about?
- Before you listen to each extract, read the two questions. Underline the key words in each question or question stem.
- The words in the options may not be the same as the words in the text. Listen for the overall message.
- Most questions will be about people's ideas, opinions and feelings.
- Listen to find the answer to the question, then decide which of the options is closest to what you've heard.
- If you don't know the answer, guess. No marks are deducted for wrong answers.

Part 2

- Before you listen, look at the instructions. Who is talking? Where? Why?
- Before you listen, read the sentences. Think about the type of information which is missing.
- The questions follow the order of the text.
- The words you need are on the cassette, but not in the same sentences as in the questions.
- Most answers will be single words, numbers or very short phrases of 2–3 words.
- Check that your word or phrase fits the sentence grammatically and makes sense.
- Check your spelling. Incorrect spelling is penalised.
- If you don't know the answer, guess. No marks are deducted for wrong answers.

Part 3

- Before you listen, look at the instructions. Who is speaking? Where? Why?
- Before you listen, read the questions. Underline the key words in each question or question stem.
- The questions follow the order of the text.
- The words in the options may not be the same as the words in the text. Listen for the overall message.
- Many questions will be about people's ideas, opinions and feelings.
- Listen to find the answer to the question, then decide which of the options is closest to what you've heard.
- If you don't know the answer, guess. No marks are deducted for wrong answers.

Part 4

In this part, there are two main speakers, one male and one female, although a third person may set up and redirect the discussion.

- Before you listen, look at the instructions. Who is speaking? What are they talking about?
- Before you listen, read the questions. Underline the key words in each question.
- The questions are a list of statements which refer to people's opinions and feelings.
- Both speakers will talk about the points raised in the statements, so you are not listening for who mentioned each point, but rather for whose point of view it reflects.
- Listen for typical ways of agreeing and disagreeing in spoken language.
- If you don't know the answer, guess. No marks are deducted for wrong answers.

Note:

As you listen, you record your answers on your question paper. You will then have five minutes at the end of the examination to copy your answers from the question paper on to the separate Answer Sheet.

Guide to Paper 5 Speaking

General information

- Paper 5 tests candidates' **ability to use spontaneous spoken language in order to communicate naturally**.

- The usual format is **two candidates and two examiners**. (Occasionally there may be three candidates.) Only one of the examiners interacts with the candidates. Both examiners give the candidates marks.

- Paper 5 lasts approximately **19 minutes for each pair of candidates**.

- Paper 5 accounts for **20 per cent of the total marks** in the exam.

Part	Task type and focus	Task format	Length of answer
1	General conversation between examiner and each candidate

Giving personal information, general social and interactional language | The examiner encourages the candidates to give information about themselves and express general opinions. Candidates speak mainly to the examiner. | 3 mins |
| 2 | Two-way conversation between candidates

Speculating, evaluating, comparing, giving opinions, decision making, etc. | In this collaborative task, the candidates are given visual and spoken prompts which generate a discussion. | 4 mins |
| 3 | Long turn from each candidate followed by a discussion on topics related to the long turn

Organising longer unit of discourse, expressing and justifying opinions, developing topics | Each candidate in turn is given a written question to respond to. Candidates engage in discussion in order to explore further the topics of the long turn. | 12 mins* |

* Each candidate has two minutes for his/her long turn. (2 x 2 = 4 mins)
  There are eight minutes for the discussion between candidates after the long turns.

How to approach the tasks

Part 1

In this part of the paper, the examiner asks you for your names and then some questions.

- Try to have a normal conversation. Look at the examiner and respond naturally to what he/she says.
- Do not give a prepared speech about yourself, but try to make the conversation interesting by adding information which is relevant to the questions.

Part 2

This part of the paper has two phases. In the first phase you talk together about part of the visual material for about one minute. You are generally giving your first reactions to the material and establishing the theme. In the second phase, you are given a more specific task involving all the visual material. You usually have to discuss all the images in relation to the task and work towards some kind of joint conclusion.

In both phases:

- Listen to the instructions carefully and make sure you understand what you have to do.
- Look at your partner. Listen to what he/she says and respond naturally.
- Ask your partner questions, don't just give your opinions. Find out what he/she thinks and be ready to agree or disagree politely.
- Pick up on points your partner makes by adding your own ideas.

The first phase lasts one minute — a long time when you're speaking. Don't panic, and don't go too fast.

The second phase lasts three minutes.

- Listen carefully for the context of the discussion. Make sure what you say is relevant.
- Work systematically through the visual material.
- Consider all possibilities, don't come to a conclusion too soon.
- Talk about the issues raised by the visual materials. Bring in other relevant ideas.
- Work towards a conclusion, but you don't have to agree with each other!

Part 3

In this part of the paper, there are two phases. In the first phase, each of you has to talk for about two minutes. You are given a topic and a prompt card with some ideas for you to develop. Although the topics will be thematically related, each of you will talk about a separate aspect of that theme. The listening student is asked to comment on what has been said at the end of each long turn.

In the second phase, you and your partner have a discussion on the general theme explored by the two long turns. You will be asked questions by the examiner and will be expected to develop your answers fully and to comment on what each other says.

- In the first phase, use the ideas on the prompt card or introduce your own, but do not introduce irrelevant information or make irrelevant comments.
- Two minutes is a long time when you're speaking. Don't panic and don't go too fast. Give yourself time to think and use natural pauses to gather your thoughts.
- Use the ideas on the card to organise what you say. Use each one as a heading and say everything there is to say on that aspect of the topic before moving on to the next one.
- Make it clear when you are moving on to a different points by introducing and recapping main ideas.
- Give examples of what you say. You will be more interesting and won't say 'too much too soon'.
- Don't just say what you think about a topic, but talk about other people's views, why they hold them, whether you agree with them and why (not).
- Don't just talk about now. Give the historical background to an issue, say what you think will happen in the future.
- Don't just talk about your country, age group, etc. Talk about how the issue affects all sorts of people in different places.
- Try to structure what you say. Use phrases like, for example, 'The first thing I'd like to say is …', 'Another point to consider is …', etc. These will help you organise your ideas, and also give you more time to think.
- Try not to repeat yourself.
- Think about your listeners. Try to make what you say interesting, maintain eye contact with your partner and the examiner. Talk to them, not at them.
- Listen to your partner. You have to be ready to ask and answer questions about his/her topic as well as your own.

The second phase is a general discussion, so don't be afraid to introduce new ideas as long as they are related to the topic. The examiner may ask you questions in turn or may ask you both to answer together. You don't have to agree with your partner, but don't interrupt. Let your partner finish, then say what you think.

Marking

The criteria for assessment are: grammar, vocabulary, discourse management, pronunciation, communicative ability and global achievement.

TEST 1

Reading (1 hour 30 minutes)

PART 1

For questions **1–18**, read the three texts below and decide which answer (**A, B, C** or **D**) best fits each gap. Mark your answers **on the separate answer sheet**.

Tip Strip

Remember:
- Read the text through for general understanding before you try to do the task.
- The word or phrase you choose must fit the meaning of the passage as a whole.
- Check the words before and after the gap carefully.
- Some words may form part of fixed expressions, phrasal verbs or common collocations.
- When you have finished, read through the whole text again to check.

Question 3: Which verb collocates with 'temptation' to complete the expression?

Question 6: All of these verbs have the correct meaning but only one takes the preposition 'with'.

Question 10: Only one of these words can be used to link the two parts of the sentence successfully.

Question 11: Which of these adjectives usually qualifies the noun 'succession' in the common expression?

I Will not Explode

Everyone knows what happens if you give a full bottle of coke a vigorous (**1**) ..... and then unscrew the top. So the children of Benchill primary school in Manchester dived for (**2**) ..... when visitor Kim Wade flexed her muscles. Wade, head of Manchester Schools Behaviour and Support Service, (**3**) ..... the temptation to open the bottle and let the fizz drench the pupils. She had (**4**) ..... her point; the frothing of the drink was a metaphor for the build-up and explosion of temper.

Benchill's children were having a session on anger management. There is no (**5**) ..... that they are any more angry than children at other schools in the city, and the lesson was part of a scheme intended to help children identify and (**6**) ..... with the rages that life in the classroom and playground can provoke.

1 A shake	**B** stir	**C** rattle	**D** wobble
2 A shelter	**B** cover	**C** safety	**D** protection
3 A denied	**B** rejected	**C** declined	**D** resisted
4 A given	**B** made	**C** scored	**D** won
5 A inclination	**B** reception	**C** conviction	**D** suggestion
6 A cope	**B** bear	**C** handle	**D** manage

Fashion

Fashion may be said to encompass any of four forms. First, there is a conscious manipulation of dress that (**7**) ..... for effect, a 'fashion statement' or 'fad'. Second, fashion may designate innovations in dress that are more (**8**) ..... than simple fads. Some of these changes occur abruptly, whether due to economic fluctuations, or even the sudden (**9**) ..... of certain materials; other innovations may develop more deliberately. Third is the phenomenon (**10**) ..... styles in a particular area of dress change swiftly and repeatedly, with the new ones replacing the old in (**11**) ..... succession. Finally, fashion may refer specifically to the use of such adornments as cosmetics, fragrance and jewellery, whose primary purpose is to enhance a wearer's (**12**) ..... features.

7 A attempts	**B** strives	**C** endeavours	**D** seeks
8 A eternal	**B** perpetual	**C** enduring	**D** continuing
9 A abundance	**B** overload	**C** excess	**D** crop
10 A whereas	**B** whereupon	**C** whereabouts	**D** whereby
11 A prompt	**B** rapid	**C** fast	**D** brisk
12 A naked	**B** raw	**C** commonplace	**D** natural

Tip Strip

Question 14: These are all ways of looking or seeing, but which one means 'identify' in the context of the passage?

Question 16: Which of these words means 'very complicated'?

Faces

Despite our complex language skills, the face is still our primary means of communication. It is (**13**) ..... because our faces are so complex in appearance, that we can easily (**14**) ..... a friend in a crowd or attempt to check the trustworthiness of a stranger. (**15**) ..... , our ability to recognise faces quickly, in all sorts of circumstances, is arguably our most important and remarkable visual skill. Thanks to its very elastic skin, animated by a complex musculature capable of an enormous range of (**16**) ..... movements, the human face can quickly display a whole (**17**) ..... of contrasting emotions. As a result of evolution, we can read faces, making judgements about them (**18**) ..... on our experience, without effort and without anything being said.

13	**A** pointedly	**B** singularly	**C** precisely	**D** uniquely
14	**A** peek	**B** glimpse	**C** spot	**D** glance
15	**A** Indeed	**B** Still	**C** Really	**D** Anyway
16	**A** intransigent	**B** insatiable	**C** invincible	**D** intricate
17	**A** span	**B** extent	**C** scope	**D** array
18	**A** rooted	**B** based	**C** anchored	**D** derived

You are going to read four extracts which are all concerned in some way with music. For questions **19–26**, choose the answer (**A, B, C** or **D**) which you think fits best according to the text. Mark your answers **on the separate answer sheet.**

Reflections

In November last year, I led a music weekend in Cambridge, organised by the students of a national music society. It was a very memorable event but the problem, I find, with trying to do valuable work with and for young people, is that somehow the 'production values' go down. Meaning that I find myself fighting for this work to be taken just as seriously as a concert in a famous venue, or recorded for posterity. Music, it seems, is largely in the domain of the professionals, the virtuosi and the famous. When revered conductors lined up to (quite rightly) criticise successive British governments on their dismantling of the teaching of musical instruments in schools, their main complaint was a lack of potential players for orchestras. But the problem is more deep-seated. Without music at the core of your life at an early age, you won't even want to be a member of an audience at an orchestral concert, let alone be up on stage.

Two of the best films of recent years are surely *Toy Story* and *Toy Story 2*. I didn't hear anyone arguing that the reason their production values were so high — the scripts so witty, the jokes so good and twists and turns of the narrative so touching — was that 'we'll encourage a whole generation of cinema-goers to be film-makers'. No, in the film world there is generally no difference in budget or technology between children's or adult films — the aim is to produce a sure-fire winner and an appetite for film-going.

19 What criticism does the writer have of the group of revered conductors?

   A They expected too much of young children.

   B They misinterpreted the government's intentions.

   C They didn't focus on the full implications of the government's actions.

   D They didn't appreciate the full benefit that music can bring to children's lives.

20 Why does the writer draw a comparison between musical performance and film-making?

   A to highlight the false line of reasoning among those involved in music education

   B to demonstrate the high standards that can be found in children's productions

   C to criticise the allocation of resources to popular rather than educational pursuits

   D to defend the view that the end product is what matters most to audiences

CD Reviews
Bryan Ferry

Re-released on CD:
'Another Time, Another Place'

When Bryan Ferry recorded his solo album, *Another Time, Another Place*, in 1974, he was an apparently unstoppable, inexhaustibly creative force. His band, Roxy Music, was barely two years old. During a brief and meteoric ascent, the band had released three albums and, under Ferry's close artistic guidance, refashioned the rock 'n roll experience as a weirdly costumed trip around some futuristic archive. Somewhere between global engagements with Roxy Music, Ferry had found time to launch a solo career seemingly dedicated to honouring the songs he grew up listening to.

Nowadays, albums of old hits (cover versions) are a standard career ploy, but back in 1973 such retrospective dalliance was simply not the done thing amongst rock musicians. Neither was posing for your sleeve photo in full evening dress, like a posh matinée idol from the 1940s. But loosening the iron grip of conformist rock behaviour was precisely Ferry's point, and he had more than enough musical wit and wisdom to back up these outlandish postures.

On *Another Time, Another Place*, Ferry persisted with his revolutionary notion that songs from the pre-rock era could sit side by side with those of rock giants such as the Rolling Stones. The principal agent in this imperious dissolution of time and genre was Ferry's inimitable vocal style, which assumed complete mastery over anything it got near, banishing the ghosts of the originals. In pop terms, postmodernism started here.

21 In discussing the initial release of *Another Time, Another Place*, the reviewer notes that

    A the production was remarkable for such a relatively youthful performer.

    B at the time there was little public interest in the novelty of the idea.

    C Ferry had sufficient talent to challenge contemporary views on rock music.

    D Ferry was intent on following a dual career path.

22 The reviewer believes that *Another Time, Another Place* has been a such a successful album largely because

    A Ferry is so much admired by the public.

    B the songs it features were so carefully chosen.

    C the album is an effortless mix of old and new music.

    D Ferry was able to reproduce the songs in a unique way.

Tip Strip

Question 24: We understand from the conversation that the writer has never listened to the tapes and isn't interested in this type of music, but he doesn't tell Richard (Dick) this.

Extract from a novel

I'm late to work and when I get there Dick is already leaning against the door reading a book. He's thirty-one years old, with long, greasy black hair; he's wearing a Sonic Youth T-shirt, a black leather jacket that is trying manfully to suggest that it has seen better days — even though he only bought it a year ago — and a Walkman with a pair of ludicrously large headphones. The book is a paperback biography of a 1970s songwriter. The carrier bag by his feet — which really has seen better days — advertises a violently fashionable independent record label in the USA; he went to a great deal of trouble to get hold of it, and he gets very nervous when we go anywhere near it. He uses it to carry tapes around.

'Good morning Richard.'

'Oh hi. Hi, Rob.'

'Good weekend?'

I unlock the shop as he scrabbles around for his stuff.

'All right, yeah, OK. I found the first *Liquorice Comfits* album in Camden. It was never released here. Japanese import only.'

'Great.' I don't know what he's talking about.

'I'll tape it for you.'

'Thanks.'

'Cos you liked their second one, you said. *Pop, Girls, Etc.* The one with the actress on the cover. You didn't see the cover though. You just had the tape I did for you.'

I'm sure he did tape a *Liquorice Comfits* album for me, and I'm sure I said I liked it too. My flat is full of tapes Dick has made me, most of which I've never played.

'How about your weekend anyway?'

23 The comparison between Dick's leather jacket and carrier bag reveals the author's

A frustration with Dick.

B disrespect for Dick.

C sympathy for Dick.

D indifference to Dick.

24 From his conversation with Dick, we understand that the author

A doesn't share Dick's musical interests.

B is ungrateful for Dick's suggestions.

C likes obscure rather than popular music.

D doesn't care if Dick is offended.

Tip Strip

Question 26: This question is based on the text as a whole.

Music and the Mind

Making music appears to be one of the fundamental activities of mankind; as characteristically human as drawing and painting. The survival of Paleolithic cave-paintings bears witness to the antiquity of this form of art; and some of these paintings depict people dancing. Flutes made of bone found in these caves suggest that they danced to some form of music. But, because music itself only survives when the invention of a system of notation has made a written record possible, or else when a living member of a culture recreates the sounds and rhythms which have been handed down to him by his forbears, we have no information about prehistoric music. We are therefore accustomed to regarding drawing and painting as integral parts of the life of early man, but less inclined to think of music in the same way.

When biologists consider complex human activities such as the arts, they tend to assume that their compelling qualities are derivations of basic drives. If any given activity can be seen to aid survival or facilitate adaptation to the environment, or to be derived from behaviour which does so, it 'makes sense' in biological terms. But what use is music? Music can certainly be regarded as a form of communication; but what it communicates is not obvious. Music is not usually representational: it does not sharpen our perception of the external world or generally imitate it. Nor is music propositional: it does not put forward theories about the world or convey information.

25 In discussing music, the writer states that

   A   music and art evolved at the same time.
   B   early humans were strongly influenced by music.
   C   early art forms provide evidence of prehistoric music.
   D   the first musicians date back to Paleolithic times.

26 In these paragraphs, the writer's purpose is to

   A   explore the origins of music.
   B   explain why music is important to us.
   C   describe the overlap between music and art.
   D   justify the existence of different musical tastes.

You are going to read an extract from a magazine. Seven paragraphs have been removed from the extract. Choose from the paragraphs **A–H** the one which fits each gap (**27–33**). There is one extra paragraph which you do not need to use. Mark your answers **on the separate answer sheet.**

Taking the Plunge

Paying people to take part in clinical trials is frowned upon. But in a world of risks and rewards, what's the problem, asks Julian Savulescu

Consider the following scenario. Researchers from an Australian biotech company want to enlist a family with a rare genetic mutation for a study into genetic illness. They strongly believe that they can identify one of the genes involved in the disease in this family, and if they do, the company stands to make a large amount of money. The researchers aim to persuade the family to take part in the study by offering each member $10,000. All they would have to do is give some saliva samples.

| 27 |

Such standards are rigorously enforced. But there is another way of looking at it. Pharmaceuticals and biotech companies carry out trials because they hope eventually to make substantial profits from the results. The researchers also benefit financially and through the advancement of their careers. Meanwhile, the participants in a trial barely benefit at all. Indeed, they could be said to be exploited in the interests of industry and biomedicine.

| 28 |

Now compare the trial mentioned above with a real example in which a patient is invited to take part in a study into genetic predisposition to glaucoma, a disease of the eye which can cause a person to gradually lose their sight. If she agrees, the patient will have access to a

new genetic test for glaucoma that is not available outside the study. The cost of this test is a few hundred dollars.

| 29 |

The issue becomes most acute when applied to high-risk research. Ethics committees argue that in these cases money may make people go against their 'better judgement' and take risks that they would not ordinarily take. However, not paying volunteers who take part in high-risk research makes an even greater mockery of the system.

| 30 |

In many cases such as this, the financial reward is the only thing that makes it worthwhile for a volunteer to take the risk. But why should that bother ethics committees? We make such decisions every day. Do we always make them against our better judgement?

| 31 |

Similarly, an unemployed man sees an advertisement for a construction worker's job. At the interview, the employer tells him the job involves working on high scaffolding and that the risk of dying on the site is between 1 in 2000 and 1 in 5000 higher per year than working at ground level. In compensation for this he will receive an extra $10,000 a year. He takes the job.

| 32 |

Why should they be treated as a special case? Life is all about taking considered risks. If $10,000 is the going rate for taking on a 1 in 2000 increased risk of dying then researchers should be allowed to offer volunteers the going rate. Competent rational people are quite able to weigh up the risks and benefits for themselves. I have never understood the suggestion that offering money restricts people's freedom to choose.

| 33 |

It seems to me we should allow people to take measured risks for the chance to improve the quality of their lives or their children's lives or for anything else they value. We should allow them to make that choice in any field.

Tip Strip

Remember:
- Read the main text first, ignoring the gaps, to get a general understanding of its subject matter and organisation.
- Read the text around each gap carefully. Look at the whole paragraph, before and after the gap.
- Read paragraphs A–H. Check for topic and language links with the paragraphs in the base text.
- Highlight words that refer to people and places.
- Highlight time references; this will help you to follow the development of the argument.
- Re-read the completed text to be sure it makes sense.

Question 27: Which option picks up on the scenario described in the first paragraph?

Question 30: Which option picks up the idea of risk mentioned before the gap and introduces the idea of employment developed after the gap?

Question 33: At the end of the text, the writer is stating his own opinion about the issue. In which option is this indicated?

A For example, a researcher wishes to recruit healthy, unemployed men at a local labour exchange for a study into the effects of new anti-hypertensive medications. The volunteers would have to wear a device to measure pressure in the heart. This can cause life-threatening complications, although the risk of death is 1 in 2000 and is clearly stated on the consent form, yet all the researcher can offer the volunteers is a mere $100 for their trouble.

B In many countries today such a scenario is inconceivable. Researchers are not allowed to offer significant sums of money to participants in a medical trial, even for low-risk experiments. Offering money is considered 'undue inducement' that could interfere with a volunteer's judgement on whether to take part, and turn the relationship between scientist and subject into a commercial, unethical one.

C Benefits in kind like this are permissible, and many volunteers receive them. They are not considered undue inducements, yet money is. This is paternalistic and nonsensical. It would be far more respectful to volunteers if researchers could offer them the choice.

D Could you say that either situation resulted in unsound judgements? In both cases they are effectively being paid for taking on a greater risk. There appears nothing objectionable in their decisions, yet participants in medical trials are not even allowed to make the choice.

E The crucial things are to ensure that the risk involved is reasonable compared with the benefits it will offer the participant and society, and that the participants are fully informed and give their consent freely. If the risks balance the benefits — for example if the right study is likely to save the lives of patients in the future — and the participants know all the risks and are free to make their choice, then what does it matter how much they are paid?

F Consider a couple with two young children who are contemplating buying a new car. They find one for $30,000 but if they spend an extra $10,000, they could get one with significantly better safety features such as air bags and an anti-lock braking system. The safer car has been shown to reduce the risk of death by 1 in 2000 a year. But the couple decide to buy the cheaper car and spend the extra $10,000 on a family holiday instead.

G One such ethics committee in Australia nearly rejected a proposal to pay a particular group of people the equivalent of just 10 US dollars for completing an anonymous questionnaire about their behaviour for a study on the spread of hepatitis C.

H If this is the case, surely it is only fair that they share in the rewards? Publicly funded research is perhaps more complicated, as participants may be acting in the public interest. But my main argument applies equally to commercial and non-commercial trials: researchers should be allowed to pay volunteers, and to pay them well, even for high-risk research.

I have noticed that after I publish a book people inevitably ask: 'Is there going to be a film?' They ask this question in tones of great excitement, with a slight widening of the eyes. I am left with a suspicion that most people think that a film is far more wondrous than a novel; that a novel is, perhaps, just a hopeful step in the celluloid direction, and that if there is no film, then the author has partially failed. It is as if 'the film' confers a mysterious super-legitimacy upon the writer's work.

Objectively speaking, a film's relationship to a novel is as a charcoal sketch to an oil painting, and no writer I know would actually agree that 'the film' is the ultimate aspiration. Certainly, any literary novelist who deliberately tried to write something tailor-made to film-makers would fail to produce a good book, because the fact is that books are only filmic by accident.

It is, in any case, a long journey from page to screen, because the first stage involves 'selling the option', whereby, in return for a modest sum, and for a limited time, the producer retains the right to be the first to
23 have a bash at making the film, should he get round to
24 it. It is theoretically possible to go for decades having the option renewed, with no film being made at any
26 time at all. This is money for jam, of course, but the sums are not big enough to be truly conducive to contentment. My first novel had the option renewed several times, and then finally it was dropped. This is,
30 alas, a common fate, and many a novelist remembers those little bursts of hope with a wry smile.

In the case of my second novel, however, the book eventually made it over the real hurdle, which is the 'exercising of the option'. This is the point where a more substantial fistful of cash changes hands, but regrettably even this is not enough to meet the expectations of loved ones and acquaintances, who strangely assume that you are imminently to be stinking rich for ever. More importantly, here begins the battle that takes place in the author's psyche thereafter. The hard fact is, that it is no longer your own book. Although, unusually, I was asked if I would like to do the script myself, no doubt both producer and director were mightily relieved when I declined.

Novelists, you see, rarely make good scriptwriters, and in any case I couldn't have taken the job on without being a hypocrite — I had even told off my best friend for wasting her literary energy by turning her novels into scripts when she should have been writing more novels. She has had the experience of doing numerous drafts, and then finding that her scripts are still not used. I wasn't going to put up with that, because I have the natural arrogance of most literary writers, which she unaccountably lacks.

As far as I am concerned, once I have written something, then that is the way it must be; it is perfect and no one is going to make me change it. Scriptwriters have to be humble creatures who *will* change things, and even knowingly make them worse, a thousand times and a thousand times again, promptly, and upon demand. I would rather be boiled in oil.

It is, as I say, no longer your own book. The director has the right to make any changes that he fancies, and so your carefully crafted (non-autobiographical) novel about family life in London can end up being set in Los Angeles, involving a car chase, a roof-top shoot-out and abduction by aliens. This from the writer's point of view, is the real horror of film.

When my book was eventually filmed, I did get to visit the set, however. I cannot count the number of people I met there who *a propos* possible changes to the story, repeated to me in a serious tone that, 'Of course, film is a completely different medium.' This mantra is solemnly repeated so that film-makers are self-absolved from any irritation that may be set up by altering the characters or the story. I think that it is a cliché that is really either untrue or too vague to be meaningful. There could not be anything simpler than extracting the salient points of the main narrative, and making a faithful film, which is what all readers and writers would actually prefer.

My theory is that film-makers are hell-bent on a bit of territorial marking, and each time one can only hope that they have sufficient genius to do it with flair. There are, after all, a few films that really are better than the book, and it would genuinely cause me no distress were people to say this of the one based on my own efforts.

Tip Strip

Remember the questions follow the order of the text.

- Read the text carefully. Don't worry if you don't understand every word.

- Try to answer the question, or complete the sentence, before you look at options A, B, C or D.

- Underline key words in the question stem, then find the part of the text where the answer is located and underline the key words there.

- Find the option which best matches the text. Highlight parts of the text which confirm the answer.

- Consider why the options are wrong — if you don't understand the text completely, you may still reach the right answer by a process of elimination.

Question 36: Which of these expressions suggests that the writer believes producers sometimes have no intention of making the film?

Question 39: The people he met on the film set seemed keen to justify themselves and explain things because they expected him to object. Which word best reflects this behaviour?

Question 40: Look at the last paragraph to see how the writer feels about the film made from his book.

34 What do people do when the writer publishes a new book?

    A They make wrong assumptions about his aims.

    B They draw wrong conclusions from his comments.

    C They make unfair criticisms of his writing.

    D They gain a false impression of his attitude.

35 The writer compares writing with the visual arts to support his view that

    A related art forms benefit from indirect comparisons.

    B ideas are easily translated from one medium to another.

    C an artist has no idea how an idea may develop.

    D each art form should be judged on its own merits.

36 Which phrase best reveals how the writer regards the attitude of film producers in the 'option' system?

    A 'have a bash' (line 23)

    B 'get round to it' (lines 23–24)

    C 'money for jam' (line 26)

    D 'a common fate' (line 30)

37 What problem does the author of a literary work usually face once the film option has been 'exercised'?

    A financial disappointment

    B pressure to produce a script

    C loss of authorial control

    D lack of support from film-makers

38 According to the writer, a good scriptwriter needs, above all, to

    A adopt a flexible approach towards the work.

    B ignore the arrogance of literary writers.

    C resist the unreasonable demands for changes.

    D be sensitive to the literary merits of the original work.

39 Which word best describes the attitude of the people on the film set towards the author?

    A intolerant

    B defensive

    C indifferent

    D aggressive

40 In the final analysis, the writer accepts that the film version of his literary work may be

    A a lucrative sideline to his writing.

    B an opportunity to learn new skills.

    C a chance to improve on the original.

    D a way of attracting new readers.

Writing (2 hours)

You **must** answer this question. Write your answer in **300–350** words in an appropriate style.

1 You have read the extract below as part of a magazine article on 'success'. Readers were asked to send in their opinions. You decide to write a letter responding to the points raised and giving your own views.

'Many people want to have a successful career but the problem with having a high income is that you can become handcuffed to a certain lifestyle. For example, private education for children, an expensive home, two cars or luxury holidays seem to some to be a necessary part of life. If you're not careful, you can begin to find that you see yourself purely in terms of material possessions. On the other hand, would this be a bad thing? Doesn't everybody ideally want to earn a lot of money? And shouldn't those who do, be free to spend it as they wish?

Write your **letter**. Do not write any postal addresses.

Tip Strip

In Part 1 you may be asked to write an article, an essay, a letter or a proposal. In this test you have to write a letter to a magazine editor. There is generally more information to process in the input for this task than there is in the other three questions. You are expected to produce a discursive piece of writing that addresses all the prompts given in the task.

- Begin by underlining the prompts, or 'content points', that are included in the input. In this case, they are: a) the consequences of focusing on material possessions, b) the suggestion that everyone wants to have a lot of money and c) the argument that they should spend that money as they see fit. If you fail to address any of these issues, you will lose marks.

- In order to produce well-reasoned arguments for this particular question, it is useful to consider both sides of a), b) and c) above. For example, if you consider there is nothing wrong with focusing on material possessions, why do you think this is the case? If you do feel such a focus is wrong, how might you avoid it?

- Note that you do not need to supply any postal addresses, but you are likely to use a formal register and to address your letter to the editor of the magazine, signing it 'Yours sincerely'.

- At the start of the letter, you need to indicate to the reader your reasons for writing. In this case, you would make reference to the article and you may choose to state your position on the topic immediately.

- Your points should be clearly organised into paragraphs, and it would be appropriate to conclude with a brief summary of your views, although this is not essential in a letter.

- Your examiner will expect to see a range of appropriate language, and this will include defending and/or attacking the arguments put forward in the article, the expression and support of opinions (both personal and general) and some speculation and hypothesis.

Write an answer to **one** of the questions **2–4** in this part. Write your answer in **300–350** words in an appropriate style.

2 An international magazine is planning to publish a special edition for International Friendship Week and has invited readers to contribute an article for this. Write an article explaining what you feel are the most important qualities in a friend and giving reasons for your views. Illustrate at least one of the qualities by relating a story about friendship from your own experience.

Write your **article**.

3 You have recently taken a young relative to see a local theatre company's production of a well-known children's play. You were particularly impressed by the quality of the acting and the music, which had been written for the play by the cast and the producer. Write a review of the play for the local newspaper and say why you think children's theatre is important.

Write your **review**.

4 You regularly receive an English language magazine written by and for students. The editors of the magazine have asked readers for submissions. You have decided to write a report for the magazine on *The benefits of studying in a multi-cultural environment*.

Write your **report**.

Tip Strip

You may be asked to write an article, an essay, a letter, a proposal, a review or a report.

- Read the questions carefully and think about the topic and the vocabulary you will need to use. Choose a question that you feel you are able to write about. Underline the key points in the question and make sure you address these in your answer.
- Think about the target reader. This will influence the style and tone you will need to use.
- Organise your answer carefully using paragraphs for main ideas or points.
- Use appropriate language for description, giving opinions, making recommendations, etc.
- Check your final answer for grammatical accuracy, spelling and punctuation.

Question 2
The article may be formal or semi-formal but whichever style you choose, make sure that you stick to it throughout.

- Obviously you can refer to your own experiences and to people that you know personally. Note that you must make reference to a personal experience at least once within this article.
- Make sure that you provide good links between your main arguments and the examples that you use to illustrate these. Avoid using any examples that are not quite relevant.
- You will use a variety of language, such as description and narration, evaluation and justification.

Question 3
- Again, a formal or semi-formal style may be used.
- Note that this question is about a local production; in other words, those involved in the play were not professionals.
- If you decide to relate the content of the play, do this very briefly in one sentence — or two at the most.
- You should make positive comments about the play, and specifically evaluate the quality of the acting and music. Think of some reasons as to why you might have been impressed, e.g. the age of the actors, their audibility, the appeal of the songs, etc.
- In discussing why you feel children's theatre is important, you should take a more general focus and widen the topic, giving reasons for your views.

Question 4
- This question requires a more formal approach, and should consist of a clearly structured report that has a well-focused introduction.
- Select a number of main points (for paragraphs) and then consider your supporting arguments. Students who have experience of studying in a multi-cultural environment should find that there is plenty of scope for material. Personal examples may be used for support.
- Use a range of language, e.g. description, analysis, comparison and contrast, concession, speculation.

PART 1

For questions **1–15**, read the text below and think of the word which best fits each space. Use only **one** word in each space. There is an example at the beginning **(0)**. Write your answers in **CAPITALS LETTERS on the separate answer sheet.**

Example:

0	O	N																

The Map Thief

For a couple of years, Gilbert Bland was a unique figure in the privileged world of antique map dealing. He made a 100% profit (**0**) …*on*… every map he sold, (**1**) …*not*… because he was a clever businessman, but because he was a thief. In the mid-1990s, Bland crept around libraries in the USA, armed (**2**) …*in*… a sharp razor and a baggy shirt and sliced out those ancient maps which took (**3**) …*it*… fancy. Some were worth tens of thousands of dollars, and he (**4**) ………. on to sell them through both mail-order catalogues and his shop in Florida.

(**5**) ………. Bland's historical knowledge of maps was patchy at best, his knowledge of (**6**) ………. exact location in the rare book stacks was second to (**7**) ……….. . When he heard that early maps of, (**8**) ………. , Seattle were becoming popular, he would know precisely (**9**) ………. to start slicing.

His crimes only came (**10**) ………. light when a researcher in a Baltimore library noticed that a man appeared to be tearing a page from a 200-year-old book (**11**) ………. if it were a newspaper. At (**12**) ………. , it was assumed that this was an isolated case, and the library and police were happy to (**13**) ………. Bland off with a warning. (**14**) ………. later did they (**15**) ………. across his notebooks, which contained elaborate details of all his thefts.

For questions **16–25**, read the text below. Use the word given in **capitals** at the end of some of the lines to form a word that fits in the space in the same line. There is an example at the beginning **(0)**. Write your answers in **CAPITALS LETTERS** on the separate answer sheet.

Tip Strip

Remember:
- Read the text through for general understanding before you try to do the task.
- Decide which type of word is needed for each gap (e.g. noun, adjective, etc.).
- Look at the whole sentence, not just at the line including the gap.
- You may need to:
- add a prefix (e.g. un-).
- add suffix (e.g. -able) to the base word given.
- change the form of the word (e.g. receive →receipt).
- create a compound word (e.g. wildlife).
- Be careful, some words may need negative prefixes to make sense in context.
- Check whether the plural or singular form of words is needed.
- Most answers will be longer than the base word given.
- Check that you have spelled the words correctly.

Question 16: A noun is needed here. Which suffix can be added to 'like' to form a noun which completes the expression?

Question 17: A compound word is needed here. Which word can be added to 'master' to create a compound noun which collocates with 'literary'?

Question 22: Which prefix is added to make this noun into a verb? Which form of the verb is needed?

Question 23: Which prefix is needed to make a word which fits the context of the passage?

Question 24: Which adjective fits the context better, 'imaginative' or 'imaginary'?

Example:

0	G	E	N	E	T	I	C												

Frankenstein's Real Creator

In these days of **(0)** ...*genetic*... engineering, it is not unusual to   **GENE**

hear the name Frankenstein invoked by those who fear the

consequences when humans seek to create a being in their own

(16) ....   **LIKE**

Often overlooked, however, is the fact that the tale originated, not

as a folk legend, still less as a wildly original film script, but as a

literary **(17)** .... Even today, to read the chilling story of an   **MASTER**

inventor and the uncontrollable monster he created is at once both

a thought-provoking and an **(18)** .... experience. What's   **SETTLE**

more, the **(19)** .... popularity of the novel, and its modern-   **ENDURE**

day relevance are all the more remarkable when we remember it

was written almost 200 years ago, by an 18-year-old woman

called Mary Shelley. Over the decades, **(20)** .... films have   **NUMBER**

attempted to capture the full horror of her story, but none have

come close to equalling the power of Mary Shelley's frightening

prose. Amongst **(21)** .... and commentators, *Frankenstein*   **ACADEMY**

has long been **(22)** .... as a powerful piece of gothic   **KNOWLEDGE**

fiction, representing as it does an **(23)** .... fusion of   **ORDINARY**

contemporary philosophy, literary skill and **(24)** .... vision.   **IMAGINE**

It is only recently, however, with increased media attention devoted

to the philosophical issues her novel raises, that there has been a

more general **(25)** .... of interest in Mary herself.   **REVIVE**

Tip Strip

Remember:
• Read all three sentences before thinking about what the missing word might be.
• The same word, in the same form, (e.g. a plural noun, a past tense verb, etc.) must fit all three gaps.
• In each gap, the word will have a slightly different meaning or will be used in a different context.
• In some gaps, the word will form part of a phrasal verb or longer expression.
• Look carefully at the words before and after the gaps.
• Check that your answer fits all three gaps.
• Check that you have spelled the word orrectly.

Question 26: The third sentence uses the literal meaning of this verb. Which specific verb collocates with 'portrait'?

Question 27: A verb is needed in each of these gaps. Which tense will it be in?

Question 29: The word 'jumped' fits into the first two sentences, but not into the third. Which synonym of 'jumped' is needed to complete the expression in the third sentence?

Question 30: The verbs 'turn' and 'show' both make a phrasal verb in the first sentence. But only one of them fits into the other two sentences.

Question 31: Which noun collocates with 'regular' in the context of the first sentence?

For questions **26–31**, think of **one** word only which can be used appropriately in all three sentences. Here is an example **(0)**.

0 Last year's champion is in with a .... chance of repeating his success in the grand prix next weekend.

Some of the home owners are hoping to get compensation for the poor building work, and I think they have a very .... case.

There's no point in trying to put the tent up, the wind is far too ....

Example:

0	S	T	R	O	N	G												

Write **only** the missing word **in CAPITAL LETTERS on the separate answer sheet.**

---

26 • At the end of the holiday, ... on to any unused foreign currency because it may come in handy on another occasion.

• If your call is not answered within two minutes, you're advised to .... up and dial again.

• The company decided to .... a portrait of the retiring managing director in the boardroom.

27 • After a long series of meetings with the management, the workers .... for a 3% pay increase.

• Before leaving for Australia, Ray sold his car and .... his account at the local garage.

• The contents of the jar .... during the long car journey and it no longer looked so full.

28 • It is necessary to wash clothes made from .... fibres at a low temperature.

• Negotiations between the rival factions have reached a very .... stage, with neither side willing to give an inch.

• Although it is made from various root vegetables, the dish has a very .... taste.

29 • When the commanding officer entered the room, the young cadets all .... to attention.

• They were moving steadily through the seemingly impenetrable jungle when suddenly a large animal .... at them from out of the undergrowth.

• With the arrival of the ebullient young actor, the party really .... to life.

30 • Because he failed to .... up for the job interview, Mr Garrard has been crossed off the shortlist of applicants.

• In terms of recognition, Tamsin had little to .... for all the effort she'd put into reorganising the office.

• Despite her poor reception in New York, the artist is still keen to .... her work across the rest of the USA.

31 • Many people fail to recognise that the mind needs regular .... just like any other part of the body.

• Trying to get every member of staff to take their holiday at a different time was a very frustrating ....

• Every .... in the book is designed to build up your reasoning skills.

For questions **32–39**, complete the second sentence so that it has a similar meaning to the first sentence, using the word given. **Do not change the word given.** You must use between **three** and **eight** words, including the word given. Here is an example **(0)**.

Example:

0   Immediately after winning the race, Sandy began training for the next one.

had

No .... she began training for the next one.

0   sooner had Sandy won the race than

Write **only** the missing words **on the separate answer sheet.**

32   Attendance at the additional evening lectures is not obligatory for students.
under
Students .... the additional evening lectures.

33   You must keep this door closed at all times when the red light is illuminated.
account
On .... this door when the red light is illuminated.

34   You can't find pottery like this in any other part of the country.
type
This is the only part of the country .... found.

35   Natalie's friends talked her out of going to the concert alone.
dissuaded
It was Natalie's friends .... to the concert alone.

36   As a result of the bad weather, there may be delays on some international flights.
subject
Due to the bad weather .... possible delay.

37   Lorraine was the only student to hand in her assignment on time.
exception
With .... of the students handed in their assignment on time.

38   It never crossed my mind that the studio door might have been locked.
occurred
It .... might have locked the studio door.

39   Students at the school are not allowed to go into the Rainbow Disco.
bounds
The Rainbow Disco .... students at the school.

For questions **40–44**, read the following texts about hotels. For questions **40–43**, answer with a word or short phrase. You do not need to write complete sentences. For question **44**, write a summary according to the instructions given. Write your answers **on the separate answer sheet.**

There's no such thing as a perfect hotel guide. If it is to be comprehensive, it will probably not have enough space for subjective criticism. To be high-minded and opinionated, it has to be selective. And then there is the delicate issue of independence. Is it possible to rely on a recommendation if the hotel's inclusion has been paid for?

This month sees the publication of the latest edition of the Good Hotel Guide — and with it a sideswipe by its authors against some of their rivals. Unsurprisingly, the
8 well-known glossy guide which charges hotels £2,500 for an entry is the prime target. Guides which demand payment are little more than advertising sheets, it is claimed, but it seems that very few readers appreciate the difference between a genuinely independent hotel guide and one which is not.

One alternative, in England at least, is to go to the local tourist board in the area of your choice. Each year, in return for an inspection fee, the boards award hotels in their area a grade for their facilities. But there is need for caution here too. Although hotels have to make the grade in terms of pre-set standards in order to be included, the boards don't really set out to offer observations on things like décor or the quality of the cooking, which could affect your own impression. What's more, hoteliers pay extra if they want a more lavish entry in the board's official guide, with colour photographs for example to make them stand out from their competitors.

---

40 In your own words, explain why the writer feels that even an independent hotel guide will never be perfect.

....

41 Which word, used earlier in the text, provides the context for the expression 'the prime target' in line 8?

....

All hotels look great in the brochure; tables laden with exquisite food, smiling staff, cosy lounges, softly-lit rooms, and the promise of five-star treatment. But how do you know that what you see is what you'll get? Well, firstly, when you phone to ask for a brochure, expect to find it on the doormat the day after your inquiry. That's efficiency. Although the law requires brochures to be truthful, they don't have to reveal the ways in which a hotel may fail to live up to your expectations. If there's no mention of a pool, there may not be one. And if the brochure says, 'Two minutes from the airport', check that this doesn't mean it's next to the main runway!

And if you intend to book a hotel for a very special occasion, check it out personally rather than running the risking of feeling let down on the day itself. But don't be cajoled into making an appointment to view the place; that way you may only see what they want you to see. It's better just to drop in unannounced. The most important area in any hotel is reception. I wouldn't expect to walk up to the desk without the receptionists acknowledging me, however busy they might be with other clients. Also, check that the staff really are fully occupied; at quiet times in a well-run hotel they should be busy making sure everything's up to scratch and getting ready to welcome the next wave of customers.

42 Which phrase in this text makes reference to the main topic of the first text?

....

43 Which expression later in the text echoes the idea introduced by the phrase 'fail to live up to your expectations' in line 6?

....

44 In a paragraph of between **50 and 70** words, summarise **in your own words as far as possible**, the reasons given in the texts to explain why prospective clients may be misled by the information available about hotels.

Tip Strip

Read through both texts before you begin to answer the questions.

Questions 40–43:
• Your answers to these questions do not need to be full sentences, but they must be clear to the examiner.
• Some questions will ask you to find and write down words or phrases from the text.
• Some questions will ask you to explain the meaning of a part of the text. Use your own words for these answers — don't copy from the text. Explain yourself clearly, but do not write too much.

Question 40: To answer this question you need to use information from the first paragraph of the text. Use your own words to explain briefly what the writer is saying in the first three sentences.

Question 42: The first text is about hotel guides. What system is often used to tell us the quality of hotels? Find the word in the second text which picks up on the reference.

Question 43: This phrase expresses the idea of disappointment. Which phrasal verb in the second paragraph also expresses this idea?

Question 44:
• Read the instructions carefully. Underline the important words in the task.
• Find and underline the relevant parts of the texts before you begin your summary.
• Make sure you answer the question exactly. Do not include irrelevant information.
• You may use content words from the texts, but use your own words to express the ideas. Don't copy phrases and sentences from the texts.
• Make sure you include at least one content point from each text.
• Remember you get marks for both content and language.
• Make sure your answer is within the wordlength.
• Use linking expressions to connect your ideas.
• Express the ideas simply and clearly. Don't repeat yourself.
• Check your answer for spelling, grammar and punctuation.

PART 1

You will hear four different extracts. For questions **1–8**, choose the answer (**A, B** or **C**) which fits best according to what you hear. There are two questions for each extract.

Extract One

You hear a woman telling a friend about a book she is reading.

1 What impresses the speaker about the writer called Rosie Pearson?

   A the uniqueness of her views
   B her skill in setting a scene
   C the force of her message

   1

2 On what level has the speaker benefited from Pearson's writing?

   A psychologically
   B practically
   C financially

   2

Extract Two

You hear part of a radio interview with a producer of children's television programmes.

3 What is the speaker doing when he speaks?

   A recounting a period of indecision
   B explaining how a problem was resolved
   C illustrating the drawbacks of his profession

   3

4 What was the speaker's attitude towards his 'Supercar'?

   A He was realistic about its role in the programmes.
   B He was annoyed at the way it was perceived.
   C He regretted its impact on the programme.

   4

Question 5: This is a gist question focused on the topic of the extract. Listen for the scientist's main area of concern.

Question 7: This is a gist question focused on the speaker's feelings. How did she think she would feel at the party?

Extract Three

You hear part of a radio interview with a famous scientist.

5   What is the main focus of the discussion?

   A   disease
   B   pollution
   C   conservation

5

6   The speaker reinforces his view on the topic by

   A   stating his solution to certain issues.
   B   denying that he holds other related views.
   C   listing the consequences of human ignorance.

6

Extract Four

You hear two friends talking about a birthday celebration.

7   How did the woman expect to feel during the celebration?

   A   embarrassed
   B   anxious
   C   amused

7

8   What does the woman say about the poems?

   A   Anyone could have written them.
   B   They were read in random order.
   C   She appreciated all of them.

8

You will hear a talk about Phyllis Pearsall, the creator of the London map-book known as the A–Z. For questions **9–17**, complete the sentences with a word or short phrase.

Tip Strip

Remember:
- Before you listen, look at the rubric. Who is talking? Where? Why?
- Before you listen, read the sentences. Think about the type of information which is missing.
- The questions follow the order of the text.
- The words you need are all on the tape, but not in the same sentences as in the questions. This is not a dictation.
- Write 1–3 words or a number in each space. Don't repeat the words and ideas already used in the sentence.
- Most answers will be concrete pieces of information. Don't try to paraphrase the information. Use the words you hear.
- Check that your word or phrase fits grammatically and makes sense.
- Check your spelling.

Question 11: You are listening for a number. Two large numbers are mentioned. Which one refers to streets?

Question 12: You need to listen for the actual word the speaker uses to describe Phyllis' father's attitude.

Question 14: You are listening for an adjective that describes the way Phyllis drew things. Listen for the word 'efficient' which is in the sentence and on the tape, the word you need comes soon afterwards.

Question 17: You are listening for a type of shop. Three are mentioned in the last part of the text, but which was the first to sell Phyllis' maps?

Before beginning the map project, Phyllis worked as a [*portrait artist*] **9**

Before the A–Z, most maps of London concentrated on [*geographical*] **10** features.

Phyllis covered a total of [~~3000~~ ~~3000~~ 23000] **11** streets during the project.

Phyllis' father is described as being [*unsupported* *vanguard*] **12** of the project.

Unlike other maps, the A–Z is not [*mathematics caculation*] **13** in basis.

Phyllis is described as being both efficient and [*observa* *color*] **14** in her sketching.

When cataloguing the streets she'd sketched, Phyllis used a system of cards in [*shoes box* *tea box*] **15**

The omission of Trafalgar Square from the index was noticed by the book's [*printer*] **16**

The first type of shop to sell the A–Z maps was a [*new agence*] **17**

You will hear an interview with an author called Rachel White. For questions **18–22**, choose the answer (**A**, **B**, **C** or **D**) which fits best according to what you hear.

18 What does Rachel particularly recall about her school days?

 A She was only really interested in the subject of literature.
 B She was aware that she was brighter than her classmates.
 C She was given preferential treatment by a certain teacher.
 D She disliked being considered hard working by her peers.

18 □

19 Which of the following added to Rachel's negative feelings about her essay?

 A It was not her own work.
 B Her classmates were critical of it.
 C Some of the content was misleading.
 D There was an insufficient amount of material.

19 □

20 According to Rachel, what attitude do many people have towards Jane Austen's books?

 A They lose interest in them at an early age.
 B They read them because they feel they should.
 C They believe they suit a certain type of personality.
 D They feel they should be read in certain situations.

20 □

21 Why did Rachel write the essay 'Literature and the Young Mind'?

 A in order to express a commonly-held view
 B in order to encourage young people to read literature
 C because she wanted to express her gratitude to writers like Austen
 D because she wanted to recommend certain writers to young readers

21 □

22 When discussing her own writing, Rachel highlights its

 A contemporary relevance.
 B emotional content.
 C standard development.
 D essential complexity.

22 □

You will hear two people, Alex and Mandy, talking about the experience of having an identical twin brother or sister. For questions **23–28**, decide whether the opinions are expressed by only one of the speakers, or whether the speakers agree.

Tip Strip

Remember:
• Before you listen, look at the rubric. Who will you hear? What will they be talking about?
• Read the questions and underline the key words.
• The questions are a list of statements which refer to people's opinions and feelings.
• Both speakers will talk about the points raised in the statements, so you are not listening for who mentioned each point, but rather for whose point of view the statement reflects.
• Listen for typical ways of agreeing and disagreeing in spoken language.

Question 23: Alex says that the researchers find what they want to find. Does what Mandy say next show that she agrees or disagrees with him?

Question 26: Alex thinks his job has given him lines on his face so that he no longer looks so much like his brother. What does Mandy say before this?

Question 28: Mandy talks about outdoing her twin, and Alex talks about one-upmanship. So do they agree on this point?

Write   **M**   for Mandy,
            A   for Alex,
or   **B**   for Both, when they agree.

23 I think some of the research on identical twins is unreliable.   23

24 I find the false assumptions people make about twins annoying.   24

25 I've always enjoyed exploiting the similarity between me
    and my twin.   25

26 I don't resemble my twin as much as I used to.   26

27 I appreciate the perceptions my parents had about being a twin.   27

28 I have a competitive relationship with my twin.   28

PAPER 5

Speaking (19 minutes)

You can listen to extracts from a model Speaking Test on the first of the three cassettes that accompany CPE Practice Tests Plus.

Tip Strip

Part 1
Remember:
• Try to have a normal conversation.
• Answer the examiner's questions.
• Be spontaneous, make what you say interesting.

PART 1 (3 minutes)

Answer these questions:
• What do you do? Tell us about your work or studies.
• Do you live near here? Tell us about your daily journey to work/school/college.
• What are your plans for the immediate future?

PART 2 (4 minutes)

Turn to pictures A–F on pages 162–3 which show things which influence young people.

First look at Picture A only and discuss together what the relationship between these two people might be and what might have happened before this picture was taken. You have one minute for this.

Now look at all the pictures. These pictures all suggest different ways in which young people are influenced by the world around them. Talk together about whether each picture suggests a positive or a negative influence and then decide which represents the strongest influence of all. You have about three minutes for this.

PART 3 (12 minutes)

Candidate A: Look at the question in the box. You have two minutes to say what you think about the question. There are some ideas to use in the box if you like.

> What influence does the broadcast media have on our lives? *enormous*
> • increasing number of channels *little choice*
> • coverage of world news
> • entertainment and celebrities

Candidate B: Is there anything you would like to add?

Candidate B: Look at the question in the box. You have two minutes to say what you think about the question. There are some ideas to use in the box if you like.

> How has the world changed as a result of the Internet?
> • access to information *phycological*
> • communications via e-mail
> • on-line shopping

Candidate A: Is there anything you would like to add?

Candidates A and B: Now answer these questions about communications in general.
• Do people spend too much time looking at screens these days?
• Do you think people will still read books in the future?

TEST 2

Reading (1 hour 30 minutes)

For questions **1–18**, read the three texts below and decide which answer (**A, B, C** or **D**) best fits each gap. Mark your answers **on the separate answer sheet**.

Tip Strip

Remember:
• Read the whole passage first.
• The word must fit the meaning of the whole passage.
• Read through to check once you've finished.

Question 2: Which word completes the fixed expression?

Debut Goal

No matter how serious the sporting event, once an animal becomes involved, it will almost certainly steal the (**1**) ..... . In November 1985, a football match between Newcastle Town and Chell Heath (**2**) ..... an unexpected turn after a terrier dog called Susie decided to make a contribution to the game.

Newcastle Town were leading 1–0. A Chell Heath player was (**3**) ..... a great chance of equalising, with only the goalkeeper standing between him and the goal, but the shot went wide. At that moment, Susie the dog came sprinting up the pitch, leaped up and headed the ball past the goalkeeper and neatly into the net. To the amazement of the crowd and (**4**) ..... disbelief of the Newcastle players, the referee awarded a goal.

Fortunately, Newcastle Town went on to win by three goals to two, as (**5**) ..... speaking the goal shouldn't have been allowed. Sadly, before local football scouts had a chance to (**6**) ..... her up and turn her into a star, Susie had disappeared back into the crowd, never to be seen at the stadium again.

1	**A**	highlight	**B**	limelight	**C**	footlight	**D** spotlight
2	**A**	took	**B**	made	**C**	got	**D** gave
3	**A**	out for	**B**	up against	**C**	away on	**D** in with
4	**A**	entire	**B**	whole	**C**	utter	**D** full
5	**A**	truly	**B**	rightly	**C**	precisely	**D** strictly
6	**A**	sign	**B**	enroll	**C**	join	**D** enlist

Dance for your Health

Does the thought of going jogging or joining a gym fill you with dread? If so, the answer maybe to give partner dancing a (**7**) ..... . It's good fun, healthy and can also boost your social life. Dance provides a good aerobic workout. It helps tone the muscles, whilst at the same time, improving balance, (**8**) ..... and co-ordination. What's more, because you can easily go at your own (**9**) ....., it's suitable for all ages and fitness levels. Learning new steps and keeping to time tends to be fairly (**10**) ....., so dancing is usually more effective in (**11**) ..... your mind off the cares of the day than other forms of repetitive exercise. As with all exercise, dance promotes the release of endorphins — natural chemicals that help (**12**) ..... your mood, so you come away not only fitter, but also happier for the experience.

7	**A**	shot	**B**	try	**C**	test	**D** stab
8	**A**	bearing	**B**	stance	**C**	posture	**D** standing
9	**A**	trot	**B**	pace	**C**	stride	**D** rate
10	**A**	concentrating	**B**	overwhelming	**C**	absorbing	**D** consuming
11	**A**	pulling	**B**	fetching	**C**	holding	**D** taking
12	**A**	inspire	**B**	enhance	**C**	raise	**D** foster

Stuck on You

What's the most important piece of office equipment of modern times? Not the PC, nor even the Internet or e-mail, and it certainly doesn't have a microchip (**13**) ..... anywhere within it. So what can it be? Well, it's likely to be canary yellow and the chances are that you find it indispensable. You may have several, most likely all over your computer monitor at work, plus a few at home, loitering by the phone. It's the Post-It Note, transcending office hierarchies — proving essential to busy boss and humble clerk (**14**) ..... — and prompting riots when the stationery cupboard runs (**15**) ..... .

In an age of high-tech desk managers, its enduring popularity perhaps reflects a (**16**) ..... of stubborn eccentricity in many office workers. After all, you have a choice: you can put your reminder into a complicated computer programme that will (**17**) ..... you with bleeps and on-screen fireworks should you forget it, or you can scribble it on a bit of paper and stick it on your desk, gradually making your grey workstation (**18**) ..... a field of sunflowers.

13	**A**	endowed	**B**	embedded	**C**	encircled	**D**	entrenched
14	**A**	alike	**B**	akin	**C**	aside	**D**	alone
15	**A**	empty	**B**	down	**C**	low	**D**	through
16	**A**	stroke	**B**	smack	**C**	streak	**D**	strain
17	**A**	caution	**B**	signal	**C**	alert	**D**	warn
18	**A**	recollect	**B**	reminisce	**C**	remind	**D**	resemble

You are going to read four extracts which are all concerned in some way with noise. For questions **19–26**, choose the answer (**A, B, C** or **D**) which you think fits best according to the text. Mark your answers **on the separate answer sheet.**

A Family Affair

Our little boy Sam goes to play at the next-door farm, and sometimes we collect him at the end of the meal. Whatever the weather, and however far from the farmhouse they are working, our neighbours come home at midday to their dinner and sit down at the family table. The meal is hot, exhibiting the staple diet of the English — roast meat, root vegetables, potatoes in gravy, and afterwards a fruit pie. If the children are home, they too participate, as do grandparents, siblings, nieces and nephews.

These meals are remarkable for their silence, which is a peculiar contented, sociable
8 silence, quite distinct from the silence of the lone commuter eating pizza on the train. It is laid like a cloth across the table, and provides a soft, clean background to the gentle sound of eating. Above this silence, the members of the family communicate in wordless ways — helping the children to food, passing the ketchup, grunting and nodding when the pudding appears. This speechless conversation includes the newborn and the senile, and binds the whole family in a web of mutual dependence. Isolation is overcome, and anxiety stifled in the small, including gestures of the table.

19 Why does the writer mention the commuter eating pizza (line 8)?

    A to show that it's not unusual to eat in silence

    B to underline the formality of his neighbours' meals

    C to emphasise that his neighbours choose to eat in silence

    D to show how traditions are adapted to suit the modern world

20 The writer describes his neighbours' meal to show that silence can be

    A entertaining.

    B reassuring.

    C inhibiting.

    D embarrassing.

A SPECIES THAT I WANTED TO KILL

I like to watch animals, especially rare animals in Africa. But such animals don't like loud noises. They are unanimous about it. They don't, for instance, like noisy electronic games played by adolescent boys. The scowling blond teenager with a severe haircut – let's call him Bart – glowered at me in the cool confines of the observation hut by the waterhole in the Hwange National Park. A lilac-breasted bird alighted momentarily at the water's edge, but was gone as a beeping and a deft flicking of thumbs signalled that Bart had trebled his score. In half an hour in the hide, I'd glimpsed impala, warthogs, even a giraffe, but Bart's device had seen them all off. We couldn't go on like this, it was ridiculous.

Bart was beginning to sense something from my body language. With barely contained menace, I hissed, 'What's the game?' 'I don't know, it's one of my sister's,' he volunteered breezily. Now with trembling self-control. I rehearsed with Bart the reasons in favour of ceasing to play with the Gameboy and actually watching the wildlife. Ripping open the Velcro fastener on his binocular case, a sound amplified by the acoustics of our wooden hut to a dull roar, Bart instantly complied. But by then, all there was to be seen were hoof prints in the mud.

21 Which word in the text is used to emphasise an indifference to the atmosphere in the hut?

   A 'scowling' (line 6)
   B 'glowered' (line 8)
   C 'deft' (line 13)
   D 'breezily' (line 23)

22 From the last paragraph, we understand that Bart

   A resented the writer's comments.
   B ignored the writer's advice.
   C attempted to follow the writer's example.
   D continued trying to annoy the writer.

Can't Stand the Music

Breaking point came about eight minutes into my regular evening session on the rowing machine. It was impossible to go on — but it wasn't my arms or legs that were hurting. The problem was the music. It began with a giant Black & Decker drill and ended with rapid machine-gun fire. It was probably the most superb techno-funk but it was driving me crazy.

'Any chance of changing the music?' I asked a gym instructor.

'Don't you like it?' she said. 'What would you prefer?'

Anything rather than this. Or nothing. 'Well,' I said, 'how about Van Morrison or Dire Straits?'

10   She looked witheringly at me and explained that the music policy was under review. A few weeks later, the results were announced. 'I'm sure you would agree that the new policy will provide a wider choice of music to listen to while working out,' said a note posted on the message board. 'A mixture of middle-of-the-road, pop and dance music will be played on random mode. From 6pm, more upbeat music will be selected with an increase in volume to compensate for a busier gym.'

And so it is. I've thought about asking if some equipment can be installed in the changing rooms, where I notice that laid back Van Morrison still rules supreme and no one ever complains.

23   What does the word 'witheringly' (line 10) tell us about the gym instructor?

   A   She had little respect for the writer's taste in music.
   B   She had never heard of the music the writer suggested.
   C   She had little interest in the writer's opinion of the music.
   D   She had some sympathy with the writer's reaction to the music.

24   In future, the music played in the gym at the time the writer attends will

   A   mostly be of the type he approves of.
   B   follow no particular style or pattern.
   C   reflect the intensity with which the facilities are used.
   D   be varied in accordance with the taste of its clients.

Tip Strip

Question 26: The writer talks about 'affected self-indulgence'. Which option matches this idea?

What Price Peace & Quiet?

The relatively soundless space —beyond significant road, rail, air and mining noise — where the British picnic and play and do all things green and pleasant has shrunk from 91,000 sq km in the 1960s to 73,000 sq km today. What's more, National Noise Action Day organised by a coalition of pressure groups, recently highlighted such varied stealers of silence as in-car stereos, mobile telephones and talking household appliances as things which are driving up the decibels. In town, we're even stealing it from ourselves. One recent report recorded sound levels in London restaurants which came close to the legal limits set for noise levels in the workplace.

As life gets louder, so silence becomes a commodity. Clever designers and marketers have already begun to package what was once naturally freely available. To the traditional double glazing and thick curtaining that keep external noise at bay, are now added silent washing machines and other appliances designed to keep the peace within. Other products, ostensibly designed to prevent us polluting the aural comfort zone of our neighbours, to me smack more of affected self-indulgence. One company, for example, has just added the eerily silent cello to its range of silent musical instruments; silent, that is, to everyone except the headphone-clad player.

25 In the first paragraph, the writer is

    A providing evidence in support of a proposal.

    B reporting on the effects of a day of protest.

    C apportioning blame for unrecognised problems.

    D drawing attention to a disturbing national trend.

26 The writer regards the range of silent musical instruments as

    A somewhat pretentious.

    B unnecessarily discreet.

    C completely ridiculous.

    D vaguely sinister.

A Matter of Trust

Behaviour, such as reciprocity and co-operation is not bred in the bone. Rather, it responds to incentives and experience

How much do you trust your business partners, and how much do they trust you? Even in rules-based, litigious societies, some measure of trust is essential. Contracts cannot plan for every eventuality, and outcomes are often hard to verify anyway. The issue is that much more pressing in emerging economies, whose threadbare legal systems and poor enforcement offer little assurance to investors.

27

Kenneth Clark of the University of Manchester and Martin Sefton of the University of Nottingham examine the first of these motivations in a recent paper. By having subjects play a series of simple games, the academics measured levels of trust and trustworthiness among strangers at their first encounter, and then recorded how the levels of trust changed over time.

28

There are four possible outcomes, depending on the player's actions. Should the first player to be interrogated confess, whilst the second does not, then the first is released and the second gets 20 years (or vice versa). Should both confess, then both get ten years. Should neither confess, both get two years.

29

Using money as a payoff rather than prison sentences as a threat, Messrs Clark and Sefton had student subjects play the game ten times. Players kept the same role (first or second mover) in each round, but were randomly paired with different, hidden partners.

30

The levels of mutual distrust had ratcheted up in the intervening play. This evidence belies the idea that any given person is, by nature, consistently trustful or mistrustful. The authors refined their results in two ways. They doubled the payoffs across all outcomes, and they offered far greater reward for a solitary confessor.

31

Despite the evidence that trust responds to incentives, certain situations foster trust more than others. In another game of trust, Edward Glaser of Harvard University and his collaborators paired off players, some of whom knew each other in real life. In this game, the first player received a small sum of money, of which he could give any part to the second player, hidden from view.

32

Sadly for those with a high regard for human nature, the first players sent an average of $12.41 to their partners, who returned an average of 45% of the doubled sum. First movers who declared before the game that they trusted strangers sent $2.21 more across, other things being equal, than counterparts who remembered their mother's advice on the subject.

33

Together, the studies argue that trust is shaped by experience not native personal traits. It also seems that trust is a fragile thing, prone to break down altogether. The lesson? A handshake is no substitute for ready money, or a hard-earned reputation.

Tip Strip

Remember:
• Read the whole text first.
• Read the text around each gap carefully.
• Read each of the paragraphs carefully.
• Underline references in both text and options.

Question 33: Which option talks about one of two groups of participants in an experiment?

A During initial rounds, the first mover began by trusting (not confessing) 57% of the time. In 35% of those cases the second mover followed suit, thus obtaining the trusting outcome. By the tenth round, however, only 32% of first movers were still trusting.

B The existence of a previous acquaintance also affected behaviour: both the amount initially sent, and the percentage returned by the second player, rose in proportion to the length of time the players had known each other.

C The statistics show that respondents who had recently suffered a personal setback also reported lower levels of trust. This suggests that when people revise their expectations of fellow humans, it may sometimes be for apparently irrelevant reasons.

D Simply raising the stakes had no effect. But in the second case, where the cost of trust was increased, the frequency of the trusting outcome fell substantially. Again the idea that some people are inherently trusting while others are not, appears ill-founded.

E Intuitively, at least two sets of factors are significant. For one, trust could serve as a signal of goodwill, either to secure initial co-operation or to ensure the success of a long-term relationship. On the other hand, the origins of trust might be simpler: some people might just feel good about trusting others.

F If the amount transmitted was $15, for example, this was doubled by the researchers, and the second player then sent any part he wished of the new amount back to the first player. Here, the trusting outcome is for the first player to send all $15 to the second. Then, provided that the second player is worthy of the first's trust, both can walk away with $15.

G The format each time was the 'sequential prisoner's dilemma' known more briefly as SPD, which imagines two prisoners being held separately for interrogation on their parts in an alleged crime.

H In this game, the greatest mutual trust is shown when the first player refuses to confess and the second one does the same. True, the second player might well be inclined to confess and so get off scot-free. But if the game is played several times, maintaining trust gives the best overall outcome.

The New Housekeeper

She liked to come downstairs early. She would even get up in the dark, bumping into things before she found her balance. She liked to come down, and sit, and listen to the house after her own footsteps had died away, and to the sound of the stove on which she had brewed a pot of tea. Then, she would sit and wrinkle her nose at the smell of kerosene, while she thawed out, if it were winter, or relaxed in summer after the weight of the heavy nights. Later she would start to walk about touching things. Sometimes she would move them: a goblet or a footstool. Or she would draw a curtain, cunningly, to look out at the spectacle of the morning, when all that is most dense becomes most transparent, and the world is dependent on the eye of the beholder.

She was at her best early in the morning. Except on
16 this one. She jerked the curtain. And it tore uglily. A long
17 tongue of gold brocade. But she did not stay to consider. It was the morning before the arrival of the housekeeper at Xanadu.

'A housekeeper!' she said, feeling her knuckles to test
21 their infirmity, and finding they were, indeed, infirm.

A housekeeper though was less formidable than a person and this was what Miss Hare dreaded most: an individual called Mrs Jolley, whose hips would assert themselves in navy blue, whose breathing would be heard, whose letters would lie upon the furniture addressed in the handwriting of daughters and nieces, telling of lives lived, unbelievably, in other places. It was frightening, frightening.

Naturally she found it impossible to like human beings, if only on account of their faces, to say nothing of their habit of relating things that had never happened and then believing that they had. Children were perhaps the worst, because they had not yet grown insincere, and insincerity does blunt the weapons of attack. Possible exceptions were those children who grew up in one's vicinity, almost without one's noticing, just being around; that was delicious, like air. Best of all Miss Hare liked those who never expected what they would not receive. She liked animals, birds and plants. On these she would expend her great but pitiable love, and because that was not expected it ceased to be pitiable.

'Ah, no, no, no!' she protested and whimpered in the cold early morning air.

And the house repeated it after her.

Mrs Jolley got off the bus at the post office. It could only have been Mrs Jolley, her black coat composed of innumerable panels — it appeared to be almost all seams — over what would reveal itself as the navy costume anticipated by Miss Hare. The hat was brighter, even daring, a blue blue. From the brim was suspended, more daring, if not actually reckless, a brief mauve eye-veil. She remained, however, the very picture of a lady, waiting for identification at the bus stop, but discreetly, but brightly, and grasping her brown port.

Oh dear then it must be done, Miss Hare admitted, and sighed.

Mrs Jolley was all the time looking and smiling, at some person in the abstract, in the rather stony street. At one corner of her mouth she had a dimple, and her teeth were modelled perfectly.

'Excuse me,' began Miss Hare at last, 'are you the person? Excuse me,' — and cleared her throat — 'are you expected at Xanadu?'

Mrs Jolley suppressed what could have been a slight upsurge of wind.

'Yes,' she said, very slowly, feeling her way. 'It was some such name, I think. A lady called Miss Hare.'

The latter felt tremendously presumptuous under Mrs Jolley's glance, and would have chosen to postpone her revelation.

But Mrs Jolley's white teeth — certainly no whiter had ever been seen — were growing visibly impatient. Her dimple came and went in flickers. Her expression, which might have been described as motherly by some, became suspect under the weight of its suspicion.

'I am Miss Hare,' said Miss Hare.

'Oh yes?' replied the disbelieving Mrs Jolley.

'Yes,' confirmed Miss Hare. 'I am she.'

'Mrs Jolly scarcely believed what she was hearing.

'I hope you will be happy,' continued the object, 'at Xanadu. It is a large house but we need only live in bits of it. Move around as we choose, for variety's sake.'

Mrs Jolley began to accompany her mentor over the stones, in shoes which she had purchased for the journey. Black. With a sensible strap. The sound of the two women's breathing would intermingle distressingly at times. Each wished she could have repudiated the connection. Miss Hare had grown tense, as if, at the back of her mind, there was something dreadful she could not remember.

They went on.

'We shall arrive soon now,' she encouraged.

Tip Strip

Remember:
• Read the text carefully.
• Underline key words in the question stem.
• Try to find the answer before you look at the options.

Question 39: Miss Hare says, 'Oh dear then it must be done.' What is her attitude?

34 Which of the following best describes Miss Hare's activities on waking?

   A romantic

   B habitual

   C secretive

   D reserved

35 Which word is used to reveal the uncharacteristic nature of Miss Hare's mood that morning?

   A 'jerked' (line 16)

   B 'tore' (line 16)

   C 'tongue' (line 17)

   D 'infirm' (line 21)

36 What thought does Miss Hare find 'frightening'?

   A the possibility that Mrs Jolley will have personal habits that she will find difficult to live with

   B the knowledge that she can no longer live in her home without the assistance of Mrs Jolley

   C the realisation that Mrs Jolley's life and relationships will inevitably intrude upon her own

   D the prospect of having to make new acquaintances as a result of her employment of Mrs Jolley

37 What is Miss Hare's opinion of children?

   A They are more convincing to listen to than adults.

   B They are tolerable if kept at a distance.

   C They indulge in make-believe more than adults.

   D They are innocent of adult crimes.

38 In describing Mrs Jolley's clothes, the writer's tone is

   A neutral.

   B mocking.

   C critical.

   D appreciative.

39 On deciding to present herself to Mrs Jolley at the bus stop, Miss Hare's attitude is one of

   A indifference.

   B defiance.

   C resignation.

   D self-importance.

40 As the two women walk towards the house, it is evident that

   A Mrs Jolley is not the typical housekeeper.

   B Miss Hare is concerned about the state of her house.

   C they feel more at ease with each other than they did at first.

   D they regret the circumstances that have brought them together.

PAPER 2 · Writing (2 hours)

You **must** answer this question. Write your answer in **300–350** words in an appropriate style.

---

1 You made the notes below while listening to a lecture on the subject of 'dress in the workplace'. Your course tutor has asked you to write an essay giving your personal views on these points and providing specific examples to support your views.

Dress in the Workplace

Historical perspective (global)
- Have attitudes changed?
- Where? To what extent?

A company/professional code (personal view)
- Is it desirable? In which jobs?
- Why? Why not?

Uniforms (local/home country)
- Are they necessary?
- For whom? Where?

Write your **essay.**

Write an answer to **one** of the questions **2–4** in this part. Write your answer in **300–350** words in an appropriate style.

2   You have a part-time job at a city centre music and book shop. In recent months, sales at the shop have fallen. The manager has asked staff to think of ways to reverse the situation and has expressed interest in receiving written suggestions. Write a proposal providing ideas on how to improve the physical appearance of the shop and the methods of advertising used. Suggest at least one new activity that might encourage more people to visit the store.

Write your **proposal**.

3   The owners of the company that you work for want to provide sports and leisure facilities for employees but have a limited amount of money to spend. Write a report stating which facilities would be most appropriate for your staff and suggesting an economical means by which these might operate.

Write your **report**.

4   You have recently heard about a plan to build a complex in your neighbourhood that will include a multi-screen cinema and nightclub. Some local residents are concerned about the impact this will have on the environment. You have decided to write a letter to the town planners outlining what these concerns might be. In your letter, suggest how some of the potential problems might be avoided and request at least one piece of relevant information.

Write your **letter**.

Tip Strip

Question 2
- A proposal that is written for an employer, or someone who is in a position of superiority to the writer, must have a formal style.
- It is often appropriate — as in this case — to divide a proposal into sections, which may or may not have headings.
- Note that recommendations are required for two areas: the shop's appearance and the advertising used. Also you need to recommend an activity to help promote the shop.
- Think of popular shops or retail outlets that you are familiar with; this may help you with ideas.
- Make sure that you use appropriate language for making recommendations and suggestions.

Question 3
- This report should be formal as it is being written for an employer.
- Note the areas that have to be covered in the report and the fact that they might easily be turned into headings. You can then end the report with the recommendation.

- Form ideas by thinking of courses that you have attended yourself.
- If you make negative comments you should explain why you are being critical (e.g. by drawing comparisons with other courses you have attended). A balanced view, with negative and positive comments, often reads better than a one-sided view.

Question 4
- An impersonal opening would be appropriate here; e.g.' To Whom it may Concern'. The style should be formal.
- Consider some realistic concerns that residents might have, such as parking, noise, etc.
- As you are also being asked to suggest solutions, a moderate, impartial tone would be appropriate here. This should be reflected in your choice of language for making proposals/ recommendations.
- Remember to ask for some information and ensure that this request relates to one of the points you have made.

PAPER 3

Use of English (1 hour 30 minutes)

For questions **1–15**, read the text below and think of the word which best fits each space. Use only **one** word in each space. There is an example at the beginning (**0**). Write your answers in **CAPITAL LETTERS on the separate answer sheet**.

Tip Strip

Remember:
• Read the text through first.
• Check the words around the gap carefully.
• Make sure your answer fits the sense of the whole text.
• Check your spelling.

Question 1: A modal verb is needed in this gap.
Question 14: Which word is needed to complete the linking expression?

Example:

0	I	N															

Science Fact and Science Fiction

When writers attempt to anticipate the future, they often only succeed (**0**) ...*in*.... providing an interpretation of the present. This (**1**) .... be seen in the fantasies produced by science fiction writers in the middle of the twentieth century. Almost nothing has turned (**2**) .... the way that these writers expected. Although they (**3**) .... manage to predict intelligent robots, they completely (**4**) .... to anticipate the developments in communications technology that would make them possible. This (**5**) .... that science fiction written before 1980 now seems absurdly dated, and what strikes you most (**6**) .... the curious absence of personal computers, e-mail and the Internet. Science fiction writers, it seems, were remarkably (**7**) .... on the uptake when (**8**) .... came to grasping the extent to (**9**) .... the nature of communications would change.

Instead, their focus was (**10**) .... much on rocket technology and space travel. For they (**11**) .... not to know that the lunar landings, so exciting at the time, would actually lead nowhere. There are no human colonies on the Moon, (**12**) .... alone on Mars and the idea that people might eventually populate the cosmos seems even (**13**) .... within the realms of possibility now than it did then, despite half a century of bewilderingly rapid technological progress. What's (**14**) .... , scientists have even begun to ridicule the notion, fundamental to much science fiction, that one day we just (**15**) .... encounter intelligent aliens.

For questions **16–25**, read the text below. Use the word given in **capitals** at the end of some of the lines to form a word that fits in the space in the same line. There is an example at the beginning **(0)**. Write your answers in **CAPITAL LETTERS on the separate answer sheet**.

Tip Strip

Remember:
• Read the text through first.
• Look at the whole sentence, not just the line with the gap.
• Is the word: singular/plural? positive/negative?
• Check your spelling.

Question 18: The new word needs both a prefix and a change of verb form.

Example:

0	A	S	S	O	C	I	A	T	I	O	N	S						

Meditation

People are often put off meditation by what they
see as its many mystical **(0)** _associations_ . Yet meditation is a   **ASSOCIATE**

(16) .... technique which merely involves sitting and resting   **STRAIGHT**

the mind. In addition to its **(17)** .... , meditation offers   **SIMPLE**

powerful help in the battle against stress. Hundreds of studies have

shown that meditation, when **(18)** .... in a principled way, can   **TAKE**

reduce hypertension which is related to stress in the body. Research has

proved that certain types of meditation can **(19)** .... decrease   **SUBSTANCE**

key stress symptoms such as anxiety and **(20)** .... In fact,   **IRRITABLE**

those who practise meditation with any **(21)** .... see their   **REGULAR**

doctors less and spend, on average, seventy per cent fewer days in

hospital. They are said to have more stamina, a happier

(22)................ and even enjoy better relationships.   **DISPOSE**

When you learn to meditate, your teacher will give you a personal

'mantra' or word which you use every time you practise the technique

and which is **(23)** .... chosen according to your needs. Initial   **SUPPOSE**

classes are taught individually but **(24)** .... classes usually   **SEQUENCE**

consist of a group of students and take place over a period of about

four days. The aim is to learn how to slip into a deeper state of

(25) .... for twenty minutes a day. The rewards speak for   **CONSCIOUS**

themselves.

Tip Strip

Remember:
• Read all three sentences.
• The word must fit all three gaps in the same form.
• Check your spelling.

Question 27: A simple verb is needed in these gaps. Which one?

For questions **26–31**, think of **one** word only which can be used appropriately in all three sentences. Here is an example **(0)**.

Example:

0   Last year's champion is in with a .... chance of repeating his success in the grand prix next weekend.

Some of the home owners are hoping to get compensation for the poor building work, and I think they have a very .... case.

There's no point in trying to put the tent up, the wind is far too ....

| 0 | S | T | R | O | N | G | | | | | | | | | | | | | |

Write **only** the missing word in **CAPITAL LETTERS on the separate answer sheet**.

26 • The politician insisted that she was addressing the audience in her .... as a mother and not as a Member of Parliament.

• The pop group were delighted to discover that they were playing in a hall that was filled to ....

• Since animals lack the .... for reproach, our relationships with them tend to cause us less concern than those with our fellow human beings.

27 • Helen rubbed her carpet as hard as she could but the stain still wouldn't .... out.

• I'm afraid people don't .... much meaner than my neighbour; she even re-uses her old tea bags!

• Matt has gone out this evening to try and forget how badly his presentation went, but in the cold light of day it'll .... back to haunt him.

28 • Everyone was surprised to discover that the young man was eligible to .... for president.

• The factory closure became such a contentious issue that even the national newspapers decided to .... a series of articles on it.

• The supervisor had to .... through the safety guidelines several times before she was convinced that all the staff had understood.

29 • There are many jobs that my sister could do but she seems unwilling to .... herself to anything.

• The varnish will not have a smooth finish if you .... it too liberally.

• I was attempting to complete the whole form until I realised that half the questions didn't .... to me.

30 • The children looked up to see their father entering the room .... gifts from foreign countries.

• Glancing in his rear-view mirror, the learner driver was horrified to see a large articulated lorry .... down on him.

• .... in mind everything you've told me, I think we should postpone our trip until later in the year.

31 • The toddler looked up pitifully at his mother, aware that he had not received a fair .... when the cake had been handed out.

• The manager informed his staff that despite the economic downturn, there was every reason to believe that the forthcoming .... would go ahead as planned.

• It's a sad fact that in every newspaper there's a good .... of material that you can flick through mindlessly.

PART 4

Tip Strip

Remember:
• Read both sentences carefully.
• Include all the information in the second sentence.
• Use no more than eight words.
• Contractions count as two words
• Check your spelling

Question 37: This answer includes the verb 'suggested'. What other changes are needed to allow this?

For questions **32–39**, complete the second sentence so that it has a similar meaning to the first sentence, using the word given. **Do not change the word given.** You must use between **three** and **eight** words, including the word given. Here is an example **(0)**.

Example:

0   Immediately after winning the race, Sandy began training for the next one.
   had
   No .... she began training for the next one.

0   sooner had Sandy won the race than

Write **only** the missing words **on the separate answer sheet**.

---

32   You may be dismissed if you fail to observe the company's dress code.
   result
   Failure to .... your dismissal.

33   It wasn't Melanie's fault that she ended up breaking the law.
   own
   Through .... ended up breaking the law.

34   The offer of a job will only be confirmed following a successful medical examination.
   completed
   Once .... , the offer of a job will be confirmed.

35   It is as yet unclear whether a new sports centre is being planned or not.
   seen
   It .... are any plans for a new sports centre or not.

36   Decisions about the exact contents of the college magazine will be left to the students.
   up
   It will .... what the exact contents of the college magazine will be.

37   The suggestion to increase the entrance fee at the disco came from Tony.
   should
   It was Tony .... increased at the disco.

38   One seldom has the opportunity to meet a famous celebrity.
   get
   Rarely .... meeting a famous celebrity.

39   Miranda is rumoured to be about to sign a new contract with the film studio.
   verge
   Rumour has .... signing a new contract with the film studio.

For questions **40–44**, read the following texts on writing novels. For questions **40–43**, answer with a word or short phrase. You do not need to write complete sentences. For question **44**, write a summary according to the instructions given. Write your answers to questions **40–44 on the separate answer sheet.**

Tip Strip

Remember:
• Keep your answers short but clear.
• Underline the key words in the summary task.
• Make sure you only include relevant information.
• Use your own words.
• Don't write too many words.
• Try to use linking expressions.
• Check your spelling, punctuation and grammar.

Question 40: Look at the time references in the first paragraph to answer this question.
Question 44: Remember to include only *practical* recommendations.

As the organiser of a national competition for unpublished novelists, I have come to realise that for most authors, the road to publication is usually a very long one. Overnight success is almost unheard of, and an author who seems to spring from nowhere, suddenly publishing a first novel which sells 500,000 copies, attracts rave reviews and wins literary awards, will more often than not have been working hard at his or her chosen craft for years.

So how can an unpublished novelist gain success? One approach is to ask yourself some hard questions, to which you may not like all the answers. First of all, are you enjoying writing your novel? Of course it is hard work, but this does not mean it cannot be fun. At the end of a writing day you might feel tired and drained, but you should also feel happy. If you are miserable and exhausted, you may be writing the
12 wrong sort of novel, and believe me it will show.

Ask yourself — is the novel I am working on a story I need to write? Am I possessed by the people in my work, and am I living their lives? If, at the end of a writing session, you need a few minutes to return to the reality of daily life, the answer is probably yes. But if you turn off the computer with a sigh of relief, and collapse in a heap on the sofa, you should probably be writing a different book.

40 State briefly in your own words, what message the writer is giving to unpublished novelists in the first paragraph.

....

41 Explain in your own words what the writer means by the phrase 'and believe me it will show' in line 12.

....

Only by an author getting inside a character's head can that character come alive on the page. To know something about psychology in general can be a great asset to a novelist. By focusing on a character's psychology, you determine their inner conflicts. You learn what makes them tick and why they act as they do.

Too many authors fail because their characters are too stereotyped or too one-dimensional. By the time we reach adulthood our attitudes and beliefs are coloured by our past experiences. This affects how we react to present and future events. Similarly, a character's history and past experiences will be reflected in how they deal with their present life and any crises they must face. This is true of everyone, even identical twins. Only by knowing a character's past can you bring them alive on the page and once you know about your character's psyche, you will know how they will react to future situations.

Do not be daunted by psychology or feel it is a complicated science. There are many books to read which make the subject easily accessible and fascinating. Some are best sellers and are invaluable to an author in
18 understanding how the mind works. Recommended easy reading: *I'm OK, You're OK* by Thomas A Harris, *Men are from Mars, Women are from Venus* by John Gray, and *Women who run with the wolves* by Clarissa Pinkola Estes.

42 Which **two** expressions used earlier in the passage introduce the idea of 'understanding how the mind works' (line 18)?

....

43 In your own words, explain the main point that is exemplified by the reference to identical twins in the second paragraph?

....

44 In a paragraph of between **50 and 70** words, summarise **in your own words as far as possible**, the practical recommendations put forward in the texts that are aimed directly at helping novelists to be more successful.

Listening (Approximately 40 minutes)

You will hear four different extracts. For questions **1–8**, choose the answer (**A, B** or **C**) which fits best according to what you hear. There are two questions for each extract.

Tip Strip

Remember:
- Read and listen to the rubric.
- Underline key words in the question stems.
- Listen for the overall message.

Question 5: The speaker says, 'It's my muse' about the river. Which option does this correspond to?

Extract One

You overhear two people, May and Peter, discussing a newspaper article.

1 What point do they agree on?

    A Living without jeans is hard to imagine.
    B Jeans are associated with a certain lifestyle.
    C It's surprising that jeans date back to the 1800s. \

                                                     1

2 When May comments on Peter's jeans he appears

    A indignant.
    B determined.
    C / apprehensive.

                                                     2

Extract Two

You hear someone introducing a radio programme about a type of tree called a monkey-puzzle tree.

3 What does the speaker suggest is most striking about the monkey-puzzle tree?

    A It has a variety of uses.
    B It has an unusual appearance.
    C It has nothing living on it.

                                                       3

4 What is the programme going to be about?

    A the threats to the tree's survival
    B the natural environment in which the tree grows
    C the importance of the tree to those living nearby

                                                       4

Extract Three

On the radio, you hear an artist talking.

5 What is she talking about when she mentions the river?

    A how she spends her non-working time
    B how she gets inspiration for her work
    C how she deals with problems in her work

5

6 In her work, the artists says that she tries to

    A paint places which are recognisable.
    B keep to one well-defined style.
    C respond to her changing surroundings.

6

Extract Four

You hear a young pop musician being interviewed on the radio.

7 How does he feel about having a famous father?

    A He appreciates there are some drawbacks to it.
    B He regrets not having succeeded on his own.
    C He doubts he will ever be as good as his father.

7

8 What does he say about his relationship with his father?

    A It is better than it used to be.
    B It is based on mutual admiration.
    C It has a positive effect on the band's performance.

8

You will hear a radio report about coral, a type of marine creature. For questions **9–17**, complete the sentences with a word or short phrase.

Tip Strip

Remember:
• Read and listen to the rubric.
• Read the sentences carefully. Think about the type of information that is missing.
• Write 1–3 words or a number.
• Write words you hear – don't try to paraphrase.
• Check that the word fits grammatically.

Question 9: You are listening for another adjective.
Question 17: What type of people could damage coral in the sea? Try to predict the answer.

The speaker describes British coral as both [*splendid* | **9**] and colourful.

The speaker notes with surprise that [*jellyfish* | **10**] are closely related to coral.

Members of the coral family defend themselves whilst [*tiny* | **11**] by firing poisonous threads.

What's called 'cup' coral is unusual because it does not live in a [*colony* | **12**]

The rarest type of cup coral is called the [*gold* | **13**] coral.

One type of soft coral gives underwater cliffs a [*w* | **14**] appearance.

The soft coral known as [*red finger* | **15**] is commonly found on the southwest coast.

Sea fans are described as resembling [*brushes* | **16**] because of the way they grow.

Sea fans are easily damaged by the actions of people such as [*souvenir hunter* | **17**] and fishermen.

PART 3

You will hear an interview with a man who for many years worked as a television newsreader. For questions **18–22**, choose the answer (**A, B, C** or **D**) which fits best according to what you hear.

Tip Strip

Remember:
• Read and listen to the rubric.
• Underline key words in the question stems.

Question 19: John mentions 'shuddering' in connection with 'glitches'. Which option matches this idea?

18 Why did John agree to extend his contract as a newsreader?

  A Audiences had asked to have him back.
  B Another channel was keen to appoint him.
  C He thought he'd miss being in the public eye.
  D His suggested replacement was unpopular.

      18

19 What does John say about the early days of newsreading?

  A News programmes occurred less frequently.
  B A news reader's job was more straightforward.
  C Audiences focused on style and presentation.
  D Mistakes were sometimes embarrassing.

      19

20 In John's view, competition between news programmes is something which

  A irritates the viewing public.
  B affects their outward appearance.
  C detracts from the quality of the content.
  D reinforces negative views about news programmes.

      20

21 In considering how opinions are formed, John points out that

  A reporters may present a biased view.
  B people sometimes misinterpret the facts.
  C there are pros and cons to watching the news.
  D television operates under certain constraints.

      21

22 John implies that he finds the general public's attitude towards the news

  A disheartening.
  B enlightening.
  C surprising.
  D appreciative.

      22

You will hear two people Georgia and Jack, talking about a business which their friend Amelia runs. For questions **23–28**, decide whether the opinions are expressed by only one of the speakers, or whether the speakers agree.

Write   **G**   for Georgia,

         J   for Jack,

or   **B**   for Both, when they agree.

23 To improve profits, Amelia needs to re-focus her efforts. | 23 |

24 Amelia is right to feel she has too much local competition. | 24 |

25 It's worth suggesting to Amelia that she updates some aspects of her business. | 25 |

26 Advice is best sought from experienced business people. | 26 |

27 Some irregularity in turnover is to be expected. | 27 |

28 Amelia is able to deal with the current challenge her business presents. | 28 |

PAPER 5

Speaking (19 minutes)

Tip Strip

Part 2:
Remember:
• Listen to the instructions carefully.
• Talk to your partner.
• Pick up on your partner's ideas.
• Agree and disagree.
• Have a natural conversation.

PART 1 (3 minutes)

Answer these questions:
• How long have you been studying English?
• How much do you like the area you live in? Are there any drawbacks to living there?
• Do you have any unfulfilled ambitions in life?

PART 2 (4 minutes)

Turn to pictures A–E on pages 164–5, which show various means of transport.

First look at Picture A only and discuss why you think this situation has arisen and how the people are feeling. You have about one minute for this.

Now look at all the pictures. An environmental organisation is publishing a book which will highlight the need for good public transport systems in the world's largest cities as a way of reducing pollution. These photographs have all been suggested for the front cover. Talk together about the environmental and practical issues raised by each of the photographs, and decide which would make the most appropriate cover for the book. You have about three minutes for this.

PART 3 (12 minutes)

Candidate A: Look at the question in the box. You have two minutes to say what you think about the question. There are some ideas to use in the box if you like.

> What role does music play in our lives?
> • social role of music
> • entertainment and relaxation
> • fashion and culture

Candidate B: Is there anything you would like to add?

Candidate B: Look at the question in the box. You have two minutes to say what you think about the question. There are some ideas to use in the box if you like.

> What role do museums have in modern society?
> • education
> • preservation
> • research

Candidate A: Is there anything you would like to add?

Candidates A and B: Now answer these questions about culture in general:
• How important is it to preserve the cultural differences between the world's peoples?
• Is the study of history relevant to the modern world?

TEST 3

PAPER 1

Reading (1 hour 30 minutes)

Tip:

Take no more than 20 minutes to do this part.

For questions **1–18**, read the three texts below and decide which answer (**A, B, C** or **D**) best fits each gap. Mark your answers **on the separate answer sheet**.

In Praise of Face to Face Communication

Homo sapiens is a communicative creature and in our ordinary life, if we want something, we tend to communicate automatically and directly in order to obtain it. As a species, we have developed very sophisticated methods by which we can communicate with (**1**) ..... ever-increasing ease. Unfortunately, it seems that sometimes we are so dazzled by the brilliance of the technology we have at our (**2**) ..... that we overlook the fact that the simplest, and often the most effective, means of communication is talking face-to-face to our target audience. (**3**) ....., very often the more sophisticated the means of communication, the less effectively the message itself may be (**4**) ..... . After all, if we are face to face with a person, we can use body language to emphasise our (**5**) ....., and check that we have been interpreted correctly. This is a far more effective way of communicating than using the underlining of words in a memo or (**6**) ..... type in a report.

1 A	efficiently	**B**	actually	**C**	apparently	**D**	eventually
2 A	request	**B**	availability	**C**	convenience	**D**	disposal
3 A	Indeed	**B**	Otherwise	**C**	Conversely	**D**	Nonetheless
4 A	imparted	**B**	inscribed	**C**	intoned	**D**	imposed
5 A	aspects	**B**	points	**C**	issues	**D**	positions
6 A	dark	**B**	bold	**C**	strong	**D**	heavy

Home Security

Home: it's one of the most emotive words in any language. The place itself has (**7**) ..... people with privacy and security ever since individual dwellings first appeared nearly two million years ago. But nowadays, that sense of security has a twist. (**8**) ..... safe people feel at home, when they are away, they worry their home will be broken into. What's more, this fear is far from (**9**) ..... . In spite of falling burglary rates in the UK, a recent survey found that a house left unoccupied for a month a year is 43 per cent more likely to be burgled than an identical one that is never empty at night. Having someone (**10**) ..... during the day is no (**11**) ..... either: about 55 per cent of domestic burglaries happen between 6pm and 6am. At the same time, people are spending longer away, on business and on holiday. Many are, therefore, prepared to (**12**) ..... a little privacy, employing professional housesitters to live in their homes in their absence.

7 A	produced	**B**	offered	**C**	provided	**D**	donated
8 A	Regardless	**B**	Nonetheless	**C**	However	**D**	Albeit
9 A	groundless	**B**	aimless	**C**	faultless	**D**	clueless
10 A	look over	**B**	check out	**C**	call on	**D**	pop in
11 A	restraint	**B**	deterrent	**C**	hindrance	**D**	impediment
12 A	withhold	**B**	sacrifice	**C**	deny	**D**	refrain

Ballet Shoes

When they are new, ballet shoes are interchangeable until the dancer (**13**) ..... them in and decides which shoe goes best on which foot. In fact, ballet shoes are best when they are old and professional dancers are (**14**) ..... to breaking their shoes down by any means, even hitting them with a hammer, until they reach a comfortable (**15**) ..... of pliancy.

There are soft ballet shoes and point shoes. Soft shoes are (**16**) ..... worn by male dancers. Made of leather and lined with canvas, the under sole is much smaller than the sole of the foot. In this (**17**) ....., the dancer's toes and part of his heel stand on the soft upper leather. In point shoes, the toe is (**18**) ..... with an extra layer of canvas, hardened with paste, to provide a little flat area for the dancer to balance on.

13	**A**	smoothes	**B**	wears	**C**	bends	**D**	forms
14	**A**	accustomed	**B**	familiar	**C**	known	**D**	adjusted
15	**A**	grade	**B**	scale	**C**	degree	**D**	extent
16	**A**	significantly	**B**	vitally	**C**	appreciably	**D**	essentially
17	**A**	respect	**B**	means	**C**	fashion	**D**	way
18	**A**	reinforced	**B**	augmented	**C**	replenished	**D**	aided

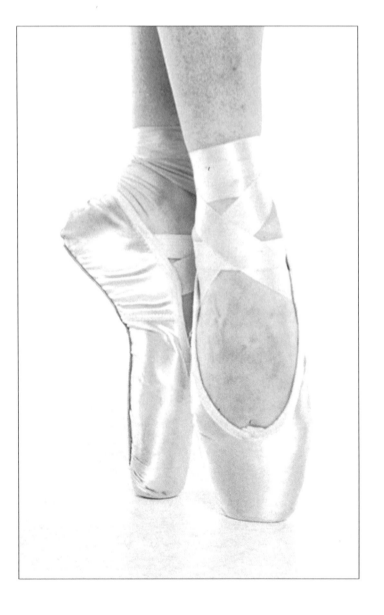

PART 2

Tip:
Take no more
than 20 minutes
to do this part.

You are going to read four extracts which are all concerned in some way with primates. For questions **19–26**, choose the answer (**A, B, C** or **D**) which you think fits best according to the text. Mark your answers **on the separate answer sheet.**

F a n a n a

We had set off that morning from the shores of Lake Tanganyika, climbing up into Tanzania's Mahale Mountains National Park. After less than an hour, the high-pitched hoots of distant chimpanzees brought smiles to our faces. We were walking through beautiful dry deciduous forest, a tangle of vines, palms, creepers and trunks snake-patterned by lichens.

Suddenly, a scream fled from the forest, followed quickly by a chorus of hoots from both the ground and up in the trees. Branches cracked and whipped and leaves rattled as two black shapes hurtled through the foliage. In front, the smaller figure squealed in panic while the larger animal behind became increasingly agitated. For a few moments they disappeared into the undergrowth. Amid a crescendo of shrieks the bigger chimpanzee emerged, swaggering like a triumphant gunslinger out of a western saloon. He moved arrogantly towards the path, his frenzy growing, his black hair standing on end. As he came, he first slapped and then swung powerfully on the trunks of the trees on other side as if taking part in some eccentric country dance.
15 Then, point made, his temper subsided and he went back to feeding with the rest of his group. But Fanana, the alpha male, left none of us in any doubt as to who was the boss.

19 The words 'point made' in line 15 refer to Fanana's

    A competitive nature.

    B assertion of authority.

    C dislike of being observed.

    D display of anger.

20 How does the writer help us to visualise Fanana's behaviour?

    A by describing how other animals reacted to it

    B by discussing her own feelings about it

    C by describing changes in the animal's physical appearance

    D by drawing parallels with comparable human behaviour

The Ape & the Sushi Master:
Cultural Reflections
of a Primatologist

By Frans de Waal

There must be a hundred books comparing ape and human behaviour, so why read this one? Hasn't it all been said? Thankfully, no. This book needs to be read for at least three reasons: the unusual viewpoint of the author, the timely content and the fact that it is almost three books in one. A Dutch primatologist, Frans de Waal has decades of experience with the behaviour of our nearest relations in captivity. He spans divides: Europe-America, field-laboratory, monkey-ape, chimpanzee-bonobo. He is the author of five books, counting this one, and each has been better crafted than the last. From *Chimpanzee Politics* (1982) onward, de Waal has been holding our primate cousins up for us to view.

Targeted at the educated layperson, the three themes of *The Ape and the Sushi Master* are how we see other animals, the nature of culture, and how we see ourselves. Each theme occupies a third of the book. The first of the book's 11 chapters is a masterful prologue. Other chapters range from autobiographical musings, to natural history essays, to elegant treatises on topics such as morality, technology and teaching.

In checking the website of one online bookseller, I found De Waal's book listed among the cookbooks. This is understandable, given the title (which alludes to the fact that the skill of making sushi is acquired through observation rather than formal instruction), but do not be misled. It is an intellectual feast!

21 What does the reviewer say about de Waal in this extract?

   A He writes in an objective style.

   B He favours a broad approach to the subject.

   C He is increasingly admiring of his subject matter.

   D He is keen to build on the theories of other scientists.

22 What does the reviewer say about de Waal's book?

   A It can be read without specialist knowledge.

   B It is every bit as good as his other books.

   C The style is consistent throughout the book.

   D The title accurately reflects the content.

Too Much Monkey Business

Over a three-year period in the mid-fifties, Dr Desmond Morris, a famous anthropologist, supervised a chimpanzee named Congo in the production of several hundred 'monkey paintings'. A small exhibition of these paintings proved an unexpected success but there was also some negative criticism from those who scorned the aesthetic worth of the end product.

In his publication *Monkey Paintings,* Thierry Lenain says that Morris's rotations of paint and paper raise the question of who decided when a given stage was finished, or when the painting as a whole was complete. 'Nothing could interrupt him (Congo) until he was satisfied with the balance of his painting, 'averred Morris. But Lenain says that 'Congo enjoyed covering a shape that he had just produced with "savage" brushstrokes; the best examples of circles produced by him were saved by removing the paper before he had completely finished.'

The question of a conscious finishing point is vital. With human activity, there is always the before, during and after of conception, execution and assessment. 'Action painting' is an attempt to elide the distinction between conception and execution — but consciously so and, therefore, vainly. With the monkey painter, however, there is only execution. This is not to say that monkeys may not be stimulated by the act of painting but to liken this to the 'joy of creation' is to abort the meaning of creation and parody that of joy.

23 In the second paragraph, the writer is questioning

- **A** the definition of the term 'painting'.
- **B** the human influence on Congo's paintings.
- **C** the honesty of those supervising Congo's painting.
- **D** the similarity of Congo's brushwork to that of humans.

24 According to the writer, chimpanzees cannot be classified as 'action painters' because they

- **A** fail to appreciate their own work.
- **B** cannot be seen to finish a painting.
- **C** do not think about what they paint.
- **D** lack the necessary artistic skill.

THE CULTURE CLUB

Scientists have been investigating chimpanzees for several decades, but too often their studies contained a crucial flaw. Most attempts to document cultural diversity among groups of chimpanzees have relied solely on officially published accounts of the behaviours recorded at each research site. But this approach probably overlooks a good deal of cultural variation.

For example, scientists don't typically publish an extensive list of all the activities they do *not* see at a particular location. Second, many reports describe chimpanzee behaviours without saying how common they are. Finally, researchers' descriptions of potentially significant chimpanzee behaviours frequently lack sufficient detail, making it difficult for scientists working at other sites to record the presence or absence of the activities.

To remedy these problems, we asked field researchers at each site for a list of all the behaviours they suspected were local traditions. With this information, we pulled together a list of 65 candidates for cultural behaviours. Then we distributed our list to the team leaders at each site. In consultation with their colleagues, they classified each behaviour in terms of its occurrence or absence in the chimpanzee community studied.

The extensive survey turned up no fewer than 39 chimpanzee patterns of behaviours that should be labelled as cultural variations, including numerous forms of tool use.

25 In these paragraphs, the writer is

   A rejecting research findings.
   B itemising research subjects.
   C providing a rationale for research.
   D detailing the conclusions to research.

26 What was the unique feature of the writer's research project?

   A its intensive approach
   B its impartial focus
   C its short-term objective
   D its comprehensive nature

You are going to read a newspaper article about happiness. Seven paragraphs have been removed from the extract. Choose from the paragraphs **A–H** the one which fits each gap (**27–33**). There is one extra paragraph which you do not need to use. Mark your answers **on the separate answer sheet.**

Happy as your genes allow

The true key to happiness, says researcher David Lykken, lies in our genes. To many of us, this notion might seem absurd. Humans seem to be on an emotional roller coaster, the ups and downs of which often appear to be determined by fate. We feel good when we win an award or make a new friend; bad when we have to face one of life's inevitable setbacks.

27

Lykken's interest in happiness was sparked by his earlier research into its possible determinants. Scientists have tried for years to identify a link between contentment and marital status, socioeconomic position, professional success and other factors. Yet they invariably come up empty handed. 'I was intrigued by the way that things like beauty, wealth and status never seemed to make much difference,' says Lykken, a semi-retired professor at the university of Minnesota.

28

As part of the comprehensive research on the siblings, Lykken had asked his subjects a range of questions about how happy they felt. He decided to revisit those studies to see if he could establish a genetic connection. The results, says Lykken, were surprising. He found a very high correlation between happiness and genes as revealed by the similarities in the twins' responses to questions, irrespective of whether they had been raised together or apart.

29

Nine years on, therefore, he decided to ask the same subjects the same questions. The evidence Lykken found suggested that their contentment was 90 per cent genetic. Both a twin's previous responses and those made almost a decade later enabled the answers of the other twin to be predicted with a high level of accuracy. Lykken's first reaction was to label the pursuit of happiness as a futile exercise.

30

In his own life, Lykken concentrates on completing small tasks that give him a great deal of satisfaction. 'I've just spent the morning writing, which is something I like and that I'm pretty good at,' he says. 'This afternoon, I'll bake some loaves of bread, because I need that for my morning toast. I just discovered that the American Psychological Association wants to give me an award, and that makes me feel good, but maybe not as good as that daily baking.'

31

The demeanour of those we live with is another vital factor. Teenagers with happy parents tend to be happy themselves. It's not until they leave home that they find their own set point. Likewise, a husband or wife's inner contentment has a large bearing on that of their spouse. Marrying an upbeat person is probably the best mood enhancer around.

32

In the science fiction work *Brave New World*, for example, people who took 'happy pills' were incapable of seeing life as it truly was. Fans of Woody Allen, the perpetually depressed actor and film maker, will remember the scene in the film *Annie Hall* in which he asks a strolling couple why they are so happy. 'Because we are so shallow and mindless,' they reply.

33

Lykken is sceptical. 'Even if you can speak their language, they might not have the same psychological vocabulary for expressing how they feel at any given moment,' he says. Lykken refuses to believe that there is any correlation between the state of a society's technical or intellectual development and personal happiness. In fact, he argues that good humour is probably favoured by evolution. 'The gloomiest probably don't do very well in the romance stakes,' he theorises. 'So, as a human race, we're probably getting slightly happier over time.'

A 'Then I began to ask myself whether those findings may have been influenced by how people were feeling on a certain day — if they had just cut themselves, for example, or had trouble finding a parking space,' he says.

B Lykken also advocates control of anger as another regular way of boosting happiness quotients. 'People would rather feel anger than feel scared,' he says. 'When we are angry we feel strong, but in the long run, I believe it's more harmful to happiness than anything else.'

C The surest way to do this, Lykken believes, is to lose sight of our purpose in life. He described the case of a Californian firefighter — the patient of a friend — who recently retired from the service and quickly became depressed. His mood picked up quickly when he discovered that many widows in the neighbourhood needed to have things fixed round the house.

D Some philosophers question whether humans should actually be seeking such happiness inducing arrangements in the first place. Joy is sometimes associated with ignorance, they argue, causing happy people to 'see the world through rose-tinted glasses'.

E According to Lykken, however, each person possesses a 'happiness set point' — the level of contentment to which we return after the impact of such specific events is absorbed. While humans teeter wildly around that point during their lives, experiencing moments of extreme elation or depression, in the long run they gravitate back to their pre-set happiness level.

F 'I said at the time that trying to be happier might be the same as trying to be taller,' he recalls, but he no longer views his research in that light. While the individual's sense of well-being might be 90 per cent predetermined, people still have substantial leeway to control their emotions. Lykken believes humans can — and should — aim to achieve happiness slightly above their pre-set level.

G In the late 1990s, the psychologist realised that he might be able to shed some further light on the subject. 'That was a happy moment,' he jokes. Over a long period of time, Lykken had been following the progress of 300 pairs of identical twins. Identical twins help scientists differentiate between the effects of the environment and heredity. Because twins' genetic make-up is the same, small differences between them argue in favour of heredity. Large divergencies point to the environment as the greater determining factor.

H Some people would rule out even this possibility, insisting that happiness is inconsistent with modern times. Contemporary lives are so stressful, they say, that joy becomes elusive. Primitive tribes are better off. We should all feel nostalgic for 'simpler' times when we felt content with so much less.

PART 4

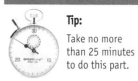

Tip:
Take no more
than 25 minutes
to do this part.

You are going to read an essay on the subject of intellectual property. For questions **34–40** choose the answer (**A, B, C** or **D**) which you think fits best according to the text. Mark your answers **on the separate answer sheet.**

The Sound of Silence

Twenty people — specialists, experts, thinkers — sit around a seminar table. They might be discussing education, the stock market or one of a whole range of issues. Although people are speaking, no one is saying anything. At least half of the participants have an original idea at the front of their mind. But they do not share it because it is too valuable. They are afraid that one of the others will steal the idea and use it, publish it or sell it before they do. Their intellectual property is at risk.

Images of the so-called 'new economy', that much talked about product of the 'age of information' are of
13 complexity and hubbub. You get the sense that it is a noisy place. In fact, however, such is the fear of being
15 intellectually gazumped that people who you might think of as being in the driving seat of that new economy are becoming rather cagey, and as a result, it echoes to the
18 sound of silence as received wisdoms are recycled.

There has always been a reluctance to share new ideas in professions linked to the media, but it's a phenomenon that seems to be spreading, especially into the world of policy. It is finding its way into government departments and the 'think tanks', those groups of intellectuals and academics whose job it is to inform and inspire
25 government policy. On an individual level, hoarding and
26 hiding make good sense, but collectively it impoverishes conversation — potentially to the detriment of good policymaking.

This new intellectual coyness highlights the peculiar quality of information and ideas in a market economy. The essential problem is this: you cannot know the value of a piece of information, still less an original idea, unless you know what it is. But once gleaned, it cannot be returned to its originator intact. In other words, you cannot feel the quality of an idea before deciding whether to buy it or not. This means that ideas make bad commodities. Pricing, in the usual economic sense, is impossible because the value of the product is not physically captured — at least, not immediately.

This is why intellectual property lawyers are licking their lips, and why one academic has just taken out the first-ever patent on an idea. But legal and contractual approaches to the problem are of limited use. Many of the best ideas come out of a conversation between two people. Who, then, do they belong to? And the danger of legally based approaches is that they will make us more guarded, not less so.

On the face of it, the argument that we are becoming intellectual misers flies in the face of current developments. Isn't the Internet democratising knowledge? And what about the free software at the heart of cyberspace? Far from living in monastic silence, aren't we being bombarded with ideas and information?

Well, yes. But most of the information we receive is of limited value. How many people who have a truly innovative idea will broadcast it on the web? Some, but
57 not many. With so much guff all over the place, the value of an original idea is all the more worth guarding.

All this means that intellectual generosity is becoming rarer and much more precious. It also elevates the role of trust. If my colleague gives me an idea, and I pass that idea on, either in print or through conversation, it's critical that I 'tag' it as hers, rather than succumbing to the temptation to pass it off as my own. Such a system of tagging would mean that my colleague continues to reap the rewards of her intellectual labour, making her more willing to share her ideas with others in the future, and it would also mean that our conversations would be free of the fear of theft. In short, she will trust me, and vice versa, thus ensuring a free flow of information.

There are issues for employers here, too. When someone's ability to add value rests on their skill at coming up with ideas, how do managers ensure that they are working as hard as they should be? Maybe they are storing up the best stuff for the online consultancy they run from home. In most cases, the desire of workers to be recognised as talented, to win promotion and gain greater financial rewards is sufficient incentive, but managers need to ensure that good ideas are credited properly through tagging, to keep the best minds on board.

So if we want to encourage intellectual generosity, as well as fostering an atmosphere of co-operation rather than distrust, we need to tag ideas to the person they originally came from. So how about it? As John Knell puts it: do you dare to share?

34 According to the writer, the people in the meeting described in the first paragraph are

    A   lacking in original ideas to share.
    B   unnecessarily distrustful of their colleagues.
    C   overvaluing ideas which they regard as their own.
    D   too cautious for any worthwhile discussion to take place.

35 Which phrase, used later in the essay, refers to the behaviour of the people in the meeting?

    A   'complexity and hubbub' (line 13)
    B   'intellectually gazumped' (line 15)
    C   'received wisdoms' (line 18)
    D   'hoarding and hiding' (line 25–26)

36 In the third paragraph, the writer makes the point that

    A   good policies arise out of open discussion.
    B   government departments need to co-operate with each other.
    C   government policies need to be discussed in the media.
    D   economic principles should apply to policymaking.

37 Which reason does the writer give for not favouring a legal approach to the problem of intellectual property?

    A   It would exacerbate existing trends.
    B   It would be expensive for academics.
    C   It would tend to stifle intellectual endeavour.
    D   It would hinder the democratisation of knowledge.

38 What does the phrase 'so much guff' (line 57) refer to?

    A   an over-supply of imaginative ideas
    B   the wide availability of copious information
    C   the various ways of accessing ideas on the Internet
    D   an atmosphere of distrust between academics

39 What main advantage does the writer see in the system of 'tagging' he proposes?

    A   It will make people more productive in terms of ideas.
    B   It will foster a cooperative approach among thinkers.
    C   It will force employers to be more honest with their staff.
    D   It will ensure that unscrupulous academics are exposed.

40 Towards the end of the passage, what does the writer suggest is a concern for employers?

    A   employees who steal the ideas of others in order to gain advantage
    B   how to reward those who work hard but fail to produce ideas
    C   how to implement tagging in the business context
    D   employees who choose to withhold good ideas

PART 1

You **must** answer this question. Write your answer in **300–350** words in an appropriate style.

---

1   While reading a magazine, you come across the following letter from another reader. You decide to write a letter in response, providing your own analysis of the problem described and suggesting a number of possible courses of action that might help the situation.

> My relationship with my parents is not as good as it used to be. They always seem too busy to talk to me and when they do, it's usually to complain that I go out too often, come home too late or spend too many hours on the computer. I'm sixteen now and I feel I should be able to do what I like with my time.

Write your **letter**. Do not write any postal addresses.

2   You write a column for a local newspaper. A new restaurant has opened in your town and you ate there recently with a group of friends. While some features of the restaurant were impressive, others left room for improvement. As a result of this experience, you have decided to write a review of the restaurant for your next column.

Write your **review**.

3   You write articles for a popular magazine. Your employer recently paid for you to attend a short evening course at a local college on 'descriptive writing'. The Editor has asked you to write a report in which you evaluate the course content, organisation and method. She has also asked you to assess the usefulness of the course for yourself and for colleagues who might wish to attend the course in the future.

Write your **report**.

4   A local radio station has received a number of phone calls from listeners complaining about the lack of facilities for teenagers in the area. The programme producer has invited listeners to submit a proposal recommending a range of new facilities that could be provided in the future. Within your proposal you should justify the provision of these facilities and briefly explain how teenagers would benefit from them.

Write your **proposal**.

Use of English (1 hour 30 minutes)

For questions **1–15**, read the text below and think of the word which best fits each space. Use only **one** word in each space. There is an example at the beginning **(0)**. Write your answers in **CAPITAL LETTERS on the separate answer sheet**.

Example:

0	T	E	R	M	S													

Niagara Falls

Niagara Falls is Canada's foremost tourist attraction in (**0**) ..*terms*.. of the number of visitors it attracts. (**1**) ………. from the waterfall itself, however, there is precious (**2**) ………. to detain you in the area. Unless, (**3**) ………. is, you're a fan of wax museums, flashing neon lights and souvenir shops. But the *Maid of the Mist* boat ride is something not to be missed. (**4**) ………. operation since 1846, the boat takes millions of tourists a year around the base of the Falls. It's a wet ride and more (**5**) ………. than not, the raincoats they supply you (**6**) ………. prove futile against the stinging spray, but it's well (**7**) ………. the drenching. The view of hundreds of litres of water per second crashing onto the rocks right in front of you is (**8**) ………. short of breathtaking.

(**9**) ………. those who want a closer look, the journey behind the Falls also repays the price of admission, as the school groups you'll inevitably (**10**) ………. across there will be only (**11**) ………. willing to testify. You walk through man-made tunnels to an observation tower situated (**12**) ………. the very brink of the Falls. The experience (**13**) ………. only be described as surreal; you feel as though you're actually walking inside the waterfall. (**14**) ………. with the boat ride, you're guaranteed a soaking, but there again, this is a waterfall, so (**15**) ………. do you expect?

For questions **16–25**, read the text below. Use the word given in **capitals** at the end of some of the lines to form a word that fits in the space in the same line. There is an example at the beginning **(0)**. Write your answers in **CAPITAL LETTERS on the separate answer sheet**.

Example:

0	D	E	F	I	N	I	T	I	O	N								

The Invisible Profession

For many people, the job of the chartered surveyor remains something

of a mystery. The best **(0)** ..*definition*.. that we've found calls surveying   **DEFINE**

'the discipline involved in extracting, adding and maximising value

from the most important commodity there is — land.' But if we have

a mental image of surveyors at all, it is of rather quiet,

(16) .... men in hard hats, carrying something called a   **ASSUME**

theodolite,the purpose of which is largely **(17)** .... to us.   **KNOW**

Real life surveyors, an articulate, diverse body of men and women,

view this misperception with **(18)** .... and amusement in   **WEARY**

equal measure. For surveying is a vastly varied field, with several

distinct and **(19)** .... stimulating careers within it. A chartered   **INTELLECT**

surveyor may be found setting up **(20)** .... property deals; he   **COMMERCE**

or she may equally be discovered in a wet suit, making an

(21) .... of the seabed for an oil company. Many are   **ASSESS**

managers and experts in the construction industry, whilst others

(22) .... in areas such as environmental   **SPECIAL**

(23) .... The financial wizard with the laptop,   **APPRAISE**

simultaneously phoning his contacts with statistical information is a

surveyor, too. For there's another little secret about chartered

surveying. Salary **(24)** .... of £100,000 in your mid-thirties are   **PACK**

by no means a **(25)** .... , plus there's the chance to go into   **RARE**

property development and make millions.

For questions **26–31**, think of **one** word only which can be used appropriately in all three sentences. Here is an example **(0)**.

0 Last year's champion is in with a .... chance of repeating his success in the grand prix next weekend.

Some of the home owners are hoping to get compensation for the poor building work, and I think they have a very .... case.

There's no point in trying to put the tent up, the wind is far too ....

Example:

0	S	T	R	O	N	G														

Write **only** the missing word in **CAPITAL LETTERS on the separate answer sheet**.

---

26 • The children were surprised to hear the tree branch .... as they sat down on it.

• Barry realised that he needed to .... out of his despondent mood if he was going to have any chance of getting a job.

• 'I think you'd better go back to bed if all you can do is .... at me first thing in the morning!' Amy's mother said.

27 • Clarissa's bad temper .... something of a shadow over the whole meeting.

• One of the director's main responsibilities is to .... the show before rehearsals begin.

• The opposing sides in the dispute agreed to .... aside their differences and work for the common good.

28 • Although students on the course should be familiar with the basic theories of economics, they are not expected to have any great .... of understanding.

• In the company of such well-known figures as the town's mayor and a presenter from the local radio station, Paula felt out of her .... , and so remained quiet.

• When planting asparagus, it is necessary to dig a trench of sufficient .... to ensure that the roots will be entirely covered.

29 • I was on the .... of my seat during the grand prix because it was such a close race.

• If you drink a glass of water before each meal, you'll find that it takes the .... off your appetite.

• Jean appeared to be rather on .... during the evening and the other guests wondered if she was worried about something.

30 • In their desperate struggle to get a conviction, the police succeeded in .... the blame for the murder on an innocent bystander.

• If the actress persists in marrying a wealthy man more than twice her age, she will be .... herself open to the obvious criticisms.

• At the end of the event, the organisers are .... on a meal to thank all those who have helped.

31 • The assistant .... me to believe that the equipment would operate in any country, but that just wasn't the case.

• After the presentation, a panel of experts .... a half-hour discussion, during which time the audience was able to ask a number of questions.

• A series of police raids in the early hours of the last Friday morning .... to several arrests being made.

For questions **32–39**, complete the second sentence so that it has a similar meaning to the first sentence, using the word given. **Do not change the word given.** You must use between **three** and **eight** words, including the word given. Here is an example **(0)**.

Example:

0 Immediately after winning the race, Sandy began training for the next one.
had
No .... she began training for the next one.

0   sooner had Sandy won the race than

Write **only** the missing words **on the separate answer sheet**.

---

32 When a novel is made into a film, the author may have to tolerate changes to his or her original work.
put
When a novel is made into a film, the author may have no choice
.... being made to his or her original work.

33 The newspaper article said that the runner wasn't old enough for international competitions.
too
The newspaper article described .... internationally.

34 Owing to the company's financial problems, several of their retail outlets were closed.
resulted
Financial problems .... several of the company's retail outlets.

35 Rumour has it that the famous couple are about to announce their engagement.
verge
The famous couple are said .... their engagement.

36 You can borrow Dad's car, but don't blame me when it breaks down.
hold
You can borrow Dad's car but .... breaking down.

37 It's unfortunate that I came to see him when he wasn't here.
going
If I .... here, I wouldn't have come.

38 In order to discover how the disagreement had started, Mary talked to each child separately.
one
Mary talked to the children .... attempt to discover how the disagreement had started.

39 Kim hasn't had as much success with her project as she had hoped.
liked
Kim .... more successful.

For questions **40–44**, read the following texts on science. For questions **40–43**, answer with a word or short phrase. You do not need to write complete sentences. For question **44**, write a summary according to the instructions given. Write your answers to questions **40–44 on the separate answer sheet.**

In both its beauty and its power, science is mankind's greatest achievement.
2 The triumphs of art, for all their immense intrinsic significance, touch
3 minorities only, and even at their most potent are diffuse and indirect in their effects. But science, particularly through its technological applications, affects everyone directly, for better or worse.

Furthermore, art seems to flower and decline at the whim of the age. It is cyclical, each phase existing for itself alone — whereas science, since its crucial discoveries of the 17th century, seems to expand, progress, rise in a
9 strong upward line, each phase building on the last and then superceding it, harvesting newer and greater abundances of knowledge each time. The efficacy of science and its cumulative character go together; we seem constantly to be learning more about the world — and knowledge is power.

Admittedly, the appearance of smooth progress in science can be a trifle misleading. It has its false starts and wrong turns just as other human endeavours do, and it is as susceptible as they are to prejudice and folly, to personality clashes and egoism, to the lust for fame and reward which prompts dishonesty or dishonourable behaviour. But in practically every case of advance in scientific knowledge, the basic fuel has been co-operation, whether willing or not; for science cannot move forward unless the results of investigations are shared by the scientific community, so that they can be used in the next stage of research.

---

40 In your own words, explain what the writer means by 'touch minorities only' (lines 2–3)?

....

41 Which phrase used later in the second paragraph, echoes the idea of each stage of scientific discovery 'building on the last' (line 9)?

....

Our level of reliable knowledge about the world and our ability to make predictions have never been greater. The reach and scope of what we know, moreover, is unmatched in history. Yet for all that, we hear again and again that the world is becoming an increasingly uncertain place. Things are moving so fast that it seems impossible to know what the future will look like, even in a generation.

That's breathtaking, but also a little frightening. And herein lies a paradox: the very knowledge that we acquire about the world increasingly allows us to change it, and in changing it, we seem peculiarly adept at making it incomprehensible again. Think how many of the big issues of our time relate to this idea. Is nuclear power safe? Will pesticides make us all ill? What caused the hole in the ozone layer? Questions like these continue relentlessly. In some cases, the problems that we face may be so remote and complex that even the experts have trouble grasping them.

The past 100 years brought an explosion of new scientific disciplines. Consider the extraordinary interdisciplinary effort of physicists, meteorologists, geographers, and computer scientists, among others, in assessing the likely outcome of the increased carbon dioxide in the global atmosphere. Unfortunately for us, this is where we face, if not a paradox, at least an irony. Contemporary knowledge — as broad and deep and voluminous as it may be — is astonishingly fragmented, and the more we know collectively, the less capable an individual seems to be at interpreting matters outside his or her area of expertise.

42 Which sentence echoes the point made about science in the second paragraph of the previous text?

....

43 Explain briefly how the question 'Is nuclear power safe?' illustrates the paradox referred to by the writer.

....

44 In a paragraph of between **50 and 70** words, outline **in your own words as far as possible**, the positive and negative aspects of science as outlined in the two texts.

P A R T 1

You will hear four different extracts. For questions **1–8**, choose the answer (**A, B** or **C**) which fits best according to what you hear. There are two questions for each extract.

Extract One

You hear someone calling a radio phone-in programme where a national museum is being discussed.

1 According to the caller, the museum is losing visitors because of

    A a failure to update its image.
    B a lack of financial investment in its upkeep.
    C a resistance to public involvement in its future.

    ☐ **1**

2 What does the caller criticise the museum's managers for?

    A their lack of appropriate qualifications
    B their failure to take account of expert advice
    C their unwillingness to consider public opinion

    ☐ **2**

Extract Two

You hear a woman talking on the radio about a part she is playing in a film.

3 Overall, what is she doing when she speaks?

    A accounting for people's reactions to the story
    B explaining why she was chosen to play the part
    C comparing herself with the character that she plays

    ☐ **3**

4 What does she say about being the inspiration for a fictional character?

    A It has altered her perception of herself.
    B People have preconceived expectations of her.
    C She is unsure of her own feelings about it.

    ☐ **4**

Extract Three

In a radio play, you hear two people talking.

5 Where are they?

  A in an office
  B in a sports club
  C at someone's home

5

6 How is the woman feeling?

  A amused
  B anxious
  C frustrated

6

Extract Four

You hear a journalist being interviewed on the radio.

7 What does she say about her lifestyle?

  A She would like it to be more varied.
  B Her attitude towards it has changed.
  C Some aspects of it are better than others.

7

8 What does she feel is the purpose of her work?

  A to inform people
  B to expose things
  C to protest about things

8

You will hear someone giving a talk about careers in the fire service. For questions **9–17**, complete the sentences with a word or short phrase.

Careers in the Fire Service

Like all her colleagues, Debbie is involved in ⟨ area fire **9** prevention ⟩ as well as dealing with emergencies.

Debbie explains that most emergency calls turn out to be ⟨ false alarm **10** ⟩

Debbie's first experience of a big fire was when a ⟨ vast warehouse **11** ⟩ near London caught light.

At her first big fire, Debbie was positioned on a piece of equipment called a ⟨ **12** ⟩

After a major fire, the firefighters meet for what's known as a ⟨ **13** ⟩

Debbie is especially useful when someone is needed to work in a ⟨ **14** ⟩ in an emergency.

To become a firefighter, Debbie had to undergo tests of fitness, ⟨ **15** ⟩ and strength.

Debbie blames an unfair ⟨ **16** ⟩ for preventing women from joining the service in the past.

Finally, Debbie reminds us that the job is not as ⟨ glamorous **17** ⟩ as it might appear on TV.

You will hear an interview with a couple who work as photographers in Africa. For questions **18–22**, choose the answer (**A, B, C** or **D**) which fits best according to what you hear.

18 Why do Bob and Hilary find it hard to organise their photographic trips?

    A Ceremonies take place at irregular intervals.
    B The information they receive is unreliable.
    C The precise timing of events is unpredictable.
    D Important messages may not reach them in time.

                18

19 Hilary feels that she and Bob are accepted by the communities they visit because

    A they don't rush into things.
    B they make influential friends.
    C they avoid getting involved with them.
    D they are able to explain their aims to them.

                19

20 When living with a group of people in a remote area, Bob and Hilary

    A avoid adopting local eating habits.
    B make a point of dressing in local clothes.
    C depend on the hospitality of their hosts.
    D take a supply of basic provisions with them.

                20

21 Hilary explains that they gain access to very private ceremonies thanks to

    A their persistent requests.
    B changing attitudes in Africa.
    C their long-term relationships with people.
    D an acceptance of their role in the ceremonies.

                21

22 Bob and Hilary feel that the significance of their work is that

    A it will prevent certain traditions from dying out.
    B it portrays traditional ceremonies in a positive way.
    C it encourages young Africans to appreciate their heritage.
    D it allows comparisons with similar traditions elsewhere.

                22

You will hear two well-known singer-songwriters, Cathy and Paul, talking about their approach to writing songs. For questions **23–28**, decide whether the opinions are expressed by only one of the speakers, or whether the speakers agree.

Write   **C**   for Cathy,

                P   for Paul,

or   **B**   for Both, when they agree.

23 Many of my songs have never been recorded. | 23 |

24 I have to view songwriting as a job. | 24 |

25 I rarely have difficulty in coming up with new songs. | 25 |

26 I don't allow myself to waste time on a song that is hard to complete. | 26 |

27 I've been surprised by the success of some of my songs. | 27 |

28 I need to have an idea before I can write a song. | 28 |

PAPER 5

Speaking (19 minutes)

Tip Strip

Part 3
Remember:
- Don't panic!
- Take your time.
- Use the prompt card to help you.
- Keep your listeners interested.
- Listen to your partner.

PART 1 (3 minutes)

Answer these questions:
- What opportunities are there for people of your age in this area?
- How useful will English be in your chosen career?
- What do you think life will be like in ten years' time?

PART 2 (4 minutes)

Turn to pictures A–F on page 166–167, which show images connected with student life.

First look at Picture A only and discuss how the objects in the picture relate to young people who leave home to go away and study. You have about one minute for this.

Now look at all the pictures. A bank has been using Picture A in its advertising leaflets aimed at encouraging students to open bank accounts. The bank is now planning a new leaflet and is looking for two new images. Talk together about how effective each of these images would be in attracting young clients, and then choose the two that the bank should use in its leaflets. You have about three minutes for this.

PART 3 (12 minutes)

Candidate A: Look at the question in the box. You have two minutes to say what you think about the question. There are some ideas to use in the box if you like.

```
Is it fair to keep wild animals in zoos?
• animal welfare
• educational role of zoos
• preservation of endangered species
```

Candidate B: Is there anything you would like to add?

Candidate B: Look at the question in the box. You have two minutes to say what you think about the question. There are some ideas to use in the box if you like.

```
Is it right to try and prevent the economic development
of remote parts of the world?
• ecological considerations
• rights of local people
• opportunities for doing research
```

Candidate A: Is there anything you would like to add?

Candidates A and B: Now answer these questions about the environment in general:

- On balance, has mankind had a positive or negative effect on the planet?
- Who should be responsible for managing the world's resources in future?

TEST 4

PAPER 1 — Reading (1 hour 30 minutes)

PART 1

Tip:
Take no more than 20 minutes to do this part.

For questions **1–18**, read the three texts below and decide which answer (**A, B, C** or **D**) best fits each gap. Mark your answers **on the separate answer sheet**.

Happy Landings

The technique honeybees use to land smoothly could, it seems, be an ideal way to control pilotless planes as they (**1**) ..... down. A team of Australian scientists monitored the flight (**2**) ..... of six bees and found that, as the bees descended, their flying speed was always proportional to their height — and this gave the scientists the (**3**) ..... to the simple trick they were using to land safely.

As you travel along, the closer an object is, the faster it seems to pass. It's the same for bees: if they flew at a constant speed (**4**) ..... descending, the ground would appear to hurtle by faster and faster. They ensure that the image of the ground always crosses their field of (**5**) ..... at the same rate, and so they automatically slow down as they land, (**6**) ..... their speed close to zero as they reach the ground.

	A		B		C		D	
1	touch	**B**	bring	**C**	set	**D**	put
2	road	**B**	line	**C**	path	**D**	route
3	indicator	**B**	insight	**C**	clue	**D**	hint
4	during	**B**	while	**C**	for	**D**	as
5	view	**B**	scene	**C**	focus	**D**	vision
6	having	**B**	bringing	**C**	causing	**D**	leading

The Death of Languages

The death of languages has been repeated many times in history. Localised disasters such as great floods or warfare have (**7**) ..... a part, but in the modern era the increased international movement of people has greatly (**8**) ..... the destruction. Local languages may be overpowered by a metropolitan language, thus increasing the pressure to neglect ancestral tongues in (**9**) ..... of the new one, which is seen as the key to prospering in the (**10**) ..... culture. Children may be forbidden to use their mother tongue in the classroom, as has occurred to many groups, including the Welsh and Aboriginal Australians. The death of a language is not only a tragedy for those directly affected, but also an (**11**) ..... cultural loss for the world. Through language, each culture expresses a unique worldview. Thus, any effort to (**12**) ..... linguistic variety implies a deep respect for the positive values of other cultures.

		A		B		C		D
7	A	done	B	made	C	adopted	D	played
8	A	speeded	B	accelerated	C	urged	D	hurried
9	A	favour	B	preference	C	support	D	choice
10	A	foremost	B	major	C	leading	D	dominant
11	A	invaluable	B	irretrievable	C	inimitable	D	irrepressible
12	A	champion	B	hold	C	preserve	D	collaborate

Old Friends

'Dear Davina and Simon,' began the letter from Debbie, 'A visit from your family wouldn't be complete without a subsequent visit to the Post Office. I'm pleased to say that this time you've left only a minor item that didn't (**13**) ..... me in fretting over who wasn't going to be able to clean their teeth or explain to a teacher about a missing homework book.'

(**14**) ..... of how often I entreat the kids to pack up their own stuff, or how (**15**) ..... I search the bedrooms and bathroom, we always leave something behind.

We've known Debbie and Andrew since before any of our children were born. Debbie and I had our first babies at around the same time, and lent each other lots of moral and practical support. What you (**16**) ..... then, I suggest, bonds you to those you (**17**) ..... the experience with. When we lived round the corner from each other, all this leaving behind of possessions never (**18**) ....., but since they moved 70 kilometres away the leavings have had to be posted back.

		A		B		C		D
13	A	entail	B	involve	C	imply	D	oblige
14	A	Despite	B	Considering	C	Provided	D	Regardless
15	A	diligently	B	disconcertingly	C	despicably	D	dependably
16	A	put up	B	get by	C	go through	D	stand for
17	A	cope	B	share	C	deal	D	bear
18	A	bothered	B	minded	C	fussed	D	mattered

PART 2

Tip:

Take no more
than 20 minutes
to do this part.

You are going to read four extracts which are all concerned in some way with people who are away from home. For questions **19–26**, choose the answer (**A, B, C** or **D**) which you think fits best according to the text. Mark your answers **on the separate answer sheet.**

The Thinking Person's Hotel

There's an old saying about the cobbler's children having no shoes. In a similar vein, and from personal experience, I can add that economists tend towards chaotic personal finances and philosophers rarely use the words 'happiness' and 'meaning of life' in the same sentence. But in the Netherlands, people take pride in cutting across type and the country certainly has one happy and practical philosopher. Dr Ida Jongsma runs the Hotel de Filosof, a little-known haven of apparent eccentricity in Amsterdam. In between lecturing and running seminars on her subject, Ida applies philosophy to the amusement of mankind. A hotel is not a bad forum for this kind of philanthropy. Checking in at the hotel is a relaxed affair—the staff tend to be 'resting' thinkers, musicians and writers — but it's also a gentle test of foundation-course philosophical knowledge. Each room is decorated according to different schools of thinkery, and you're expected to make a reasoned choice. The hotel is a place for people to relax and talk, albeit not too seriously, and I'd certainly rebook on the strength of the late-night conversation alone. 'A philosopher,' they say, 'is someone who knows the square root of a jar of pickles, but can't get the lid off.' The Filosof seems to be a place where you might just manage both.

19 In the first paragraph, the writer gives the impression that Ida Jongsma

    A   is unlike other philosophers he's known.

    B   lacks commitment to the business she runs.

    C   has an eccentric view of philosophy.

    D   is untypical of people in the Netherlands.

20 His stay at the hotel left the writer feeling

    A   more interested in philosophy than previously.

    B   intimidated by its intellectual pretensions.

    C   stimulated by the company he had kept.

    D   disappointed by its level of seriousness.

Extract from an autobiography

One bright June morning, when I was nineteen, I packed all I had on my back, left my native village, and walked up to London looking for gold and glory. I've been here on and off ever since, and I shall probably stay here for the rest of my life. Yet in spite of all that, I still can't think of myself as a Londoner, nor ever will, nor ever want to. For years, I have lived in the flats, rooms and garrets of this city, the drawers in the human filing-cabinets that stand in blank rows down the streets of Kensington and Notting Hill. Yet when I talk of my home I still think of that damp green valley where I was brought up. The boys I went to school with have long since grown, got married and gone bald, and they would probably have to give me a very long look before they recognised me if I turned up there again. But that is my home, and the image of it the day I left it is still more real to me than the long years in this crowded capital city.

Now why does one become an exile in the first place? And if one does, why be obstinate about it? Furthermore, if one is forced to be as disloyal about the place of one's adoption as I am going to be about London, why not simply go back home?

21 In his description, the writer paints a picture of London as

    A a captivating place.

    B a disappointing place.

    C a disorienting place.

    D an anonymous place.

22 From the last paragraph, we understand that the writer fears that he may be

    A unfair in his analysis of London.

    B unqualified to write about London.

    C hypocritical in his attitude towards London.

    D biased in his assessment of London.

Hitching a Ride

If the hitch-hikers are American, I usually stop for them. One can generally tell. They try harder for their lifts, holding up well-lettered destination signs and offering
3 ingratiating smiles. Not for them the mechanical jerk of the thumb while looking the other way; they are in the lift-getting business, and they do the job properly.

When they are on board, they generally work for their keep, too. They do not sit there slumped and morose, like so many travellers of other nationalities. They tell me all about themselves, they learn all about me, although I always hope I'll be spared a
8 lecture on the social customs of my own country, or that they'll refrain from kindly
9 correcting me when I appear to them to be going the wrong way. They are generally willing to oblige. 'Are you going to Scotland?' one young man asked me when I stopped for him just outside London. 'No, I'm going to Wales.' 'OK, make it Wales'.

In many ways, these people epitomise the pleasures America has given me through
13 life. I am not entirely deceived by them. I know their charm is partly delusive, and that
14 sometimes, if I decide against picking one up, he makes a rude gesture at me from behind, but I don't hold this against them.

23 What does the writer appreciate most about the American hitch-hikers she picks up?

    A   their sincerity

    B   their sociability

    C   their generosity

    D   their seriousness

24 Which phrase from the text reveals a slight irritation on the part of the writer?

    A   'ingratiating smiles' (line 3)

    B   'kindly correcting' (lines 8–9)

    C   'partly delusive' (line 13)

    D   'a rude gesture' (line 14)

Steak and Chips

Experience has taught me that food guides are not wholly to be trusted. The gestation period between research and publication means that there is a strong likelihood of the establishment about which you read having changed hands, chefs or managers in the meantime. But I might have been forgiven for thinking that in the case of the small organic café I visited on Tuesday, I stood some chance of sampling the same delights as its reviewer. In the previous Friday's London *Evening Standard* magazine, a journalist had been dispatched to discover the whereabouts of the best steak and chips in town and this place had won; it had received five stars. As I was on business in the city and at a loose end, I decided to give it a try.

The café itself is plain: wooden floors, wooden tables and chairs, and it was empty. At length, a waitress arrived and I ordered steak and chips. 'Not at lunchtime, anyway we ran out of organic steak over the weekend because of that advertisement.' I asked if I might just try the chips? No chips; they didn't usually do chips but if I came back that evening there would be sautéed potatoes.' Perhaps I could see the chef? The chef came, explained that it was his day off, he had come in only for stocktaking. I managed not to ask him how one took stock when one had run out of ingredients, asked instead how he cooked chips. He did not cook chips, not at the moment; difficulty in getting the floury potatoes you need.

25 What led the writer to visit the organic café?

    A his faith in the publication which featured it

    B the type of food for which it is renowned

    C his belief that he'd read a reliable review of it

    D the range of people who had recommended it

26 In describing the restaurant, the writer's tone is

    A ironic.

    B indignant.

    C dismissive.

    D affectionate.

PART 3

Tip:
Take no more
than 25 minutes
to do this part.

You are going to read an extract from a magazine. Seven paragraphs have been removed from the extract. Choose from the paragraphs **A–H** the one which fits each gap (**27–33**). There is one extra paragraph which you do not need to use. Mark your answers **on the separate answer sheet.**

Give Pennies a Chance

**They're derided as worthless, thrown into landfill sites and left to fester behind sofas.
Is it time to rehabilitate copper pennies?**

A few years ago, when a convention of American lawyers was held in London, the organisers issued delegates with advice about the host country. It was full of all the predictable tourist stuff about tipping, strange food and so on. When it came to dealing with the currency, the delegates were naturally told all about British banknotes and silver coinage, but advised in an aside to 'throw away the lowest denomination coins, those made of the brown metal, copper. They are worthless.'

27

Copper coins are irritating when they weigh your pockets or purse down, but they do have monetary value, and I felt that I was putting them to their best possible use. One day, I would have enough to buy something tangible and long lasting — I had a painting in mind — as a permanent memorial to my thrift.

28

Keen to make the acquisition sooner rather than later, I even started raiding my wife's purse for pennies, ostensibly as a service — 'You don't want to be lugging all that about' — but really to add to my penny mountain. In idle moments at work, I would attempt to calculate how much I had. It had to be £300, I concluded one July day about five years after beginning the collection. It was time for the big count. It took most of the morning. I ended up with blackened, smelly hands and a grand total of £78.

29

The conundrum remains, however, of what people should do with the 8,459 million 1p and 5,102 million 2p coins which, according to the Royal Mint, the body which controls Britain's currency, are out there somewhere, festering in jars and boxes or weighing down the darkest depths of our pockets and handbags.

30

Yet if you're not one of the people who spends it as you go, and you want to avoid either philanthropy or saving it for years then counting for days and being ultimately disappointed, the solution to your burdensome stash may have arrived in the form of a new machine just over from the US, the Coin Star.

31

Those responsible for the innovation argue that it helps the economy by releasing this small denomination of buried treasure from its captivity in the nation's piggy banks, jam jars and bottom-of-handbag recesses. Apparently the amount of small change waiting to be liberated and do its bit by being spent on consumer goods staggers the imagination.

32

Other equally mind-boggling stories abound and it is claimed that after four years in operation, Coin Star is bringing into circulation more than the US Mint issues in a year. And the Coin Star company's market research also uncovered some interesting attitudes to small change. For example, it's not as simple as throwing it in the bin, but if someone finds a penny while sweeping up, they won't bother to bend down and pick it up. It goes out with the rubbish; the number of copper coins in landfill sites is frightening.

33

But I can see how the rich, and more so, the famous, might not see things in quite the same light. If you were well known and were observed going to great lengths to count out 37 pence, the seven in 1p pieces, someone would be bound to say, 'Oh, I saw so-and-so in a shop *fiddling with his change*.' And so in a way you can't win.

A With deft precision, it sorts out your change, tots it up and spits out a shopping voucher in exchange, less a 6.9 per cent handling charge. Leading supermarkets in the UK have been testing it in a few branches and it's been a considerable hit with change-rich, pocket-heavy shoppers who invariably have more in their jars of coins than they think.

B Ultimately though, isn't there an alternative to heaving bags of brown coins into the supermarket? One journalist says the answer is never to allow your change to accumulate. 'I try to use them as I go along by giving shopkeepers the correct money — that's what pennies are for. It's polite and sensible; throwing them away is vulgar and wasteful.'

C Even with such a miserable yield, it still took half an hour and an extremely good-natured counter clerk to deal with it. As you can imagine, my small change fixation was now fixed. My belief in that silly saying 'penny wise, pound rich' had evaporated, and brown coins regained their rightful status as a nuisance, ending up down the backs of sofas.

D Having said that I try to spend coppers as I get them; I'm not that set against a pocket full of change. I can remember when my father's friends used to come round and they'd stand and talk in the garden, all jingling their change in a way that I came to regard as rather grown up.

E Research estimates that 66 per cent of the UK population hoards coins, and that there's about £10.5 billion worth of hoarded change, from pennies to £2 coins, in people's homes across the UK. In the US, where there are now machines in 7,500 supermarkets, one man lugged in a suitcase of change containing $8,000.

F The tale was reported with amusement on national radio, but it caused me, and I suspect a lot of other people on the quiet, some concern. For the previous year, I had been assiduously collecting one and two penny pieces in a box in my office.

G Putting the most minuscule of small change in charity collecting boxes is one way out, but it does seem a bit cheap, and there's always the worry (for a penny collector at least) that the box is a fake, and that the person responsible is secretly hoarding coppers to pay for exotic holidays, albeit cheap ones.

H Hence I began to display the signs of a minor obsessive: it was a moment of rare satisfaction when the collection became too hefty to lift without real effort; I realised that I was actually pleased when a shop assistant decided to palm me off with a pile of brown fiscal shrapnel for change instead of silver.

PART 4

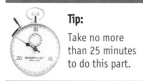

Tip:
Take no more
than 25 minutes
to do this part.

You are going to read a book review. For questions **34–40** choose the answer (**A, B, C** or **D**) which you think fits best according to the text. Mark your answers **on the separate answer sheet.**

The Other Side of Eden

Hunter-gatherers, Farmers and the Shaping of the World

By Hugh Brody

The anthropologist Hugh Brody has spent most of his working life studying, filming, living among, and campaigning for, hunter-gatherers. He has written a number of books on the subject — including the intriguing *Maps and Dreams*. He has made documentaries, and sat on advisory committees established to protect these isolated peoples from the rampant expansion of a more acquisitive way of life. *The Other Side of Eden* (part ethnography, part autobiography, part manifesto) has the sense of distilling all that experience and knowledge. It is a big book in every way, a paean for a vanishing version of ourselves. Brody sets it up as nothing less than a 'search for what it has meant, and can mean, to be a human being'. Reading such a claim at the beginning of a book, you tend to think 'uh-huh...' — and wait for it to fall short. But it does not. It is wonderfully persuasive, deeply felt and as exhilarating as an Arctic sky.

Brody's first brush with hunter-gatherers was with the Inuit of Hudson Bay. Equipped with little more than caribou skins, some hard biscuits, a burgeoning stock of Inuktitut words and a well-honed relativism, he set off across the ice on week-long expeditions of genuine hardship. His guide and mentor was a man named Anaviapik, who later came to London in his seal-skin boots and was amazed by the apartment blocks: how, he asked, could people live in cliffs?

It was Anaviapik who taught Brody the early lesson that the word 'Inuktitut' is a synonym for the Inuit language from which it comes and also for the 'way of being' of the people themselves. In this lay the two themes that have driven his work: the importance of language and the essential integration of hunter-gatherer society. Over the coming years, Brody revisited the Inuit many times, as well as the Nisga'a and Dunne-za of northwestern Canada. If his portrait of them appears at times a little rosy, he would probably claim that that view in itself is merely ethnocentric; that looking for the 'flipside' is a habit of our own dualistic worldview. Traditionally, he tells us, hunter-gatherers live in prosperity, in harmony with their environment, free from infectious disease. They display a calm self-confidence and wisdom. They respect their elders and in their relationships are open and honest. Inuit parents, for instance, openly talk in front of their children about which one of them they love most. Far from creating neurosis, claims Brody, such candour means that hunter-gatherer groups remain largely immune to the kind of mental anguish that arises from half-truths.

That all changes when they encounter us. We — the scions of agriculturalists—have ridden roughshod over their pristine lands. We have plucked their children from them, sent them to residential schools, drummed their language from them. We have 'settled' them — and anyone who has witnessed settlements around the areas they once depended on, will know just what that can mean: alcoholism, confusion and a pathetic lassitude.

At the heart of Brody's ideas about hunter-gatherers is this contrast with agriculturalists. In this, is an inversion of the popular wisdom that hunter-gatherers are nomadic, while herders and grain-growers are settled. In fact, he claims, the opposite is true. Hunter-gatherers always have a profound and dependent relationship with a single area. They tend to keep small families and are demographically stable. It is agriculturalists, on the other hand, who have wandered the earth. With larger families, they have developed the habit of expansion – and in their constant colonising of new land they have left only those hunter-gatherers who inhabit areas unfit for agriculture. Here lies the problem with such theorising. If there was a pre-agricultural period in which all humans were hunters and gatherers, then they must also have occupied much more favourable land than they do now. Those who do survive may not be typical. In better land, for instance, they may have had large families, may also have developed rudimentary 'agricultural' techniques independent from each other.

As an anthropologist, Brody shows less respect for his discipline than for the people he studies. This is very welcome. Like most social sciences, ethnography has been hobbled by an attachment to methodology. In the debates between other theorists, essential questions have often been forgotten. But Brody breaks the rules by writing well and saying what he thinks. He evokes the landscape of the Inuit with shivering accuracy. He employs a clear aphoristic style ('to equivocate is to refuse absolutes ... words are the beginning of the end of nothingness ... verbal untruth has the power to render us neurotic'). A book that could have been leaden and dry has been transformed by good prose into one that glitters with universal ideas. *The Other Side of Eden* is a potent elegy to marginalised societies. But in managing to convey the complexities of an alien cosmology, Brody highlights attitudes that, in our post-agricultural society, have a renewed urgency — the importance of knowing nature, the integral power of language and a mystical respect for place.

34 What main point does the reviewer make about *The Other Side of Eden* in the first paragraph?

    A The claims Brody makes about it are justified.
    B The reader's expectations of it are realised.
    C It is the long-awaited sequel to *Maps and Dreams*.
    D It presents hitherto unknown facts about its subject.

35 When Brody first visited the Inuit in Hudson Bay, he

    A appreciated the need to learn the language beforehand.
    B was deprived of any luxury on the trip.
    C decided he could no longer assume the role of an observer.
    D realised he had made some false assumptions about their lifestyle.

36 In the third paragraph, the reviewer suggests that Brody

    A overplays the positive features of a hunter-gatherer lifestyle.
    B oversimplifies the challenges of a hunter-gatherer lifestyle.
    C draws too many parallels between different hunter-gatherer societies.
    D underestimates the reader's understanding of hunter-gatherer societies.

37 Which of the following does Brody claim is a feature of hunter-gatherer society?

    A humility
    B equality
    C physical awareness
    D psychological well-being

38 Which of the following phrases is used in the article to evoke a sense of cruel injustice?

    A 'ridden roughshod' (line 46)
    B 'pristine lands' (line 47)
    C 'pathetic lassitude' (line 52)
    D 'demographically stable' (line 59)

39 In questioning Brody's theories, what does the reviewer suggest about hunter-gatherer societies of today?

    A They must be the strongest genetically.
    B They must have migrated from more barren areas.
    C They cannot be assumed to be entirely representative.
    D They cannot be held responsible for their current living conditions.

40 In his approach to studying hunter-gatherer societies, the reviewer feels that Brody has

    A supported the work of others in his field.
    B failed to address some important issues.
    C reached a successful synthesis of ideas.
    D made a healthy break from tradition.

Writing (2 hours)

You **must** answer this question. Write your answer in **300–350** words in an appropriate style.

1 You have read the following advertisement in a geographical magazine:

Propose a Friend

Do you know someone who meets the following criteria?

- Has a keen interest in other cultures
- Can be self-financing for six weeks
- Is able to work as part of a team
- Has a range of practical skills (indoors or outdoors)
- Is willing to endure unfamiliar environmental conditions

An international aid team is looking for people to help out with a voluntary work scheme in undeveloped rural areas in the third world.
If there is someone you would like to recommend for this, please submit a formal proposal to the magazine, clearly addressing the criteria above and outlining the contributions that you feel this person would be able to make to a project of this kind.

You have a close friend who is keen to take part in this project and whom you feel would be very suitable. Write your **proposal**.

Write an answer to **one** of the questions **2–4** in this part. Write your answer in **300-350** words in an appropriate style

2   A weekly magazine about the environment has invited readers to write to the editor, giving views about how governments and individuals can cooperate to protect the global environment.

Write your **letter**.

3   A national newspaper is running a special weekly insert on careers, and has invited readers to contribute an article entitled *Key Considerations for the School Leaver.* Write an article stating the issues that you feel are most important for young people when they are deciding on a career path. In your article, recommend at least one course of action that a school leaver might take in order to help clarify their career goals.

Write your **article**.

4   You belong to an Internet discussion group that exchanges views on current affairs. In order to help select topics for discussion, each member of the group has agreed to write a review of a documentary film that was particularly memorable and that they feel would provide the basis for future discussion.

Write your **review**.

For questions **1–15**, read the text below and think of the word which best fits each space. Use only **one** word in each space. There is an example at the beginning **(0)**. Write your answers in **CAPITAL LETTERS on the separate answer sheet.**

Example:

0	P	A	R	T															

The Sensual Shopper

How can retail stores encourage customers to (**0**) ...*part*.... with their money? Here's how the good stores do (**1**) .... We were performing a study for RadioShack just (**2**) .... the chain had decided to try to become America's favorite phone store. We watched countless shoppers approach the wall of telephones on display, look them all (**3**) .... , check out the prices and then, almost (**4**) .... exception, pick up a phone and hold it up to an ear. What were they hoping for? Nothing, probably – it's just a reflex action, I think. (**5**) .... else do you *do* with a phone? On what other basis do you compare phones but (**6**) .... how they feel in your hand and (**7**) .... your ear.

Well, we reasoned, if the first principle (**8**) .... trial is to make it as lifelike as possible, you can complete the experience by putting a voice in that phone. We advised RadioShack to connect the phones to a recorded message that (**9**) .... be activated when a receiver (**10**) .... lifted. Once that happened, the stores were alive (**11**) .... shoppers picking up display phones, listening (**12**) .... moment and then holding the receivers out for their companions to hear – (**13**) .... was a bonus, because that would provide some basis (**14**) .... discussing the purchase, which greatly increases the chances that something will (**15**) .... bought.

PART 2

For questions **16–25**, read the text below. Use the word given in **capitals** at the end of some of the lines to form a word that fits in the space in the same line. There is an example at the beginning (0). Write your answers in **CAPITAL LETTERS on the separate answer sheet**.

Example:

0	R	E	C	O	G	N	I	S	E	D									

Ventriloquism

Ventriloquism is a (**0**) ..recognised.. art throughout the world. It is **RECOGNISE**

defined in most dictionaries as the practice of making the voice appear

to come from somewhere other than its source. It is, in short, a vocal

illusion.

The word 'ventriloquist' is a (**16**) .... of the Latin *ventriloquus*, **DERIVE**

meaning 'belly speaker'; however, the name is (**17**) .... **LEAD**

because the ventriloquist does not speak from the stomach, but

(**18**) .... his stomach muscles in the same manner as a singer **UTILITY**

does, to assist the diaphragm to give volume and tonal strength to the

voice. In fact, contrary to popular belief, ventriloquism can be acquired

through the (**19**) .... of basic principles and practice. **APPLY**

Ventriloquism takes advantage of a common human failing, the

(**20**) .... to measure the distance of sound. We can only judge **ABLE**

the distance that sound has travelled, by making (**21**) .... to **REFER**

previous experiences of similar sounds. The use of a speaking doll

further exploits the potential for such (**22**) .... between sound **ASSOCIATE**

and distance.

In (**23**) .... recent years, the ventriloquist's dummy has **COMPARE**

become the (**24**) .... point of performances and the art itself **FOCUS**

has produced some very accomplished (**25**) .... **PRACTISE**

For questions **26–31**, think of **one** word only which can be used appropriately in all three sentences. Here is an example **(0)**.

Example:

0 Last year's champion is in with a .... chance of repeating his success in the grand prix next weekend.

Some of the home owners are hoping to get compensation for the poor building work, they have a very .... case.

There's no point in trying to put the tent up, the wind is far too ....

Example:

0	S	T	R	O	N	G													

Write **only** the missing word in **CAPITAL LETTERS on the separate answer sheet**.

---

26 • Jenny realised that she had become so engrossed in what she was doing that she had lost all .... of time passing.

 • There is no .... in trying to persuade someone to give up smoking if they don't really want to.

 • Just sitting in this old building gives me a real .... of history and culture.

27 • After six months' hard work at a town centre restaurant, Kevin eventually succeeded in .... together enough money to go on a trip round the world.

 • With so many labour-saving devices on the market Kate finds it irritating that her mother continues .... the skin from potatoes with a blunt knife.

 • The social worker asked Mrs Timmins how she was managing financially and the old woman had to admit that she was barely .... by.

28 • Quite a number of families in the area have decided to .... from electric to gas central heating.

 • If you should detect a leak, ... off the mains water supply and call a plumber.

 • Tanya is bilingual in Welsh and English and can .... effortlessly from one language to the other.

29 • The policeman was subjected to a .... of abuse when he asked what the young men were doing on the roof of the building.

 • Sensibly, Mick decided to postpone his purchase of a CD player until the recently advertised models came on ....

 • When Jenny returned to school after the holidays, she was surprised to find that she had been placed in a higher .... for maths.

30 • Although they've tried dozens of local restaurants, Jenny and her husband still .... that Richard's Place is the best.

 • After retirement, many old age pensioners find it difficult to .... their previous standard of living.

 • Families in Britain are not as close as they used to be and very few people .... regular contact with relatives outside their immediate family group.

31 • Because of a lack of adequate regulation, the system whereby students supposedly have equal access to the college computer network is .... open to abuse.

 • The company's estimates of how quickly demand for their products would rise have tended to be rather .... of the mark.

 • Although she hadn't slept very well, Hayley was feeling .... awake and ready for the day ahead.

PART 4

For questions **32–39**, complete the second sentence so that it has a similar meaning to the first sentence, using the word given. **Do not change the word given.** You must use between **three** and **eight** words, including the word given. Here is an example **(0)**.

Example:

0 Immediately after winning the race, Sandy began training for the next one.
had
No .... she began training for the next one.

0   sooner had Sandy won the race than

Write **only** the missing words **on the separate answer sheet**.

---

32 Few ways of exploring the countryside are as rewarding as mountain biking.
one
Mountain biking is .... exploring the countryside.

33 David is colour blind, which means that red and green look the same to him.
tell
David is colour blind, which means that he is not ....
red and green.

34 I'm afraid that I get a terrible rash every time I eat seafood.
brings
I'm afraid that eating .... a terrible rash.

35 Most people are more aware of other people's faults than they are of their own.
identify
Most people are .... they are those of others.

36 The building had been extensively repaired and looked as good as new.
undergone
The building .... and looked as good as new.

37 Nick said that the swimming lesson cost £11, but was well worth it.
fact
Nick said that .... , the swimming lesson
was well worth it.

38 Jane said she was unlikely to be going to the reunion that evening.
of
Jane said there .... to the reunion this evening.

39 'If my brother doesn't improve his appearance, he'll never get a girlfriend,'
Miranda said.
about
Miranda said that if her brother .... , he'd never
get a girlfriend.

For questions **40–44**, read the following texts on effective communication. For questions **40–43**, answer with a word or short phrase. You do not need to write complete sentences. For question **44**, write a summary according to the instructions given. Write your answers to questions **40–44 on the separate answer sheet.**

I'd better put my cards on the table right from the start and admit that about the only qualification I have for calling myself a conversationalist is a lifetime spent being paid to say other people's lines. Not that I am ungrateful for this opportunity, quite the reverse. Because I can honestly say that, over the years, one or two of the tricks of the trade have rubbed off on me. And by far the most important thing I've realised is that there's a world of difference between talking and conversation. Talking is like the mirage that faces a parched man as he staggers through a desert in search of water. Conversation is the oasis that eventually quenches his thirst. As soon as he tastes the water, he knows the difference between the real thing and the image. Let me give you an example of the real thing:

'Ladies and gentlemen,' said Sir Thomas Beecham, the famous orchestral conductor, to one of his audiences, 'In fifty years of concert-giving before the public, it has seldom been my good fortune to find the programme correctly printed. Tonight is no exception to the rule, and therefore, with your kind permission, we will now play you the piece which you think you have just heard...'

Beecham must have drunk from his first oasis very early in life. For in my opinion that display is a wonderful example of conversation. Of course you can argue that technically only Beecham was speaking. But the way he spoke implied that the audience was joining in with him. And what he was saying was succinct, full of good humour and, above all, supremely effective.

40 Quote the part of the text that gives us the best indication of the writer's profession.

....

41 Which word in the first paragraph contrasts with 'parched'?

....

When a conversation doesn't go well at work, one of two things has usually happened. You may not have thought an issue through very well, and in the middle of the conversation, this can become all too apparent. It may cause no lasting damage, other than embarrassment, as you scramble to retrieve something of value from the conversation without losing any more face than you already have. If you choose the unfortunate strategy of continuing to talk until you can think of something to say, you may end up just digging yourself into a deeper hole.

The other way a conversation might not go well is much more hazardous to relationships and credibility. However emotional you may feel about an issue, it is important not to let your emotions get the better of you. Some people may be able to think clearly in the heat of anger, but many people find that they cannot. You may start out with the intention of discussing an issue professionally, but if emotions rise, you can soon find yourself saying unnecessary and possibly hurtful things and the communication will eventually break down.

When you go to bed at night, of course, and replay these conversations over in your mind, they may seem totally different. Rather than responding impulsively to something, you may envisage yourself giving a calm, collected response to a difficult question and, in return, receiving praise from your colleagues for the insight you have shown. Such imaginary conversations go exactly the way you would like to see them go. Unfortunately it is then far too late to change anything.

42 Which phrase in the text echoes the 'embarrassment' referred to in line 4?

....

43 In your own words, state what is unfortunate about the strategy described at the end of the first paragraph?

....

44 In a paragraph of between **50 and 70** words, summarise **in your own words as far as possible**, the suggestions made by the writers as to how communication can be made more effective.

Listening (Approximately 40 minutes)

You will hear four different extracts, For questions **1–8**, choose the answer (**A, B** or **C**) which fits best according to what you hear. There are two questions for each extract.

Extract One

You hear part of a radio programme about rock music.

1 The presenter regards the group called *Fluxx* as

    A overrated by their fans.
    B unimaginative in the material they produced.
    C undervalued by people in general.

1

2 How did the lead singer feel about the group in the end?

    A constrained by it
    B sentimental about it
    C bored by it

2

Extract Two

You will hear two people describing the type of work they do.

3 Where do they work?

    A in a shop
    B on the telephone
    C in people's homes

3

4 How do they feel about the type of customers they are describing?

    A sympathetic
    B antagonistic
    C indifferent

4

Extract Three

You hear the introduction to a discussion programme on the radio.

5   According to the presenter, people today are likely to find the quote he reads out

    A amusing.

    B disturbing.

    C patronising.

5

6   Today's programme will go on to discuss

    A commercial awareness.

    B methods of research.

    C attitudes to children.

6

Extract Four

You hear an artist talking about her work.

7   What makes her particularly fond of the piece of work she describes?

    A the material it is made from

    B the effect it had on her career

    C the circumstances in which it was produced

7

8   How does she feel about working at home?

    A determined

    B frustrated

    C resigned

8

You will hear a radio report about a wildlife holiday in the Yellowstone National Park in the USA. For questions **9–17**, complete the sentences with a word or short phrase.

Michela describes the man she met in Canada

as being [**9**] by his experience.

As a species, the wolf is now officially

classed as [**10**] in North America.

It is thought that as many as [**11**] visitors

have seen the reintroduced wolves at Yellowstone.

On Michela's first evening in Yellowstone, a [**12**]

gave visitors a talk about wolves.

Coyotes, which have longer ears and [**13**] colouring,

are often mistaken for wolves.

Michela's personal guide originally trained to be a [**14**]

Around half the wolves in the park are now fitted with

[**15**] to help people locate them.

Ken advised Michela to look for wolves on hillsides where

[**16**] could be seen through the snow.

Michela used a particularly good [**17**]

to study the wolf she eventually saw.

You will hear an interview with a woman called Tansy Burton, who runs a company which makes beauty products. For questions **18–22**, choose the answer (**A, B, C** or **D**) which fits best according to what you hear.

18 To what does Tansy attribute her success as a businessperson?

    A It was a family tradition.
    B It reflects her early training.
    C It grew out of a desire to please people.
    D It's something which came naturally to her.

| | 18 |

19 What was Tansy's main role in setting up the production company?

    A drawing up a business plan
    B attracting sufficient investment
    C responding to customer preferences
    D establishing administrative systems

| | 19 |

20 According to Tansy, her fragrances are successful because they

    A are elegantly packaged.
    B appeal to a wide range of people.
    C suggest an expensive lifestyle.
    D reflect changes in consumer taste.

| | 20 |

21 Increasingly, Tansy sees people's choice of fragrances as a reflection of the wearer's

    A social standing.
    B taste in other products.
    C emotional state.
    D financial situation.

| | 21 |

22 In the future, Tansy expects to see

    A a wider use of fragrances in society.
    B fewer companies involved in producing fragrances.
    C single products fulfilling a range of functions.
    D increasing profitability for producers of fragrances.

| | 22 |

You will hear two media critics, Mathew and Daniella, talking about a recently released film. For questions **23–28**, decide whether the opinions are expressed by only one of the speakers, or whether the speakers agree.

Write   **M**   for Mathew,
           D   for Daniella,
or   **B**   for Both, when they agree.

23 The film presents a new approach to an old theme.   `23`

24 The use of a narrator voice makes a positive contribution to the film.   `24`

25 The main character features too much in the film.   `25`

26 Many of the character types in the film are easy to recognise.   `26`

27 The viewer has high expectations of the film.   `27`

28 The film is targeted at a young audience.   `28`

PAPER 5   Speaking (19 minutes)

PART 1   (3 minutes)

Answer these questions:
- Where do you live? Tell us about your house or apartment.
- How has your life changed in recent years?
- How do you think you will use your English in the future?

PART 2   (4 minutes)

Turn to pictures A–G on pages 168–9 which show different faces.

First look at Picture A only and talk together about how this photograph makes you feel and what you think it represents. You have about one minute for this.

Now look at all the pictures. These photographs have all been entered for a competition on the theme of facial expressions. Talk together about the type of facial expression captured in each photograph, saying how well the photographer has caught the person's mood or character in each case. Then decide which photographs should win first, second and third prizes. You have about three minutes for this.

PART 3   (12 minutes)

Candidate A: Look at the question in the box. You have two minutes to say what you think about the question. There are some ideas to use in the box if you like.

> Why are people becoming increasingly concerned about their diet these days?
> - effects of modern lifestyles on health
> - fresh vs. packaged foods
> - questions over food safety

Candidate B: Is there anything you would like to add?

Candidate B: Look at the question in the box. You have two minutes to say what you think about the question. There are some ideas to use in the box if you like.

> How is the role of agriculture changing in modern society?
> - competition for use of land
> - mechanisation of farming
> - globalisation of world economy

Candidate A: Is there anything you would like to add?

Candidates A and B: Now answer these questions about nutrition in general:
- Do we reward those who provide us with our food and drink adequately?
- How can the world's food resources be shared more equally?

TEST 5

Reading (1 hour 30 minutes)

Tip:

Take no more
than 20 minutes
to do this part.

For questions **1–18**, read the three texts below and decide which answer (**A, B, C** or **D**)
best fits each gap. Mark your answers **on the separate answer sheet**.

Beauty from the Beast

Our cashmere sweaters are made (**1**) ..... of the purest, whitest cashmere in the world. It
comes from the rugged goats that (**2**) ..... the dry, barren, windswept plains of Inner
Mongolia. Grazing is (**3**) ....., even in the summer months, and winter temperatures drop
down to 30 degrees below freezing with the (**4**) ..... that the goats grow a unique protective
fleece. A fraction of the width of a human hair, it's the rarer downy underhairs growing
closest to the goat's body that are the most (**5**) ..... — and the only fibres used in our
sweaters. Why? Well, for a start, they're the longest, and longer fibres yield softer, stronger,
more consistent yarns which can be knit tighter to aid longevity. And (**6**) ..... even the finest
cashmere grows in several natural shades, we use only white. White fibres hold dyes better
to give our sweaters a rich, natural hue.

1	**A**	especially	**B**	extensively	**C**	effectively	**D**	exclusively
2	**A**	roam	**B**	ramble	**C**	trample	**D**	trek
3	**A**	slim	**B**	scanty	**C**	sparse	**D**	skimpy
4	**A**	recourse	**B**	reward	**C**	result	**D**	response
5	**A**	honoured	**B**	prized	**C**	gifted	**D**	awarded
6	**A**	unless	**B**	whilst	**C**	providing	**D**	despite

'Chasing Science: Science as Spectator Sport'
by Frederick Pohl

Frederick Pohl's book flits light-heartedly from continent to continent, mixing travelogue with
gentle scientific explanation. This unusual (**7**) ..... gives Mr Pohl the freedom to
(**8**) ..... into an extraordinarily diverse range of topics, including the physics of rainbows, and
how to search for fossils in the marbled halls of downtown banks. It is all good fun, yet
among the anecdotes and curious facts the scientific content is deceptively (**9**) ..... . And
along the way Mr Pohl makes a serious point. (**10**) ..... it is not necessary to be an athlete to
enjoy sport, his book suggests, it is not necessary to be a scientific expert to
(**11**) ..... science. By pointing out where science is most apparent in the world, Mr Pohl
entertainingly demonstrates that it is not some (**12**) ..... activity, but is instead everywhere;
that science is, in the end, a world view.

7	**A**	accent	**B**	approach	**C**	manner	**D**	means
8	**A**	delve	**B**	rummage	**C**	investigate	**D**	explore
9	**A**	considerable	**B**	grand	**C**	ample	**D**	high
10	**A**	Just as	**B**	Besides	**C**	Whereas	**D**	Even if
11	**A**	attain	**B**	appreciate	**C**	appeal	**D**	endear
12	**A**	abject	**B**	obsolete	**C**	arcane	**D**	obtuse

Television

Television is such a seductive medium, and entertainment programmes are so prevalent, that it is easy to miss the serious stuff altogether. (**13**) ..... the famous cry: 'There's nothing on television.' What this usually means in practice is that there is nothing on the main terrestrial channels when we happen to (**14**) ..... up from our newspaper or mid-evening snack, apart from soap operas, games shows and variety programmes. (**15**) ..... if you look around the margins and (**16**) ..... your eye on the less used networks, there is actually a remarkable quantity of serious, even high–minded, material. To (**17**) ..... some of it, you may need to set the timer on the video recorder — a task which a (**18**) ..... number of adults are still unable to perform — unless you happen to be a night owl.

13	**A**	Therefore	**B**	Hence	**C**	Thereby	**D**	Hereby
14	**A**	glimpse	**B**	glower	**C**	glance	**D**	glare
15	**A**	Yet	**B**	So	**C**	Even	**D**	Thus
16	**A**	get	**B**	hold	**C**	put	**D**	keep
17	**A**	grab	**B**	catch	**C**	pick	**D**	snatch
18	**A**	faltering	**B**	blistering	**C**	sobering	**D**	staggering

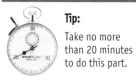

PART 2

You are going to read four extracts which are all concerned in some way with the future. For questions **19–26**, choose the answer (**A, B, C** or **D**) which you think fits best according to the text. Mark your answers **on the separate answer sheet.**

Futurology

Back in 1985, a British inventor called Clive Sinclair made quite a splash with his electric tricycle which was widely predicted to be the answer to the traffic problems of the world's big cities. Despite the hype, his dream of a new form of motorised transport proved to be no more than so much hot air; the idea, for a whole variety of reasons failed to catch on. His experience is by no means uncommon, and that's because futurology, the task of predicting trends at the intersection of technological advance and consumer taste, can be a tricky business.

Futurology is a hybrid discipline; a blend of science and creative insight, and the futurologist must always take account of the resources which we already have before he begins to factor in his range of variables: everything from the pace of economic change to political developments to the spontaneous convulsions of fashion and the popular aesthetic. In the hands of its most enthusiastic advocates, however, the discipline begins to suffer from in-built inflationary tendencies because, as Sinclair found to his cost, no chief executive or television producer is going to pay good money to be told that things will remain much as they are.

19 According to the writer, what must futurologists do?

    A have faith in their own instincts

    B keep in touch with social trends

    C ignore the whims of changing fashion

    D accept that theirs is an imprecise science

20 In the writer's view, Sinclair's electric tricycle became a victim of

    A inadequate technical research.

    B inappropriate marketing strategies.

    C unwarranted media attention.

    D unexpected changes in consumer taste.

Hypermobility

Fifty years ago, the average Briton travelled about 5 miles a day. Now it is about 28 miles a day, and forecast to double by 2025. Prodigious technological efforts are being made to solve the problems of congestion and pollution caused by this increased motorised mobility. Let us suppose for a moment that they succeed. Imagine that scientists invent a pollution-free perpetual motion engine. Imagine further, that they succeed in developing the ultimate computerised traffic control system. Finally, imagine a world in which computers are universally affordable and access to the internet is too cheap to meter; pollution-free virtual mobility is vigorously promoted as an important part of the solution to the problems caused by too much physical mobility.

21 At present, the lion's share of time and money devoted to finding solutions to the problems caused by motorised travel 24 is being spent on such technical fixes. But if successful, these will actually lead to further increases in physical mobility. Cleaner and more efficient engines will weaken existing constraints on the growth of travel, making it cheaper and removing environmental reasons for restricting it. Intelligent highway systems promise to reduce greatly the time cost of travel by eliminating congestion. And virtual mobility, while replacing many physical journeys, is more likely to serve 36 as a net stimulus to travel: by freeing 37 teleworkers to join the exodus from city centres to places where population, and related services, are more widely dispersed, and average daily travel will, therefore, increase yet further.

21 By the end of the passage, it becomes clear that, in the first paragraph, the writer is describing

A   an ideal situation from his point of view.
B   an alternative solution to existing problems.
C   the underlying weakness of current thinking.
D   the logical conclusion of current research.

22 Which phrase best reveals the writer's attitude towards the efforts being made to solve the problems of congestion and pollution?

A   'the lion's share' (line 21)
B   'such technical fixes' (line 24)
C   'a net stimulus' (line 36)
D   'join the exodus' (line 37)

Extract from a novel

Life is a journey punctuated with crossroads and side turnings. One wrong decision and the traveller may find there is no space for going back, though there may be an opportunity, further ahead, to take a lane leading away from the false trail he has been pursuing. Perhaps it will convey him, by a longer route, to the destination which was his aim, but perhaps it will lead him to a dead end or along confusing byways until he has lost his way completely. The choice may not always be his; life can throw obstacles into his path — a fallen tree, a mandatory alternative route — and he must look for signs to guide him in the right direction.

Alice's choice had been to use Godfrey as a means to change her own monotonous existence and escape the bondage to her parents which ordained her life. She had never before met a man who showed any lasting interest in her. She had lost touch with her few school friends, and did not win new ones at the secretarial college. Alice was not someone people remembered or sought out. Her colleagues at work found her quiet, dull, and dependable; as her duties at the museum lay behind the scenes, she rarely came in contact with the public, so her social skills did not improve. When she and Godfrey met, she was on the prowl, desperately seeking someone who would rescue her.

23 Which phrase best summarises the view put forward in the first paragraph?

   A Most people make their own luck.
   B Don't waste the opportunities offered to you.
   C It isn't possible to control your life completely.
   D It's never too late to make a new start.

24 Which word best describes Alice's frame of mind?

   A resigned
   B ambitious
   C frustrated
   D indifferent

Memo to the Future

A paradox of human civilisation is that the older its records, the longer they tend to last. We can read the shopping lists of the ancient Minoans from 3000 years ago; but our own memos are unlikely to last a generation. The more information we generate, it seems, the less we leave for posterity; and the process is accelerating. Technology prefers efficiency to durability. So it was that clay and stone gave way to parchment, papyrus and paper, less robust materials, but still more enduring than today's electronic and photographic means. Much of the data collected in the 1960s and 1970s has already been lost, either because the material it is stored on has decayed or because the machines needed to access it have become obsolete.

This makes us an amnesic civilisation with a short-term memory. But surely, there are things that our far-off descendents will want, or perhaps need, to know about us. Although it's difficult to stand far enough back from the whirlwind of modern life to make the assessment of exactly what is worth recording for them, finding a way to talk to the future is not just a flight of fancy. If we really want to leave a record, somebody has to make such decisions, as well as developing the technology that will assure its long-term survival and eventual retrieval.

25 According to the writer, the trend described in the first paragraph is

   A gathering pace all the time.
   B nearing its natural conclusion.
   C no longer serving current needs.
   D a result of outdated technologies.

26 What is the writer's purpose in these paragraphs?

   A to question certain widely-held assumptions
   B to provide the historical context for a current debate
   C to propose a remedial course of action
   D to re-evaluate the role of technical change

PART 3

Tip:
Take no more
than 25 minutes
to do this part.

You are going to read a newspaper article about a circus school. Seven paragraphs have been removed from the extract. Choose from the paragraphs **A–H** the one which fits each gap (**27–33**). There is one extra paragraph which you do not need to use. Mark your answers **on the separate answer sheet.**

Pain and Pleasure under the Big Top

Despite bruises and blisters, our reporter was bowled over
by an introductory course in circus skills

We stood in a large circle and took each other in. Who were these people taking an introductory class in circus skills in the deserted city of London on a Saturday afternoon? Well, there were all sorts — young and old, fit and unfit — who had learned of this little-advertised opportunity to try out flying trapeze, acrobatic balancing, *corde lisse* and the inevitable juggling at Circus Space in Old Street. We split into smaller groups; Mark, Sophie and Annie were to be my classmates. We would have different trainers for the various activities, but Lee would be our main tutor.

27

It was an entrepreneurial unicyclist who a decade ago founded the charity known as Circus Space, hollowing and decking out an imposing disused power station to create a London circus-training venue. It has since come of age, training young people to become acrobats for prestigious aerial shows amongst a range of other similarly high-profile achievements.

28

Most of the group had already tried juggling before, of course, in one form or another, and so we were more than a little bemused when Lee showed off with four balls, but declined five. None of us managed more than three as it turned out and it was certainly much slower going than any of us had anticipated. Hours of practice, it seemed, were needed to achieve better flight control.

29

The fittest of our group, Annie, stepped quickly up the steel ladder and took her place on the standing board suspended from the ceiling by cables anchored to the floor. She was strapped into the safety harness and on the trainer's word held the bar with both hands, stepped down and swung free across the width of the building. It looked exciting, tiring, graceful — and easy. But the board seemed much higher than it did from the ground, and the space ahead much bigger.

30

I stepped into the harness, held the bar and swung free. A delightful feeling of lifting flight as I travelled through the space turned into real pleasure at correctly sensing the apparently all-important 'beat'. It was tiring though, and simple, and it was over quickly.

31

Circus people accept pain as an occupational hazard. The problem with this is that they give almost no warnings about what turn out to be the inevitable range of trapeze bruises and rope burns. After all, what did we expect?

32

Annie, who had again volunteered to be the guinea pig, was the first to try, allowing herself to be guided and steadied by our powerful trainer. She was, of course, an example to us all. She'd got it down to a fine art within minutes, achieving an impressive 'flag' position.

33

Lee showed us how straightforward it was before watching us as we ascended slowly and uneasily only to balance stylelessly, with more than half an eye on the blue mats beneath. We attributed our rather lacklustre performance to fatigue, an explanation that Lee, ever encouraging, was only too keen to accept with hurried apologies for perhaps pushing us too far. But he needn't have worried. Afterwards, everyone agreed to come back for more, although no-one was yet volunteering to take the plunge and consider trading in their job for the all-round insecurity of a high-wire act. Time will tell, I suppose.

A Sophie was to go before me and as I stood beside her up there, she was saying she couldn't do it. She was shaking, making the equipment shudder violently. The trainers vainly reassured and cajoled. It is curious how one's own nerves are calmed by seeing another's and perceiving them to be irrational.

B More prosaically, some City companies have found the activities at Circus Space provide excellent opportunities for exercises in corporate team-building. Certainly our group was delighted when Sophie, having a second attempt at the activity which had foiled her previously, stepped right into it and looked like a natural.

C Not so with the flying trapeze. Here the problem is reversed — progress is heavily front-loaded. By being led through the correct movements, instant success, of a sort, is possible. But advancing beyond the simple requires a serious level of fitness, stamina and willingness to suffer pain.

D It's worth noting that Britain was seriously lagging behind the rest of the world during the rebirth of the circus in the 1980s, when Cirque de Soleil and Archaos were doing in the west what the Russian and Chinese state circuses had never stopped doing in the east.

E Only when Mark took his turn did we see how crucial it is to arch the body at the furthest extents of the arc. This adds elegance, but also prevents hitting the small of the back on the board. Mark's mistiming led to a strangled cry and a sore coccyx.

F But without equivalent experience to build on, it was hard for us to create stability in anything but the most basic moves. The laborious *corde lisse*, a single hanging rope which performers climb attractively and balance from perilously, presented us with a further challenge.

G We turned to acrobalancing, an activity that depends on the strength of one person to act as a base for the balancing movements of another. We found positions that appeared complex were strikingly easy to achieve with a degree of flexibility — and a good trainer.

H Circus Space is still lacking in some areas. There are no decent changing rooms, no lockers and no cafe at the weekends. The trainers, on the other hand, are experienced circus professionals and their Saturday class gives a whistle-stop tour of basic circus skills for absolute beginners.

PART 4

Tip:
Take no more
than 25 minutes
to do this part.

You are going to read the beginning of a novel. For questions **34–40** choose the answer (**A, B, C** or **D**) which you think fits best according to the text. Mark your answers **on the separate answer sheet.**

I rarely attend international conferences since I am neither particularly enchanted with air travel nor with the discomfort of staying in overheated hotels, trying to make myself understood in languages I do not speak, eating junk food I abhor. I content myself with contributing research papers, encouraging my students to take the podium in my stead whilst I remain in my laboratory, getting on with the work.

There are, of course, occasional exceptions. One such was an invitation I received some yeas ago, to give a keynote lecture at an important symposium in Japan. This I considered an honour as well as international recognition of my work. Nonetheless, that might have been insufficient to tempt me, but when I realised that the conference was to be held in Kyoto, a city Amy particularly longed to visit, I agreed. There was also the matter of a couple of first-class return air tickets, which swung the balance. Venal perhaps, but I make no apologies. Twelve hours sardined into the economy section of an aircraft at my age can seriously damage your health.

My original plan was to attend the conference on the first couple of days only, give my talk and see a few people in the same line of research. Afterwards Amy and I would do a little sightseeing and fly home. But it turned out to be an enormous international gathering of many disciplines, and I found myself more involved and excited than I'd expected. What I didn't bargain for was that one lecture would change my life; radically and utterly.

On the second evening, a friend from the Netherlands happened to mention that a group in Oxford was doing some excellent work on the musculo-skeletal system which was reasonably close to my own research. As luck would have it, the leader of the team was scheduled to give a lecture, late the following afternoon. Since Amy and I had arranged a visit to the Sacred Spring Garden of Shinsen-en next day, which I was reluctant to cancel, I said I would try to make it if I got back in time. In many ways, I wish I had stayed longer in that beautiful, reflective place, but alas I did not. Instead, I left my companion to return to the hotel with the rest of the tour, and took a taxi back to the conference hall.

I arrived only a minute or two before the lecture was scheduled to start. In the half-light, the auditorium looked vast. Rows of seats, each with a folding writing-flap attached to the

43 arm, horseshoed a low rostrum. As I entered, a stooped figure
44 mounted the podium. He was a fidgety individual who fumbled nervously with his notes while he gathered his thoughts. He cleared his throat three times and was about to start when he
47 looked up and blinked rapidly against the strong glare of the spotlight which was trained on his face. 'Can you dim that a little?' he asked irritably. Then: 'Is the projector properly

loaded?' From somewhere at the back of the hall, a disembodied voice answered in the affirmative and immediately the light transferred to the screen behind the speaker, leaving him in half-shadow.

Still he couldn't seem to get started, but continued fiddling with his papers until a crouching figure scurried up to the front row and switched on the lectern reading light. Effusive thanks from the speaker were interrupted by a member of the audience who asked impatiently if they could begin. Immediately, a slide bearing the name of both lecture and lecturer flashed on to the screen.

I had just entered the hall and was standing behind the back row of seats, from where I watched the proceedings with only half an eye. There was an unusually large audience. As soon as I had adjusted to the dim light of the auditorium, I looked around for a seat and eventually found one of the very few places at the end of the second row from the rear. I gingerly edged past the plethora of wires and cables which snaked off from the powerhouse at the back of the hall. As I struggled with the armrest, my neighbour turned to me impatiently, but apart from several loud shushes, mercifully retrained himself from comment.

Thus I missed the speaker's opening remarks. These I assumed to have been amusing, since laughter and applause rippled through the room. Although the subject of the lecture wasn't precisely in my own area of interest, it was near enough, and I soon became absorbed. But it went on too long. The day was hot and the lecture hall, allegedly air-conditioned, rapidly became stuffy.

I do not know at what stage I began to concentrate on the speaker rather than on what he was saying. He made a dull enough spectacle. Though he had an occasional amusing turn of phrase, his delivery was poor and he seemed more concerned with accuracy than with performance. He seldom looked up and when he did, it was to blink in the light of the projector. But his illustrations were extremely innovative. To underscore his theme, he superimposed computer images of the human locomotor system over slides of well-known paintings. I was enchanted. But I remember with infinite precision the moment when a particular juxtaposition sent my mind spinning, spinning back to the past. I leaned forward and must have given an involuntary cry of surprise because he raised his hand to shade his eyes as he scanned the room for where the sound had come from.

My mind had cleared, I did not miss a single other word and by the time the lecture ended I was won over – in a manner of speaking – to his point of view. I was determined, now, to shift the emphasis of my own line of research.

34 How does the writer generally regard attending international conferences?

    A as beneath his dignity

    B as a duty he can delegate

    C as a necessary inconvenience

    D as an occasional treat

35 What convinced the writer to attend the conference in Kyoto?

    A the prestigious nature of the event

    B an incentive which was offered

    C a desire to please other people

    D the opportunity to promote his ideas

36 What surprised the writer about the conference?

    A how stimulating it was

    B how well his lecture was received

    C how much was expected of him

    D how challenging he found it

37 On reflection, how does the writer feel about the visit to the Sacred Spring Garden?

    A He wishes he'd allowed more time to see it all.

    B He regrets not taking it more seriously.

    C He recognises that he should have cancelled it.

    D He admits it would have been better to have extended it.

38 Which word from the text gives us an impression of the lecturer's physical appearance?

    A 'stooped' (line 43)

    B 'fidgety' (line 44)

    C 'fumbled' (line 44)

    D 'blinked' (line 47)

39 At the beginning of the lecture, the writer

    A is disconcerted by the attitude of the audience.

    B is unimpressed by the state of the electrical system.

    C is prevented from giving the speaker his full attention.

    D is puzzled that the lecturer chooses to begin with a joke.

40 What suddenly changed the writer's view of the lecture?

    A a chance remark

    B a convincing argument

    C a visual image

    D a glance of recognition

PAPER 2   Writing (2 hours)

You **must** answer this question. Write your answer in **300–350** words in an appropriate style.

1   Recently, a media magazine published a review of a popular drama screened on national television about a family reunion. In the review it states:

> 'Reunions of all kinds force people to confront who they are, what they were, what they hope to become and how they relate to each other.'

As a follow-up, the magazine plans to publish a series of articles on the topic of reunions and has asked readers to submit an article for possible inclusion. Write an article that gives your opinion on the purpose and value of reunions, addressing the above quotation.

Write your **article**.

Write an answer to **one** of the questions **2–4** in this part. Write your answer in **300-350** words in an appropriate style

2   A wildlife magazine is offering an award for an original and stimulating review of a non-fiction book on the natural world. The judges are looking for informative reviews that convey the writer's feelings about the content, approach and style of the book. You have decided to enter the competition.

Write your **review**.

3   You subscribe to a magazine which is devoted to a hobby that you are particularly involved in. The editors have invited regular readers to write to the magazine and explain why they prefer it to other similar publications. They are also interested to find out what readers would like to read about in future editions.

Write your **letter**.

4   As a student on a media studies course, you are regularly asked to prepare reports to be read aloud to other members of the group. On this occasion, your course coordinator has requested that you prepare a report on a significant news item in your own country that raises important issues. The report should offer a personal view on the topic and suggest a number of questions that could be discussed by members of the group afterwards.

Write your **report**.

For questions **1–15**, read the text below and think of the word which best fits each space. Use only **one** word in each space. There is an example at the beginning **(0)**. Write your answers in **CAPITAL LETTERS on the separate answer sheet.**

Example:

0	A	N	Y																

The Science of Cooking
By Peter Barham

You do not have to be a chemist to cook a meal, **(0)** ...*any*... more than you need an engineering qualification to drive a car; but a **(1)** .... technical knowledge can help when things **(2)** .... awry. That is the reasoning **(3)** .... this volume which combines the scientific principles of cooking **(4)** .... a down-to-earth guide to kitchen utensils, some experiments to try at home and **(5)** .... random collection of recipes.

As well as learning technical details, **(6)** .... why potatoes become translucent when they are boiled, you get a sprinkling **(7)** .... really useful tips. For instance, the best way to work **(8)** .... how long to roast meat is to measure it, not weigh it. But **(9)** .... said, the recipes themselves are uninspiring and you might be wiser **(10)** .... to let children try the riskier experiments on their own: **(11)** .... involves placing a light bulb in the microwave, another boiling water in a balloon **(12)** .... a naked flame!

Gastronomy is an art. If it **(13)** .... merely a science, this book would contain most of what you need to know to rustle **(14)** .... a palatable meal. In the final analysis, the message seems simple: **(15)** .... a scientist ask you to dinner, find out who's cooking!

For questions **16–25**, read the text below. Use the word given in **capitals** at the end of some of the lines to form a word that fits in the space in the same line. There is an example at the beginning **(0)**. Write your answers in **CAPITAL LETTERS on the separate answer sheet**.

Example:

0	C	O	M	M	U	N	I	C	A	T	I	O	N					

Preface to 'Guide to Handwriting Styles'

Almost as if in response to the age of **(0)** *communication* technology   **COMMUNICATE**

in which we now all live, the last few years have seen a widespread

(16) .... of interest in the ancient art of handwriting. It seems   **AWAKE**

that the individuality and freedom of expression implicit in the

craft of penmanship are waging their own counter revolution

against the faceless **(17)** .... of the word processor.   **PERSON**

Graphologists, those people who are directly involved in the study

and analysis of writing styles, claim that an individual's handwriting

is almost as good a way of distinguishing one person from another

as taking their **(18)** ....   **FINGER**

There are, however, so many basic styles of handwriting that it would

be **(19)** .... to expect any one person to be   **REASON**

an authority on all of them. Consequently, unlike other books on this

subject, we have **(20)** .... the advice and   **SEEK**

(21) .... of several notable practitioners in penmanship, each   **EXPERT**

of whom has written about those aspects of the craft for which they

have gained professional **(22)** .... We have not attempted to   **RECOGNISE**

establish a **(23)** .... textbook of rules, but rather to provide an   **DEFINE**

introduction to the craft, with a set of practical **(24)** ....   **GUIDE**

which will be of interest to anyone who would like to learn how to

write more **(25)** ....   **ATTRACT**

PART 3

For questions **26–31**, think of **one** word only which can be used appropriately in all three sentences. Here is an example **(0)**.

Example:

0   Last year's champion is in with a .... chance of repeating his success in the grand prix next weekend.

Some of the home owners are hoping to get compensation for the poor building work, and I think they have a very .... case.

There's no point in trying to put the tent up, the wind is far too ....

Example:

0	S	T	R	O	N	G													

Write **only** the missing word in **CAPITAL LETTERS on the separate answer sheet**.

---

26 • The quiz contestant ran out of time and was unable to .... for the jackpot question.

• Although his career was progressing well, the young journalist knew he had a long way to .... before he would be ready for promotion.

• Keeping animals in captivity may .... against your principles, but it is the only way to preserve some species.

27 • Tom and Anna have reached the .... in their relationship where they feel ready to make a commitment to each other.

• The planning of the summer sports event has reached a critical .... , and certain financial decisions cannot be postponed any further.

• Negotiations to buy the building have reached an advanced .... and an announcement is expected shortly, which will reveal the identity of its new owners.

28 • The onions should be .... chopped and then sprinkled on top of the dish.

• The argument is really quite .... balanced, and it is as yet unclear what the final decision will be.

• The engine has been .... tuned to give the best possible performance.

29 • On .... of their meal, hotel guests are invited to retire to the lounge for coffee.

• The work on the new extension to the museum is nearing .... and a date for the reopening of the building will soon be set.

• Following successful .... of the introductory course, students will be invited to sign up for the options of their choice.

30 • At the moment, the evidence .... to John being guilty of the murder.

• The bibliography at the end of the book .... readers in the direction of further reading on the subject.

• Mrs Bell generally .... out any discrepancies between what was recorded in the minutes and what was actually discussed at the meeting.

31 • Shopkeepers have noticed that business has been .... since parking was banned in the High Street.

• At first, Melanie was .... to take in the full implications of what her manager was saying to her.

• Darren blamed his late arrival on the fact that the clock in his office was running ....

For questions **32–39**, complete the second sentence so that it has a similar meaning to the first sentence, using the word given. **Do not change the word given.** You must use between **three** and **eight** words, including the word given. Here is an example **(0)**.

Example:

0 Immediately after winning the race, Sandy began training for the next one.
had
No .... she began training for the next one.

0 sooner had Sandy won the race than

Write **only** the missing words **on the separate answer sheet.**

---

32 Personal history plays a role in determining how willing you are to participate in group activities.
effect
Personal history .... your willingness to participate in group activities.

33 It is important to know the difference between a joke and an insult.
draw
It is important to know .... between a joke and an insult.

34 Initially the Gregsons had trouble getting their business off the ground, but the situation eventually improved.
going
Initially the Gregsons found it .... , but the situation eventually improved.

35 'If it means that I can watch the film on the television, I'd rather stay in,' Sarah said.
being
Sarah admitted that she'd rather stay in if .... watch the film on television.

36 Julia is very nice but I find it impossible to understand most of what she says.
single
Though I like Julia, I can barely .... says.

37 There is no evidence that the famous legendary character Robin Hood ever existed.
prove
There is nothing .... of the famous legendary character Robin Hood.

38 When people are under stress they easily succumb to everyday illnesses such as the common cold.
prone
When people are under stress they tend .... everyday illnesses such as the common cold.

39 The loud music coming from her neighbour's house didn't bother Lucy at all.
way
Lucy .... the loud music coming from her neighbour's house.

PART 5

For questions **40–44**, read the following texts on e-shopping. For questions **40–43**, answer with a word or short phrase. You do not need to write complete sentences. For question **44**, write a summary according to the instructions given. Write your answers to questions **40–44 on the separate answer sheet**.

When organisations use the letters 'www' in their advertisements, we are supposed to be impressed. 'How very modern,' we are conditioned to think. And how convenient that, instead of phoning up a real person to get more information, we are now able, thanks to the magic www, to do the research ourselves. What they don't tell you, of course, is that this will involve a half-hour struggle with the 'imaginative' web design and a further half hour spent fighting through the jungle of ill-expressed and incomplete information, while all the time the phone bill rachets up.

And when it comes to trying to buy a product on line, you can be assured that this lengthy tussle will culminate in that definitive 21st century moment: you hit the 'Buy' button, only to be told that your order cannot be completed until you have entered, not just your name, address and credit card number (for you have these ready beside you), but all manner of seemingly irrelevant personal details that, of course, you do not have immediately to hand. Naturally, they need to assure themselves that you are who you say you are, and possibly they need to establish for certain that you do indeed have the funds to make the proposed transaction. I wonder, however, how many other people are tempted to give up at this point, irritated by the fact that the companies concerned seem to go out of their way to make it as difficult as possible for you to part with your money. For me at least it's a case of 'Thanks world of commerce, for the don't-we-look-groovy website. We were doing fine without it.'

40 In your own words, explain why, according to the author, companies like to include the letters 'www' in their advertising.

....

41 Which phrase in the second paragraph refers back to the idea conveyed in 'fighting through the jungle' (line 6)?

....

Shopping on the Internet just has not lived up to its early promise of convenience and time-saving at the click of a mouse. For many people the technical complexity of modem, WAP phone and interactive digital TV is decidedly off-putting, not to mention downright expensive in terms of the hardware alone. But this is nothing compared with the potential annoyance caused when the last link in the e-commerce chain proves to be doggedly low-tech. You wait for hours for the goods to arrive, pop out to buy a paper, and return to find a note which reads: 'We tried to deliver, but you were not in. Please pick up your goods from our depot.' The feeling of frustration and
10 disappointment is enough to send you straight back to a conventional shopping centre.

This last setback could, however, soon be a thing of the past. Internet companies have finally come up with some solutions, and, as is often the way with solutions, the most promising to date is breathtaking in its simplicity; what could be easier than picking the stuff up from a shop? Not just any old shop, but the nearest late-opening retail outlet, be it a street corner grocery, a petrol station or a newsagent; indeed anywhere which has long opening hours and which enough people are likely to pass on the way home from work or school may end up taking part in the proposed scheme. The e-commerce companies will vet likely outlets in each area and, if the premises are deemed suitable, the shops will hold your goods until you are able to pop in and pick them up.

42 Which phrase, used earlier in the text, introduces the idea that e-shopping can lead to 'disappointment' (line 10)?

....

43 Which two verbs in the second paragraph indicate that only certain shops will be allowed take part in the proposed scheme?

....

44 In a paragraph of between **50 and 70 words**, summarise **in your own words as far as possible**, the disadvantages of shopping over the Internet which are outlined in the texts.

PAPER 4

PART 1

Listening (Approximately 40 minutes)

You will hear four different extracts. For questions **1–8**, choose the answer (**A, B** or **C**) which fits best according to what you hear. There are two questions for each extract.

Extract One

You hear a man reviewing a book which he has read.

1 From his comments, we understand that he

    A shares the author's environmental concerns.
    B comes from a different background to the author.
    C regards the author's viewpoint with suspicion.

1

2 According to the speaker, the main strength of the book is

    A the thoroughness of the research.
    B the quality of the writing.
    C the underlying message.

2

Extract Two

You hear a man talking about cycling in London.

3 What is he doing when he speaks?

    A providing a counter argument
    B responding to an accusation
    C defending an unpopular point of view

3

4 According to the speaker, the type of cyclist he describes

    A deliberately sets out to annoy drivers.
    B claims to represent the views of all cyclists.
    C is insensitive to the needs of other road users.

4

Extract Three

You hear a woman talking about shoes.

5   What point does the speaker make about shoes?

    A Well-made ones are in short supply.
    B Replacing the ones you like isn't easy.
    C They're better when not in pristine condition.

`5`

6   Which word best describes the speaker's attitude towards
   the change she is describing?

    A regretful
    B detached
    C accepting

`6`

Extract Four

You overhear two colleagues talking about a report one of them has written.

7   What is the woman's view of the man named Bill?

    A She disagrees with the opinions he expresses.
    B She doubts the relevance of his comments.
    C She disapproves of his manner in meetings.

`7`

8   In the woman's view, a lot of the jargon used in meetings

    A is designed to exclude people.
    B has already become outdated.
    C makes little sense to those who use it.

`8`

You will hear the beginning of a radio programme about the use of fingerprints in criminal investigations. For questions **9–17**, complete the sentences with a word or short phrase.

In England, fingerprinting techniques were widely used

from the year [**9**] onwards.

In the Deptford murders, a fingerprint left on a

[**10**] in a shop led to a conviction.

Today, fingerprints are particularly useful in

solving cases of [**11**] and crimes involving cars.

New technology means that fingerprints can now even be taken from

difficult places like [**12**] or polished surfaces.

The police officers' fingerprinting equipment at the scene of a crime

includes a [**13**], powders and gels.

NAFIS is the name of the [**14**] in the

computer system which handles fingerprints.

Matching fingerprints is likened to the game known

by the name [**15**]

The pattern on most fingerprints is either arched or comes in

[**16**] or loops.

Everyone has unique fingerprints, even people such as [**17**]

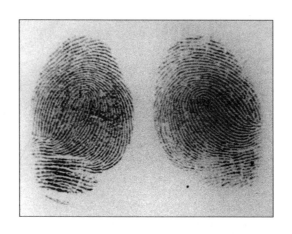

You will hear an interview with Harry Newland, a young film actor. For questions **18–22**, choose the answer (**A, B, C** or **D**) which fits best according to what you hear.

18 Harry believes his acting talent to be largely the result of

   A an inherent ability.
   B his theatrical upbringing.
   C training from an early age.
   D conscious efforts to develop it.

   [ ] **18**

19 Harry looks back on his early parts in television dramas with

   A embarrassment.
   B gratitude.
   C derision.
   D pride.

   [ ] **19**

20 How does Harry explain the attitude of other actors towards him?

   A They took great care not to offend him.
   B They appreciated his level of commitment.
   C They were keen to keep him in his place.
   D They made allowances for his difficulties.

   [ ] **20**

21 When working on big productions, Harry finds it best to

   A follow the lead of other actors.
   B bring his own ideas to the role.
   C keep the finished product in mind.
   D focus on his own performance.

   [ ] **21**

22 Looking back, Harry realises that his parents

   A put too much pressure on him on occasion.
   B may not always have had his best interests at heart.
   C were well aware of the potential pitfalls of his situation.
   D tended to be over-protective in their attitude towards him.

   [ ] **22**

You will hear two friends, Adam and Kayleigh, talking about people's attitudes to technological change in consumer goods. For questions **23–28**, decide whether the opinions are expressed by only one of the speakers, or whether the speakers agree.

Write   **A**   for Adam,
               K   for Kayleigh,
or   **B**   for Both, when they agree.

23 Most people find it hard to keep pace with technological change.   **23**

24 The government's new scheme is unlikely to be successful.   **24**

25 New technologies used to have more impact on people's daily lives.   **25**

26 New cars make less of an impression on people than they used to.   **26**

27 People are afraid of showing their ignorance about their computers.   **27**

28 Some new products are failing to reflect the needs of consumers.   **28**

PAPER 5   Speaking (19 minutes)

Answer these questions:
- What do you enjoy doing most in your free time?
- How has learning English changed your life?
- Do you think you'll always live in this part of the world? Where else would you like to live?

PART 2   (4 minutes)

Turn to pictures A–F on pages 170–1 which show various promoional images.

First look at Picture A only and talk together about how this picture makes you feel and what you think it represents. You have about one minute for this.

Now look at all the pictures. A large company is running a training course in decision-making skills for its employees and needs a striking image to put on a poster publicising the course. Talk together about how each of these images relates to the idea of decision-making and decide which one would be most effective on the poster. You have about three minutes for this.

PART 3   (12 minutes)

Candidate A: Look at the question in the box. You have two minutes to say what you think about the question. There are some ideas to use in the box if you like.

> What is the role of competitive sport in modern society?
> - motivation and rewards
> - commercial considerations
> - international competitions

Candidate B: Is there anything you would like to add?

Candidate B: Look at the question in the box. You have two minutes to say what you think about the question. There are some ideas to use in the box if you like.

> Should public services such as health and education be run according to business principles?
> - need to use scarce resources wisely
> - quality of services vs. cost of services
> - private enterprise vs. government spending

Candidate A: Is there anything you would like to add?

Candidates A and B: Now answer these questions about competition in general:
- To what extent is competition necessary for a society to function well?
- Is it possible for everyone to have equal opportunities in life?

TEST 6

PAPER 1   Reading (1 hour 30 minutes)

PART 1

For questions **1–18**, read the three texts below and decide which answer (**A, B, C** or **D**) best fits each gap. Mark your answers **on the separate answer sheet**.

The Elephant Orchestra

Some of the forty-six elephants living at the Elephant Conservation Centre near Lampang in Thailand have (**1**) ..... a new life in music. Six of the centre's elephants (**2**) ..... the Thai Elephant Orchestra by playing a variety of percussion instruments. Those familiar with Thai instruments will recognise the slit drums, the gong and the thundersheet. The only difference is that the elephant (**3**) ..... are a bit sturdier. When they play, the elephants are given a (**4**) ..... to tell them when to start; after that, they improvise. They clearly have a (**5**) ..... sense of rhythm. They flap their ears to the beat and some add to the melody with their own trumpeting. Elephant mood-music, it seems, could have a commercial future. A thirteen-track CD has been produced and anyone not knowing who the players were would simply (**6**) ..... them to be human. All profits from the sales of the CD are helping to keep the centre going.

1	**A** found	**B** settled	**C** taken	**D** opted
2	**A** put together	**B** make up	**C** play out	**D** lead off
3	**A** types	**B** replicas	**C** versions	**D** sorts
4	**A** twitch	**B** tip	**C** cue	**D** hint
5	**A** quick	**B** stark	**C** high	**D** keen
6	**A** assume	**B** attribute	**C** allocate	**D** appraise

The Pencil

The modern pencil user (**7**) ..... into one of two basic categories: the propellers and the chewers. Fans of the propelling pencil cannot be without it and have a (**8**) ..... to clip their pencils into their breast pockets with that typical (**9**) ..... of brisk efficiency. When needed, the offending object is unveiled in a flash, firmly gripped, poised and then irritatingly clicked three times. The chewers, (**10**) ....., will leave a damp legacy on every pencil that rolls innocently into their (**11**) ..... . Unconsciously, they put the unsharpened end between their front teeth and gnaw away until, eventually, graphite is (**12**) ..... through the splintered paint.

7	**A** strays	**B** falls	**C** dips	**D** drops
8	**A** tendency	**B** leaning	**C** habit	**D** liability
9	**A** state	**B** tone	**C** mood	**D** air
10	**A** by the same token	**B** in other words	**C** in the same way	**D** on the other hand
11	**A** track	**B** route	**C** path	**D** way
12	**A** revealed	**B** displayed	**C** exhibited	**D** betrayed

New Adventure

It was normal that I should feel some anxiety about my departure. Not only was I setting out to a place I had never been before, I was also (**13**) ..... on a kind of life about which I knew nothing and, what is more, stripping myself of all that was familiar to me into the (**14**) ..... . We are all, in our journey through life, navigating towards some special, dreamed-of place; and if for some reason we are (**15**) ..... off course, then we must strike out, at whatever risk, to (**16**) ..... things right. Not all of these forays need have the drastic flavour of my own leap into the unknown; some are such subtle turnings that it is only afterwards that one looks back and sees what is was all (**17**) ..... to. But to drift, blown this way and that, or for that (**18**) ..... to pursue a wrong course for the sake of fear or pride, costs time; and we none of us have too much of that.

13	**A**	escaping	**B**	exploring	**C** emigrating	**D**	embarking
14	**A**	deal	**B**	arrangement	**C** bargain	**D**	negotiation
15	**A**	spun	**B**	kicked	**C** thrown	**D**	headed
16	**A**	set	**B**	establish	**C** sort	**D**	have
17	**A**	approaching	**B**	steering	**C** going	**D**	leading
18	**A**	end	**B**	matter	**C** point	**D**	sense

You are going to read four extracts which are all concerned in some way with art. For questions **19–26**, choose the answer (**A, B, C** or **D**) which you think fits best according to the text. Mark your answers **on the separate answer sheet.**

Extract from a novel

Positano stands on the steep side of a hill, a disarray of huddled white houses, their tiled roofs washed pale by the suns of a hundred years, but unlike many of these Italian towns perched out of harm's way on a rocky eminence, it does not offer you at one delightful glance all it has to give. It has quaint streets that zig-zag up the hill, and battered, painted houses in the baroque style, but very late, in which Neapolitan noblemen led, for a season, lives of penurious grandeur. It is indeed almost excessively picturesque and in winter, its two or three modest hotels are crowded with painters who in their different ways acknowledge, by their daily labours, the emotion it has excited in them. Some take infinite pains to place on canvas every window and every tile their peering eyes can discover, and doubtless achieve the satisfaction that rewards honest industry. 'At all events, it's sincere,' they say modestly when they show you their work. Some rugged and dashing, in a fine frenzy, attack their canvas with a pallet knife charged with a wad of paint, and they say: 'You see, what I was trying to bring out was my personality.' They slightly close their eyes and tentatively murmur: 'I think it's rather me, don't you?' And there are some who give you highly entertaining arrangements of spheres and cubes and utter sombrely: 'That's how I see it!' These for the most part are strong silent men who waste no words.

19 Which of the following reflects the writer's opinion of Positano?

    A It is even more beautiful than it initially appears.

    B Its full charm is apparent only to the trained eye.

    C It does not resemble other quaint towns in Italy.

    D Its ambience suits people of a particular character.

20 In describing the varied approaches taken to painting Positano, the writer's tone is predominantly

    A admiring.

    B disinterested.

    C humorous.

    D appreciative.

ON ART

It is a remarkable fact that man was an artist before he was a maker. His urge for creativity and artistic expression was intuitive and long predated concepts of civilisation. I am profoundly impressed by the imaginative scope and able hands of the first artists, the cavemen, who depicted images of their environment, articulating ordinary human fears, hopes and dreams. They recorded their visual perception with an innocent, untutored application.

Art comes from a basic human instinct to create, which elevates the individual and, in turn, enriches society. Even if its results are tangible and intentional, we tend to think of the artistic process as something arcane and mysterious. The scope and purpose of art differs markedly in content and character among people of the world as much as the modes of visualisation. Although a work of art is as unique and as individual as its creator, its form and content are often symbolic of locale and contemporary mores. Inevitable changes in perception during the history of mankind have altered both the style and implication of paintings. The love of, and interest in, exquisitely detailed works of art have always been universal.

21 What does the writer find most striking about cave art?

    A   the degree of artistic skill it reveals

    B   the simple representation of complex ideas

    C   the record it provides of how people once lived

    D   the enduring nature of the subjects chosen

22 In the second paragraph, what are we told about art as an activity?

    A   It is inevitably restricted by ethical considerations.

    B   Its perceived complexity lies in the method, not the outcome.

    C   It produces masterpieces that transcend cultural boundaries.

    D   Its performs the same function in all areas of the world.

Pay More and You Can't See the Point!

Money matters to most artists, yet much is squandered in the traditional belief that nothing matches a brush made of pure sable. *Connoisseur* may put change in your mind and in your pocket!

This brush is a perfected blend of sable and synthetic hair which has excellent results due to the way Pro Arte have combined these materials.

Try the wash test; it loads and carries colour in the excellent way you expect from a quality brush. Then, deftly flick and it fashions easily and instantly to a perfect point for fine detail. In *Connoisseur* you have a whole range of effects at your fingertips without swapping brush sizes. This simply isn't possible to the same degree with original sable brushes — always assuming we could make them to this generous size anyway.

Equally pleasing is the price of *Connoisseur*; less than a third of sable — which, in this size, represents a staggering saving!

See the point?

Pro Arte Connoisseur

---

23 Which of the following does the advertisement presuppose of the reader?

    A an overriding need to save costs

    B an openness towards new ideas

    C a familiarity with the arguments presented

    D a loyalty towards certain well-held views

24 What advantage does the advertisement suggest a *Connoisseur* brush has over sable brushes?

    A It is easier to use and to look after.

    B It permits a higher degree of accuracy in painting.

    C Each brush looks better and lasts longer.

    D One brush would be sufficient for all your needs.

Evening Stroll

Evening Stroll is a very small oil painting by Katie Holland. The sun sinks into a reflecting sea while two convincing figures in silhouette stroll along by the water's edge. The sea has been beautifully described, with the wavelets just regular enough, and Katie has made good use of a restricted palette. The colours soften as they recede and help to give a feeling of distance. There are, however, some points that I feel need addressing. Assuming that the beach stretches fairly flatly to the groyne and beyond, the level of the beach should not rise above the horizon. Here it appears to be higher and, where it meets the groyne, is well above sea level.

The second point concerns the figures. These are well-painted and I like the way that she has shown the eagerness of the child pulling the adult along. So much can be indicated by posture. Given the lengths of their outstretched arms I feel that the child appears too far forward. The child's feet are too high compared with the adult's, giving the impression that the infant is airborne by a few inches. If the beach shelves steeply and the child is walking at a higher level, the texture lines should have reinforced this. Nevertheless, this is a good painting.

25 Which of the following aspects of the painting does the writer criticise?

    A the colour
    B the context
    C the perspective
    D the shadow

26 The writer's purpose in describing this painting is to

    A evaluate an individual work.
    B illustrate a wider point.
    C promote a certain approach.
    D defend a particular view.

PART 3

You are going to read an extract from a piece of travel writing. Seven paragraphs have been removed from the extract. Choose from the paragraphs **A–H** the one which fits each gap (**27–33**). There is one extra paragraph which you do not need to use. Mark your answers **on the separate answer sheet.**

Bombay's pedalling waiters

It's 9am on a weekday morning in the Indian city of Bombay. In most of the city's offices, staff are already at their desks, getting to grips with the first problems, enquiries or routine tasks of the day, but for another group of workers who provide them with an essential service, the official working day is just about to begin. Many of these workers, especially the younger ones, will already have commuted for up to four hours from outlying villages, but not so my guide for the day, Baba Paranvakar. He lives in the city itself, and together with his trusty Hercules has been doing this job for 20 years. Their partnership is still going strong, although Baba's legs lack their youthful vigour and Hercules' balance is not what it was.

| 27 | |

For Baba Paranvakar is a professional dabbawallah and member of the Honourable Company of Tiffinbox Carriers in Bombay, India. He is 61 years old and, with the help of his faithful thirty-something two-wheeler, still covers more than 20 miles in a normal working day.

| 28 | |

'We collect the lunch boxes from private homes all round the city, mostly from housewives, and deliver them to their husbands at their workplace,' says Baba as we make our way towards Grant Road railway station. It is rush hour and Bombay is a blizzard of people.

| 29 | |

The system of carrying lunch boxes from private homes to work places around Bombay goes back to 1890. A man named Shri Mahadev Dube was its pioneer. He used to deliver dabbas to the offices of city administrators who lived away from their places of employment. In those days, it was not the done thing to be seen carrying your lunch. Everything was delivered by bicycle and tram.

| 30 | |

Both gave up using maps a quarter of a century ago. They know Bombay like the backs of their hands and are experts at short cuts. At Grant Road, Baba's train connection is late so we chat on. 'I've had a few crashes', he reveals, 'but I have been lucky, neither Hercules nor I has ever been prevented from working as a result. Fortunately, no one steals the bicycles of dabbawallahs either. They know that they would be stealing our jobs and livelihood.'

| 31 | |

To account for this, Baba points to the obvious advantages of the system. 'Everyone prefers home cooking and at 150-250 rupees per month, depending on the distance travelled, it is still cheaper for our customers to pay for delivery from their private residences than it is for them to go to a restaurant or a street stall every day.'

| 32 | |

Some of these routes form part of chains of up to five dabbawallahs, waiting for each other at set meeting points throughout the city. Everything works like clockwork. Orders are processed centrally and records are maintained in large ledger books going back many years. Although the system may sound very complicated, there is very little chance of anything actually going wrong, as most of the routes are the same day after day and a loyal team of dabbawallahs operate them, with a pre-arranged timetable of rendezvous points. 'Grant Road is both a collection point as well as a distribution point,' explains Baba.

| 33 | |

I leave him on the platform. After lunch, Bombay's oldest dabbawallah will start retracing his route, collecting all the empty lunch boxes. By 4pm he will be back at Grant Road returning the cans. Exhausted, he will take a nap on the platform as he waits for his train home, his trusty friend Hercules by his side.

A Checking Hercules' tyres, and making an adjustment to the saddle, Baba adds, 'We are the oldest meals-on-wheels service in India and one of the oldest catering concerns in the world. I am proud to be a member of such a unique institution.'

B Baba had taken receipt of about ten cans from a gentleman with none too successful sideburns. They see each other every day and never exchange a word. After checking the coding on the cans, he swings them over his shoulder and heads for the bicycle stand.

C But despite this growing ricketiness, Baba and his 1968 touring bicycle have together clocked up more than 150,000 miles, pedalling the main streets and back ways of Bombay for a living.

D A comforting fact which applies to the 4000 dabbawallahs, like Baba and his colleague, operating every day in Bombay. They deliver 120,000 lunches throughout the city, five days a week and, Baba insists, demand for the service is growing.

E On arrival here, the cans are sorted according to the station they have to be carried to for the next leg of their journey or, if it is nearby, to their final destination. 'We are just waiters on pedal bikes,' he insists.

F Dabbas are aluminium or steel cans containing typical Indian lunch items such as rice, dal lentils, chapati bread and sometimes salad and yoghurt. The dabbawallahs are the dabba carriers and they make up the biggest food delivery relay system in the world.

G In addition to Baba and Kohindkar, there are about 30 dabbawallahs assembled with their bicycles at Grant Road this morning. As a train pulls in, they jump up and hurriedly swap the lunch boxes in their charge for other similar lunch boxes, before continuing on their rounds.

H Today, however, it is the local trains serving Bombay's sprawling suburbs which provide the main method of transportation — along with old fashioned pedal-power. Baba waves to his friend, Kohindkar, another veteran lunch box delivery man.

Turn up the light and you, too, can grow your own mind

The biggest challenge to science is to explain how the brain generates consciousness. The very concept defies formal definition, but perhaps an informal way would be to define it as the first-person, personal world as it seems to you. As such, consciousness is not just a tantalising enigma, but also an embarrassment to some scientists. If, after all, it is all about the subjective, then it could be distasteful to those of us who are trained to be impartial.

Until recently, this aversion to a phenomenology that could not be measured or shared was enough to focus most scientists on the smaller, but still awesome, problems of brain function — how the sludgy mass between our ears actually works at the nuts and bolts level. More recently, the techniques of imaging brain activity on computer and the relating of genes to specific brain properties, have given neuroscientists enough to think about.

But what has eluded us is how the brain works as a whole. Over the past few years, however, a growing band of pioneers has asked the big question of how the cells and chemicals fit together to generate mental experience. The problem has been that in our
24 enthusiasm to be objective we have thrown
25 the baby out with the bath water, and turned our backs on the very quality that perplexes the non-biologist: the first-hand feel of the subject of experience.

Perhaps a happier approach might be to ask what it is we are actually going to expect of the brain. Perhaps the mistake has been to liken consciousness to some kind of monolithic property that cannot be deconstructed. But suppose we could draw up a list of criteria for envisaging how conscious processes might be sub-served by brain tissue: what kind of issues might feature? We usually assume consciousness is all or none: you either have it or you don't. This is why the study of consciousness has proved so hard for the neuroscientists: it is very hard to peer into the human brain and find a magic property that is either there or not there. After all, science is about measurement, quantity rather than quality — so what if consciousness was quantitative, varied in degree, rather than being there as some *deux ex machina*?

What if consciousness grows as brains grow — can evolve, rather like a light bulb that is operated by an electric dimmer switch, from humble beginnings in simple non-human animals or indeed in the early foetus, and grow to become the sophisticated entities that we recognise in ourselves. Once we adopt the dimmer switch model, then two ways

A new way of thinking about the brain could give science the key to consciousness, says Susan Greenfield

forward open up. First is the possibility that our consciousness varies in degree from one moment to the next. Second, we could start to look for states in the brain that can also vary in degree.

By correlating states of consciousness along with some feature of the brain that could vary in parallel, we might open up a method for developing a way of looking at consciousness that could be expressed in scientific terms and, at the same time, respect the phenomenology beloved of philosophers.

One model that would work is that of a stone in a puddle. Imagine some kind of trigger from one moment to the next, that acted like a stone thrown onto a smooth surface of water — the ripples that resulted would depend in degree on the force at which the stone was thrown, the height from which it was thrown, its size and, of course, the competition from subsequent stones that would deform the ripples. Could it be that there are equivalent ripples in the brain?

Looking at conventional brain imaging techniques does not help. Most brain imaging is on a scale that exceeds a second, and yet we know that tens of millions of brain cells can gather into a working assembly in less than a quarter of a second. My own money goes on these highly global, but very transient, events as a possible correlate of consciousness.

In its simplest state, when there were not many connections between cells to begin with, for example in a small child, then
77 consciousness would be at its most rudimentary. Such a state could also be revisited every night in our dreams, when we are cut off from the raw input of our senses. Alternatively, in the middle of a bungee jump, where the inputs come fast and furious, this time an assembly of brain cells would be restricted due to the competition of the next set of ripples.

Connections between brain cells amazingly, can be forged
84 post-natally and, most marvellously of all, reflect individual experience. But less dramatically, every moment will leave its mark on the brain, in some change in the strengthening of one input over another. It is this growing of individuality of brain configurations that happen that I will argue is the
89 mind. For me, not some airy-fairy alternative to the banal
90 sludgy brain but rather the personalisation of it. In this sense you would grow a mind as you develop, and that mind, although it would colour consciousness, could be separated from it.

34 According to the writer, what effect has the uncertainty surrounding the nature of consciousness had on scientists?

    A   They have been reluctant to admit that they do not understand it.
    B   They have chosen to review their theoretical perspective on it.
    C   They have turned to neuroscientists for help on the matter.
    D   They have opted to study more accessible phenomena.

35 When the writer says 'we have thrown the baby out with the bath water' (lines 23–24), she means that

    A   a critical issue has been ignored.
    B   a possible solution has been rejected.
    C   too many ideas have complicated the matter.
    D   too many questions have remained unanswered.

36 In generating an image of consciousness, the writer thinks an error has been made in

    A   failing to judge the processes that it deals with.
    B   assuming that it cannot be broken down into parts.
    C   analysing the brain's role in its development.
    D   using human subjects for neurological research.

37 In the writer's 'dimmer switch model' consciousness is represented by

    A   the electricity.
    B   the switch.
    C   the operator.
    D   the light.

38 In the 'stone in a puddle' analogy, what does the stone represent?

    A   brain cells
    B   brain inputs
    C   brain imaging
    D   brain function

39 What excites the writer most about the approach she is suggesting?

    A   what it reveals about mental health
    B   how it explains the function of brain cells
    C   its application to personal experience
    D   its dependence on human development

40 Which of the following reflects the writer's lack of respect for current views on consciousness?

    A   'rudimentary' (line 77)
    B   'post-natally' (line 84)
    C   'airy-fairy' (line 89)
    D   'sludgy' (line 90)

Writing (2 hours)

You **must** answer this question. Write your answer in **300–350** words in an appropriate style.

---

1   You have read the following introductory paragraph to a newspaper article. Your course tutor has asked you to write an essay responding to the questions raised at the end of the paragraph.

> ## Trapped Cave Students Led to Safety
>
> Eight novice potholers and their teacher were rescued last night after spending three days trapped in an underground cave.
>
> The incident is not dissimilar from others that have occurred in the past few years and it has raised a number of questions: Should courses of this kind exist at all? Is it reasonable to assume that rescuers will risk their own lives in circumstances where insufficient preparations were made in the first place? What implications do these issues have for the increasingly popular range of 'dangerous' sports such as rock climbing and white-water rafting?

Write your **essay**.

Write an answer to **one** of the questions **2–4** in this part. Write your answer in **300–350** words in an appropriate style

2 You work for a local organisation that helps underprivileged and disabled children in your area to enjoy a better quality of life. The manager of your organisation has received a donation of US$1 million from an anonymous source. She has decided to consult her staff on how this money might best be spent and has asked each member of staff to submit a proposal. The proposal should suggest how the money might be allocated and give a justification for this expenditure.

Write your **proposal**.

3 A recent television documentary entitled 'The Rich and Famous' put forward the view that those who have acquired fame and wealth have done so through sheer determination and, as a result, deserve to reap the rewards of their efforts. After the programme, viewers were invited to express their opinions on the topic by writing an article evaluating the above and sending it in to the television station website.

Write your **article**.

4 A radio programme has recently announced that modern working people are losing interest in overseas holidays and showing a preference for staying at home during their leave. Listeners have been asked to write in to the programme suggesting why this might be the case and giving their views on which type of holiday is preferable and why.

Write your **letter**.

For questions **1–15**, read the text below and think of the word which best fits each space. Use only **one** word in each space. There is an example at the beginning **(0)**. Write your answers in **CAPITAL LETTERS on the separate answer sheet.**

Example:

0	A	T																	

Growing or Going?

Africa's forests are disappearing (**0**) ..*at*.. an alarming rate; a fact that (**1**) .... environmentalist you care to name will confirm. The reason, some will assert, is population growth: people are bad news (**2**) .... trees. Yet the picture that emerges (**3**) .... a growing body of fieldwork in Africa is more complex — and considerably (**4**) .... glum. It now appears that far fewer trees have been cut down than (**5**) .... previously suspected to be the case, the reason (**6**) .... that earlier estimates of tree numbers were inaccurate. The loss (**7**) .... forests has indeed been rapid but (**8**) .... so, the rate of loss is only about 40% of (**9**) .... commonly supposed.

Moroever, (**10**) .... of the forest of West Africa's past is neither as ancient nor as undisturbed (**11**) .... people generally thought. Some environmentalists maintain that large tracts of supposedly undisturbed forest were actually regrowth on areas which had (**12**) .... been intensively cultivated.

More intriguingly, researchers have drawn (**13**) .... evidence that forests are actually on (**14**) .... increase in some parts of Africa. Their fieldwork indicates that farmers often (**15**) .... with the bush fires that would otherwise destroy vegetation whilst deliberately preserving or transplanting trees that provide fruit, shelter or medicine.

For questions **16–25**, read the text below. Use the word given in **capitals** at the end of some of the lines to form a word that fits in the space in the same line. There is an example at the beginning **(0)**. Write your answers in **CAPITAL LETTERS on the separate answer sheet**.

Example:

0	U	N	I	N	H	A	B	I	T	A	B	L	E						

Life on Mars

The planet Mars is, at present, **(0)** _uninhabitable_ . Dust hangs in the   **HABITABLE**

air like a light fog, the temperature can **(16)** .... 100 degrees   **EXCESS**

below zero, the habitat is barren and humans cannot breathe

(17) .... But Dr Robert Zubrin, an astronautical   **AID**

(18) .... , believes that one day this will all change.   **ENGINE**

Although it could take hundreds of years to turn Mars into a viable

arena for the development of life, Dr Zubrin is

(19) .... by this timescale. He believes that we need the   **PERTURB**

challenge. **(20)** .... are like people, they develop in response   **CIVIL**

to challenges and a human mission to Mars would encourage every

child to learn science, develop their mind and become part of a

(21) .... new world.   **PIONEER**

More importantly Zubrin **(22)** .... , the political benefits that   **LIGHT**

life on Mars could bring to those on Earth. He sees Mars as an open

frontier where the rules have not yet been written. He believes the

most profound **(23)** .... that people can have is to make   **FREE**

their own world — one which may even have a direct

(24) .... in which everyone will vote on   **DEMOCRATIC**

(25) .... via e-mail.   **LEGISLATE**

For questions **26–31**, think of **one** word only which can be used appropriately in all three sentences. Here is an example **(0)**.

0 Last year's champion is in with a .... chance of repeating his success in the grand prix next weekend.

Some of the home owners are hoping to get compensation for the poor building work, and I think they have a very .... case.

There's no point in trying to put the tent up, the wind is far too ....

Example:

| 0 | S | T | R | O | N | G | | | | | | | | | | | | | |

Write **only** the missing word in **CAPITAL LETTERS on the separate answer sheet**.

---

26 • Leave your key with a neighbour in case anyone needs to .... access to your home whilst you're away.

• Professor Peters says that you can .... great insight into human nature by studying people as they wait in queues.

• I tried hard to convince James that he had nothing to .... by upsetting his employers, but he is very stubborn and took no notice of me.

27 • Lois has a very .... sense of humour and sometimes it's hard to know whether she is actually joking or not.

• I must stop and get some pastilles on the way to the cinema because I have a rather .... cough and don't want to spoil everyone's enjoyment of the film.

• After six months at sea, the long-distance yachtswoman was glad to be back on .... land.

28 • When the mysterious man began to sing, nobody was left in any .... as to his true identity.

• The recent heavy storms have left a .... in everyone's mind regarding the strength of the town's flood defences.

• I have no .... that Tony will go on to great things after leaving this school.

29 • The local population of blue butterflies has been almost entirely .... out thanks to the use of agricultural pesticides.

• The intruder carefully .... the door handle with a cloth to remove all traces of fingerprints.

• Chloe's mother .... a tear from her eye as her daughter received her degree certificate from the university's vice-chancellor.

30 • When we arrived at midnight, the party was already in full ....

• When you look at issues like crime and education, there has been a noticeable .... in public opinion, away from government policy.

• Amazingly, the .... which her grandfather had built in the garden for them all to play on was still there when she visited the spot fifty years later.

31 • At the end of the presentation, the speaker allowed us to .... our own conclusions from the evidence she had supplied us with.

• Despite all attempts to .... her into the argument, Polly remained aloof.

• We are fortunate to be able to .... on the experience of some eminent local scientists in setting up our research project.

For questions **32–39**, complete the second sentence so that it has a similar meaning to the first sentence, using the word given. **Do not change the word given.** You must use between **three** and **eight** words, including the word given. Here is an example **(0)**.

Example:

0   Immediately after winning the race, Sandy began training for the next one.

   had

   No .... she began training for the next one.

0   sooner had Sandy won the race than

Write **only** the missing words **on the separate answer sheet.**

---

32   The inventor never actually claimed that his idea was an original one.
   point
   At .... that his idea was an original one.

33   Her colleagues were completely surprised when the head teacher resigned.
   took
   The head teacher's .... complete surprise.

34   People can only enter the stadium if they have a pre-booked ticket.
   restricted
   Entrance .... possession of a pre-booked ticket.

35   Miranda went to Africa because she wanted to study the wildlife.
   reason
   Miranda's .... that she wanted to study the wildlife.

36   A local team has won the basketball championship for the third year running.
   succession
   For the third year .... by a local team.

37   Dawn was not the only person to notice the abandoned car that morning.
   alone
   Dawn .... the abandoned car that morning.

38   We ask passengers not to use mobile phones in this carriage.
   refrain
   Passengers are .... mobile phones in this carriage.

39   They chose that holiday resort because it was recommended in a newspaper article.
   influenced
   Their .... recommendation in a newspaper article.

PART 5

For questions **40–44**, read the following texts about four-by-four vehicles. For questions **40–43**, answer with a word or short phrase. You do not need to write complete sentences. For question **44**, write a summary according to the instructions given. Write your answers to questions **40–44 on the separate answer sheet.**

The four-wheeled drive vehicle, known as the four-by-four (4 x 4), has become increasingly popular in many parts of the world in recent years. Developed out of the Jeeps and Land Rovers of the mid-twentieth century, these vehicles were initially designed for driving over rough terrain, often in remote places where there were no proper highways, hence their appeal for those who long to escape the congestion of city streets and busy motorways and drive 'off-road'. Ironically, however, there are more of these fashionable vehicles in the London area than ever there are in more rural parts of England.

Part of the explanation for this paradox lies in the myth fostered by manufacturers addressing urban and suburban motorists that one day they might need to cross trackless moorland or cope with hazards such as floods and deep snow. In reality, practically all of these vehicles are bought to enhance a lifestyle (actual or imagined), and only a tiny minority will ever leave the highway.

A cynic would say that driving from suburban home to city-centre office in a 4 x 4 makes about as much sense as wearing green rubber boots with a business suit, yet clearly this is what happens. And there is more to it than that because many people clearly use 4 x 4s — even hefty ones the size of small lorries — for local errands such as school runs and shopping. So, the last few times I have sampled them, I have forgotten all about off-roading and treated them, as their owners seem to, as a normal car.

40 Which phrase in the second paragraph refers to the original purpose of 4 x 4 vehicles?

....

41 In your own words, explain why the writer draws parallel between driving a 4 x 4 vehicle and wearing green rubber boots.

....

When a contemporary English family decides to break free from its urban existence and go off in search of its roots in the countryside, its members opt for an appropriate vehicle to take them there. In place of the cramped saloon, with its squashed up body, its parsimonious engine and its two-wheel drive, they buy a large and greedy four-by-four, the toothy tyres of which chew the city streets as though impatient to be rid of them, and which whines along the avenues like a horse neighing for freedom and the fields.

But the fashionable status of the 4 x 4 in England can also be seen in another context. We are social creatures whose overriding concern is to impress our image
10 on others. We no longer satisfy this urge as our ancestors did – through clothes, speech and the formal gestures of a hierarchical society. These days, we are more likely to make our mark in wider society through our choice of car. Like everything else that is implicated in our social identity, cars cease, therefore, to be means and become ends in themselves. They are no longer tools, they are symbols. The 4 x 4 is the urban family's way of standing aloof from its surroundings and affirming its identity as part of the wider world.

So it is that these people subject their vehicles to a weekly outing in the green lanes of old England, carving deep ruts in those ancient byways and rendering them impassable to all other forms of transport save horses, and dangerous even for them.

42 In your own words, explain why the writer compares a 4 x 4 vehicle to a horse.

....

43 In your own words, explain what the phrase 'this urge' (line 10) refers to.

....

44 In a paragraph of between **50 and 70 words**, summarise in your own words as far as possible, the different ways described in the text in which four-by-four vehicles are used by their urban owners.

Listening (Approximately 40 minutes)

You will hear four different extracts. For questions **1–8**, choose the answer (**A, B** or **C**) which fits best according to what you hear. There are two questions for each extract.

Extract One

You will hear part of a radio programme about mirrors.

1 What point does the presenter make about mirrors?

    A Even the most sophisticated are unreliable.
    B We don't always want them to be accurate.
    C The quality of the image may change over time.

                                                         `1`

2 According to Wendy, her frames can

    A distract the attention of the user.
    B enhance the clarity of the image.
    C blend in with the owner's decor.

                                                         `2`

Extract Two

You will hear part of a report about a sports event.

3 The presenter makes the point that the race is essentially

    A nothing more than a party.
    B for the benefit of spectators.
    C a test of competitive sailing skills.

                                                         `3`

4 According to Bob, the event is popular with sailors because

    A it is relatively inexpensive to enter.
    B the prize money is generous.
    C few celebrities take part.

                                                         `4`

Extract Three

You hear someone talking about men's fashion.

5   What is he doing when he speaks about evening dress?

    A   explaining how hard it is to change a tradition
    B   encouraging us to consider it in a new light
    C   confirming our prejudices regarding certain styles

[ ] 5

6   What point is he making about evening dress?

    A   It's an opportunity to express individuality.
    B   It's better not to be seen in it too frequently.
    C   It's not something to wear half-heartedly.

[ ] 6

Extract Four

On a discussion programme, you hear two child psychologists giving advice.

7   Who is their advice intended for?

    A   parents of children
    B   teachers of children
    C   colleagues working with children

[ ] 7

8   What course of action do they recommend?

    A   specific strategies for different age groups
    B   open discussion of all problems
    C   minimum intervention in disputes

[ ] 8

You will hear part of a talk by a woman who runs a wildlife reserve in Africa, which is devoted to saving the rhinoceros. For questions **9–17**, complete the sentences with a word or short phrase.

Rhino Reserve

The land on which the rhino sanctuary

is located is also used for keeping [_____ **9**]

At first, Mary had problems finding any information

about the [_____ **10**] behaviour of rhinos.

Mary explains that a rhino largely understands the world around it

by interpreting [_____ **11**]

Mary says that the nature of mother-calf relationships suggests that

rhinos are more [_____ **12**] than is generally thought.

When a rhino moves its [_____ **13**], this often means it is alarmed.

Local agriculture has benefited from the [_____ **14**]

installed around the edge of the sanctuary.

It is hoped that visitors to the sanctuary will buy

[_____ **15**] produced locally.

At the moment, the sanctuary relies on

[_____ **16**] as a source of income.

Future plans include the building of what

Mary calls a [_____ **17**] to encourage visitors.

You will hear an interview with Simon Hemmings, who works as a fight director in the theatre. For questions **18–22**, choose the answer (**A, B, C** or **D**) which fits best according to what you hear.

18 According to Simon, during a fight scene, the audience should

    A feel the actors are really in danger.
    B see that the swords are not real.
    C be totally involved in the play itself.
    D be aware of the safety measures he adopts.

| 18 |

19 When casting the play, the theatre was looking for actors who had

    A previous experience of fighting on stage.
    B familiarity with the design of the theatre.
    C a willingness to learn a new set of skills.
    D previous training in how to handle a sword.

| 19 |

20 What does Simon say the actors must do during the performance?

    A improvise to cover up their mistakes
    B adhere closely to the agreed fight text
    C help colleagues who forget their lines
    D involve the audience as much as possible

| 20 |

21 Simon was particularly concerned that the fight scenes in this play might become

    A repetitive.
    B ridiculous.
    C inauthentic.
    D inelegant.

| 21 |

22 According to Simon, fight scenes on stage should not

    A become too violent.
    B appear over-practised.
    C be taken too seriously.
    D actually upset people.

| 22 |

You will hear part of a discussion programme in which two people, Andrew and Clarissa, are talking about airports. For questions **23-28**, decide whether the opinions are expressed by only one of the speakers, or whether the speakers agree.

Write   **A**   for Andrew,

             C   for Clarissa,

or   **B**   for Both, when they agree.

---

23 The movement of people through an airport can be compared to a manufacturing process. | **23**

24 It's surprising that people accept the check-in procedures at airports. | **24**

25 It's easier to relax once the check-in procedures are complete. | **25**

26 The time spent waiting in airports is tedious rather than unnerving. | **26**

27 Airports may be designed to take your mind off the flight ahead. | **27**

28 Airports are a good indication of what the world may look like in the future. | **28**

PAPER 5   Speaking (19 minutes)

PART 1 (3 minutes)

Answer these questions:
- Do you come from a large or small family?
- How well do you think English is taught in this/your country?
- What other skills would you like to learn in the future?

PART 2 (4 minutes)

Turn to the picture on page 172 which shows various images connected with the world today.

First look at the picture and talk together about what general image it conveys and where you might expect to find a picture like this. You have about one minute for this.

Now look at all the individual images. This picture was designed as a publicity poster to promote e-commerce on the Internet. The organisers of the publicity campaign have now decided that it is too complicated and should be simplified. Talk together about what the various images in the picture represent in the context of e-commerce, say how effective they are, and then decide which images should be kept and which removed or replaced. You have about three minutes for this.

PART 3 (12 minutes)

Candidate A: Look at the question in the box. You have two minutes to say what you think about the question. There are some ideas to use in the box if you like.

What are the qualities of a good employee?
- reliability
- resourcefulness
- personality

Candidate B: Is there anything you would like to add?

Candidate B: Look at the question in the box. You have two minutes to say what you think about the question. There are some ideas to use in the box if you like.

How has the nature of work changed for many people in recent years?
- working hours
- job security
- technological change

Candidate A: Is there anything you would like to add?

Candidates A and B: Now answer these questions about employment in general:

- Do you think people will work more or less in the future?
- How much of our lives should be devoted to work, and how much to leisure?

A

B

VISUALS FOR PAPER 5

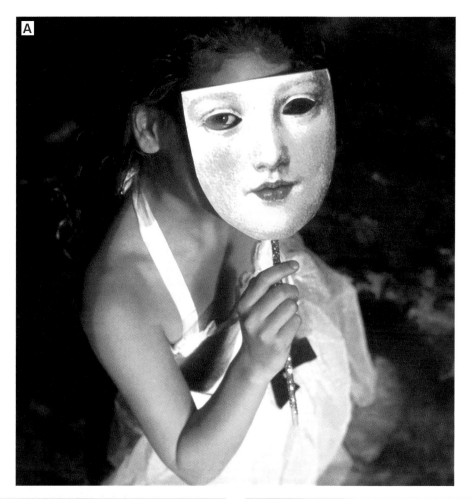

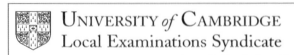
UNIVERSITY *of* CAMBRIDGE
Local Examinations Syndicate

Candidate Name
If not already printed, write name
in CAPITALS and complete the
Candidate No. grid (in pencil).

Candidate Signature

Examination Title

Centre

Supervisor:
If the candidate is ABSENT or has WITHDRAWN shade here ⬜

Centre No.

Candidate No.

Examination Details

0	0	0	0
1	1	1	1
2	2	2	2
3	3	3	3
4	4	4	4
5	5	5	5
6	6	6	6
7	7	7	7
8	8	8	8
9	9	9	9

Candidate Answer Sheet CPE Paper 1 Reading

Instructions
Use a PENCIL (B or HB). Mark ONE letter only for each question.
For example, if you think B is the right answer,
mark your answer sheet like this:

0 | A | B | C | D

Rub out any answer you wish to change using an eraser.

Part 1

	A	B	C	D
1	A	B	C	D
2	A	B	C	D
3	A	B	C	D
4	A	B	C	D
5	A	B	C	D
6	A	B	C	D
7	A	B	C	D
8	A	B	C	D
9	A	B	C	D
10	A	B	C	D
11	A	B	C	D
12	A	B	C	D
13	A	B	C	D
14	A	B	C	D
15	A	B	C	D
16	A	B	C	D
17	A	B	C	D
18	A	B	C	D

Part 2

	A	B	C	D
19	A	B	C	D
20	A	B	C	D
21	A	B	C	D
22	A	B	C	D
23	A	B	C	D
24	A	B	C	D
25	A	B	C	D
26	A	B	C	D

Part 4

	A	B	C	D
34	A	B	C	D
35	A	B	C	D
36	A	B	C	D
37	A	B	C	D
38	A	B	C	D
39	A	B	C	D
40	A	B	C	D

Part 3

	A	B	C	D	E	F	G	H
27	A	B	C	D	E	F	G	H
28	A	B	C	D	E	F	G	H
29	A	B	C	D	E	F	G	H
30	A	B	C	D	E	F	G	H
31	A	B	C	D	E	F	G	H
32	A	B	C	D	E	F	G	H
33	A	B	C	D	E	F	G	H

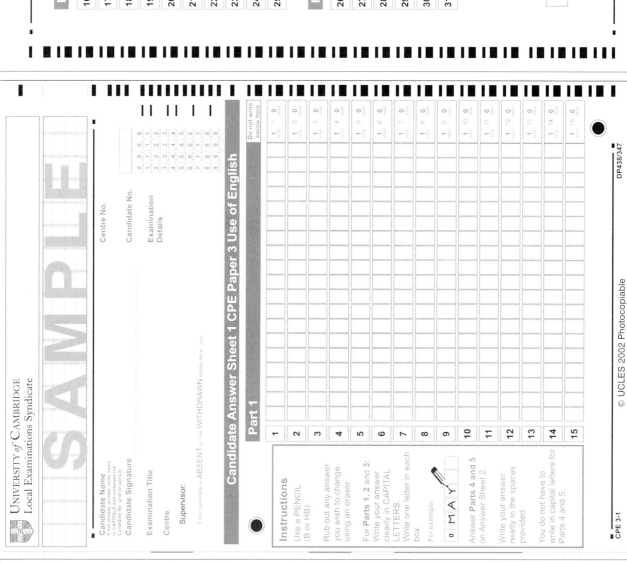

UNIVERSITY of CAMBRIDGE
Local Examinations Syndicate

SAMPLE

Candidate Name
If not already printed, write name
in CAPITALS and complete the
Candidate No. grid (in pencil).

Candidate Signature

Examination Title

Centre

Supervisor:

If the candidate is ABSENT or has WITHDRAWN shade here

Centre No.

Candidate No.

Examination
Details

Candidate Answer Sheet 1 CPE Paper 3 Use of English

Part 1

Instructions

Use a PENCIL
(B or HB).

Rub out any answer
you wish to change,
using an eraser.

For **Parts 1, 2 and 3:**
Write your answer
clearly in CAPITAL
LETTERS.
Write one letter in each
box.

For example:

| 0 | M | A | Y | | |

Answer **Parts 4 and 5**
on Answer Sheet 2.

Write your answer
neatly in the spaces
provided.

You do not have to
write in capital letters for
Parts 4 and 5.

Do not write below here: 1 0, 2 0, 3 0, 4 0, 5 0, 6 0, 7 0, 8 0, 9 0, 10 0, 11 0, 12 0, 13 0, 14 0, 15 0

CPE 3-1

© UCLES 2002 Photocopiable

DP438/347

1 7 4

Part 2

Do not write below here: 16 0, 17 0, 18 0, 19 0, 20 0, 21 0, 22 0, 23 0, 24 0, 25 0

Part 3

Do not write below here: 26 0, 27 0, 28 0, 29 0, 30 0, 31 0

SAMPLE

Continue with Parts 4 and 5 on Answer Sheet 2

© UCLES 2002 Photocopiable

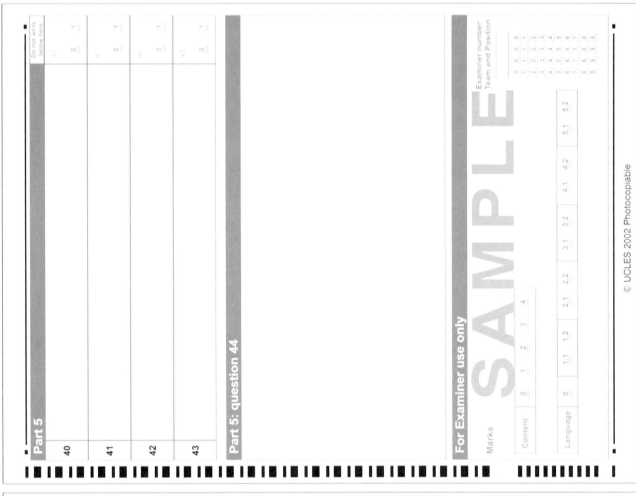

UNIVERSITY of CAMBRIDGE
Local Examinations Syndicate

SAMPLE

Candidate Name
If not already printed, write name
in CAPITALS and complete the
Candidate No. grid in pencil.

Candidate Signature

Examination Title

Centre

Supervisor:
If the candidate is ABSENT or has WITHDRAWN shade here

Centre No.

Candidate No.

Examination
Details

Answer Sheet 2 CPE Paper 3 Use of English

Part 4

Do not write
below here

32

33

34

35

36

37

38

39

CPE 3-2

DP439/348

Part 5

Do not write
below here

40

41

42

43

Part 5: question 44

For Examiner use only

SAMPLE

Marks

Content

Language

Examiner number
Team and Position

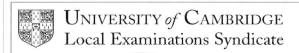

UNIVERSITY of CAMBRIDGE
Local Examinations Syndicate

SAMPLE

Candidate Name
If not already printed, write name
in CAPITALS and complete the
Candidate No. grid (in pencil).

Candidate Signature

Examination Title

Centre

Supervisor:
If the candidate is ABSENT or has WITHDRAWN shade here ▭

Centre No.

Candidate No.

Examination Details

0	0	0	0
1	1	1	1
2	2	2	2
3	3	3	3
4	4	4	4
5	5	5	5
6	6	6	6
7	7	7	7
8	8	8	8
9	9	9	9

Candidate Answer Sheet CPE Paper 4 Listening

| Mark test version (in PENCIL) | A | B | C | Special arrangements | S | H |

Instructions
Use a PENCIL (B or HB).
Rub out any answer you wish to change using an eraser.

For **Parts 1 and 3:**
Mark ONE letter only for each question.
For example, if you think B is the right answer,
mark your answer sheet like this:

| 0 | A | B | C |

For **Part 2:**
Write your answer clearly in
the space like this:

| 0 |  |

For **Part 4:**
Write ONE letter only, like this:

| 0 |  |

Part 1

1	A	B	C
2	A	B	C
3	A	B	C
4	A	B	C
5	A	B	C
6	A	B	C
7	A	B	C
8	A	B	C

Part 2

		Do not write here
9		1 9 0
10		1 10 0
11		1 11 0
12		1 12 0
13		1 13 0
14		1 14 0
15		1 15 0
16		1 16 0
17		1 17 0

Part 3

18	A	B	C	D
19	A	B	C	D
20	A	B	C	D
21	A	B	C	D
22	A	B	C	D

Part 4

		Do not write here
23		1 23 0
24		1 24 0
25		1 25 0
26		1 26 0
27		1 27 0
28		1 28 0

CPE 4

DP440/349

1 7 6

Answer Key

Test 1

Part 1
I Will not Explode

1 A: Noun with correct meaning in the context of a bottle of liquid and what you have to do to it if you want it to explode.

2 B: Correct noun in phrase 'dive for cover'.

3 D: Only verb that collocates with 'temptation'.

4 B: Correct verb in idiomatic phrase 'make a point'.

5 D: Noun with correct meaning of 'implication'.

6 A: Verb with correct meaning that takes 'with'.

Fashion

7 B: Correct verb in fixed phrase 'strive for effect'.

8 C: Only adjective meaning 'standing the test of time' that collocates with 'innovations'.

9 A: Only noun + 'of' that collocates with 'materials'.

10 D: Only adverb that leads to an explanation.

11 B: Only adjective that collocates with 'succession'.

12 D: Only adjective that collocates with 'features' to refer to the human face in general.

Faces

13 C: Only adverb that collocates with 'because' in this context.

14 C: Verb with correct meaning of 'pick out'.

15 A: Only adverb that adds correct emphasis.

16 D: Adjective with correct meaning of 'small and complex'.

17 D: Only noun meaning 'range' that collocates with 'emotions'.

18 B: Only verb that takes 'on' + noun.

Part 2
Reflections

19 C: 'But the problem is more deep-seated.'

20 A: The main idea of the second paragraph is that good films encourage 'an appetite for film-going', just as good music will encourage children to be 'up on stage'.

CD Reviews

21 C: 'he had more than enough musical wit and wisdom'; 'loosening the iron grip of conformist rock behaviour'.

22 D: 'Ferry's unique vocal style … banishing the ghosts of the originals.'

Extract from a novel

23 B: 'manfully' is sarcastic; 'really has seen better days' draws a comparison with the jacket and implies a lack of respect.

24 A: The author isn't interested in Dick's tapes (penultimate sentence). There is no indication of B, C or D.

Music and the Mind

25 C: 'bears witness to the antiquity of this form of art'. A, B and D are not mentioned in the text.

26 A: Throughout the text this is the pervading theme. B, C and D are not.

Part 3
Taking the Plunge

27 B: Link between the first paragraph and 'such a scenario'; link between B and 'Such standards' in the following paragraph.

28 H: Link between 'they could be said to be exploited' and 'If this is the case'.

29 C: Link between 'the patient will have access to a new genetic test' and 'Benefits in kind like this'.

30 A: Link between 'not paying volunteers', the example given in A and 'In many cases such as this' in the following paragraph.

31 F: Link between 'Do we always make them against our better judgement?' in the previous paragraph and the example given in F, with a further example in the following paragraph.

32 D: Link between the two preceding examples and 'Could you say that either situation resulted in unsound judgements?'

33 E: Link between 'I have never understood …' in the previous paragraph and the summary of arguments in E, ending with 'then what does it matter how much they are paid?'

Part 4

34 A: The key words in the answer are 'assumptions' and 'aims'. The writer says: 'I am left *with the suspicion* … that a novel is, perhaps, just *a hopeful step* in the celluloid direction…'.

35 D: This answer is supported by the whole of the second paragraph, ending with 'books are only filmic by accident'.

36 B: Only B expresses a negative attitude on the part of the writer towards film makers. The phrase suggests a lack of commitment.

37 C: 'The hard fact is, that it is no longer your own book.'

38 A: The key word is 'flexible'. 'Scriptwriters have to be humble creatures who *will* change things …'.

39 B: They defend the changes they make by stating that 'film is a completely different medium'. There is no suggestion of A, C or D.

40 C: The key word in the question is 'accepts'. The writer concedes to the idea expressed in C in the final sentence.

Questions 1–18	=	1 mark
Questions 19–40	=	2 marks
Total score	=	**62 marks**

PAPER 2   Writing

Part 1
Question 1
Style: Formal, probably addressed to the editor of the magazine. Register should be appropriate and arguments clearly organised.
Content: Letter should make reference to the magazine article and discuss the points raised; i.e. the consequences of focusing on material possessions, the suggestion that everyone wants to have a lot of money and should spend it as they see fit. Answer could also consider alternative ways in which money might be used and the impact of consumerism on our lives.

Part 2
Question 2
Style: Consistently formal or semi-formal, with heading for article. Points clearly marked, with personal anecdote naturally incorporated into these.
Content: Article should evaluate a number of qualities and these may be illustrated in order to account for their importance to the writer. At least one quality should be highlighted by means of a personal account.

Question 3
Style: Consistent register of formal or semi-formal nature. Review should move naturally from specific to general issues. A heading is appropriate.
Content: Review should briefly inform the reader about the play and evaluate the acting and music. It should also assess the importance of children's theatre.

Stage Theatre Company has a definite hit

Last Tuesday, I was lucky enough to be in the audience for a local theatre company's production of the classic children's story 'Cinderella'. This popular fairy tale, about a young girl and her two ugly step sisters, must be performed every winter in every town and village across the country; I admit to having seen it myself a number of times, but the Stage Theatre Company's performance was particularly memorable for many reasons.

Too often, theatrical productions are produced, directed and performed by adults. In this case, although adults were certainly involved in all three areas, the main character parts were taken by schoolchildren. My companion, a five-year-old niece, was spellbound from the moment the curtain went up. I quickly joined in with her enthusiasm because, despite the cast's lack of experience and training, the commitment and the quality of the acting were very high. In addition, I was delighted to note that I could hear every word that was spoken throughout the entire performance, which is a rare treat.

As those who are familiar with the story will know, Cinderella can be performed in many ways. The Stage Theatre Company, never short on ambition it seems, decided to make it a musical. What is more, they wrote all the songs that were included in the performance themselves. However, rather than proving dull and repetitive as so many home-penned pieces of music do, these were lively, catchy tunes that lifted the audience and the actors, who so obviously enjoyed singing them.

So full marks to a small but very promising local theatre group that will, I am sure, go on to produce even more delightful pieces for both young and old to savour. More importantly, perhaps, in an age where computers and technology are resulting in rather sedentary, information-seeking pastimes, it seems highly desirable for youngsters to be given the opportunity to participate in the type of creative, fulfilling experience that theatre can offer. The spectacle has made a considerable impact on my niece and hopefully this enthusiasm will be exploited more fully in her own school.

Question 4
Style: Formal structured report with appropriate paragraps/sections.
Content: Report should describe and analyse benefits. Disadvantages may also be referred to if they have an impact on the points being made. Some reference to personal experience may be included.

PAPER 3   Use of English

Part 1
The Map Thief
1 *not (adverb)*: part of structure 'not … but', which is used to contrast the real reason with a possible (but incorrect) reason.
2 *with (preposition)*: used with 'armed'.
3 *his (determiner)*: completes the phrase 'take someone's fancy'.
4 *went (past tense verb)*: phrasal verb 'go on' + infinitive.
5 *Although/Though/While/Whilst (conjunction)*: used to introduce a subordinate clause.

6 *their (determiner)*: referring back to 'maps'.

7 *none (pronoun)*: from expression 'second to none', meaning 'the best'.

8 *say (verb)*: used to introduce an example.

9 *where (relative pronoun)*: referring back to the location.

10 *to (preposition)*: from expression 'come to light'.

11 *as (adverb)*: from phrase 'as if', used to compare two people, things or situations.

12 *first (pronoun)*: from phrase 'at first', meaning 'in the beginning'.

13 *let (base form verb)*: phrasal verb 'let someone off', meaning 'to excuse someone from punishment'.

14 *Only (adverb)*: used to emphasise the gap in time.

15 *come (verb)*: phrasal verb 'come across', meaning 'to find by chance'.

Part 2
Frankenstein's Real Creator

16 *likeness (verb to noun)*

17 *masterpiece (noun to compound noun)*

18 *unsettling (verb to adjective by adding negative prefix)*

19 *enduring (verb to adjective)*

20 *numerous/innumerable (noun to adjective, alternative formed by adding negative prefix)*

21 *academics (noun to noun plural)*

22 *acknowledged (noun to past participle by adding prefix)*

23 *extraordinary (adjective to adjective by adding prefix)*

24 *imaginative (verb to adjective)*

25 *revival (verb to noun)*

Part 3

26 *hang (verb)*: phrasal verb 'hang on to', meaning 'to keep'; phrasal verb 'hang up', meaning 'to end a phone call'; to attach to a wall.

27 *settled (verb)*: phrasal verb 'settle for', meaning 'to accept'; to pay; to come or bring to rest.

28 *delicate (adjective)*: needing careful handling because easily damaged; needing careful or sensitive treatment in order to avoid failure or trouble; pleasing but not strong.

29 *sprang (verb)*: phrase 'spring to attention', often used in a military context, meaning 'to become quickly attentive'; to jump (from an unseen position); phrase 'spring to life', meaning 'to become lively quickly'.

30 *show (verb)*: phrasal verb 'show up', meaning 'to arrive as expected or arranged'; expression 'to show for', meaning 'as a profit or reward from'; to exhibit.

31 *exercise (noun)*: the use of any part of the body or mind so as to strengthen or improve it; any set of actions, especially when intended to have a particular effect; a question or set of questions to be answered by a student for practice.

Part 4

32 *are under no obligation to attend*: 'to be under no obligation' + infinitive.

33 *no account must you open*: 'on no account' (meaning 'under no circumstances') + modal + subject + verb.

34 *where this type of pottery can/may be found*: use of 'type' to mean 'this kind'; verb change from active to passive.

35 *who dissuaded her from going*: 'dissuade' (meaning 'to persuade not to') + someone + 'from' + -ing verb form.

36 *some international flights are/will be subject to*: 'subject' (meaning 'tending or likely') + 'to' + noun.

37 *the exception of Lorraine, none/not one*: 'with the exception of', meaning 'apart from' + pronoun.

38 *never occurred to me that someone/somebody*: 'it never crossed my mind' is replaced by 'it never occurred to me'; passive to active.

39 *is out of bounds to*: 'out of bounds' + 'to' + somebody. If a place is out of bounds to somebody, it means that they are not allowed to go there.

Part 5

40 It either says too little about a lot of hotels or a lot about a few.

41 'sideswipe'

42 '(promise of) five-star treatment'

43 '(feeling) let down'

44 The summary should include the following points:
- Hotel guide(book)s may be biased because hotels pay to be featured in them.
- Tourist boards don't cover all aspects of hotels.
- Brochures may not mention negative things.
- Hotel staff make sure that you are only shown the good things.

Questions 1–25	=	1 mark
Questions 26–43	=	2 marks
Question 44	=	14 marks
Total score	**=**	**75 marks**

PAPER 4   Listening

Part 1

1 C: 'She makes you believe' is stated twice.

2 A: 'I guess it's the notion of the indomitable spirit overcoming adversity.'

3 B: 'but the only thing we couldn't do was make them walk … So I came up with the idea for a Supercar.'

4 A: 'you couldn't get too protective about it.'

5 C: It is about 'preservation'.

6 B: 'I've never said that … Neither have I said that …'.

7 A: The man's question: 'No squirming in your seat then?' refers back to a previous comment the woman had made. She also says: 'There I was imagining all these titters of nervous laughter …'.

8 C: 'Each poem added to the next'.

Part 2

9 *portrait artist*: 'Phyllis was not a cartographer by profession; in fact she was a portrait artist'.

10 *geographical*: 'There were very few maps of London … and those there were … tended to focus on geographical features.'

11 *23,000/twenty-three thousand*: 'ended up walking … along twenty-three thousand streets'.

12 *unsupportive*: 'when she started the project he was unsupportive'.

13 *mathematical*: 'they don't have their basis in mathematical calculations'.

14 *observant*: 'As an artist she was very, very efficient … she was also extremely observant.'

15 *shoeboxes/shoe boxes*: 'arranged in shoe boxes'.

16 *printer(s)*: 'when the book got to the printers, somebody there spotted it'.

17 *newsagent*: 'a large chain of newsagents agreed to stock them'.

Part 3

18 D: She says: 'I was really keen to shake off this reputation I was getting for being a model pupil.' She also says: 'This resulted in titters all round and all the efforts I'd been making to keep a low profile were completely dashed.'

19 A: She says: 'most of it I'd pinched from a couple of books on literary criticism that I had at home.'

20 B: She says: 'I think Jane Austen is one of those writers that people like to tick off on their personal booklist … then they make a quick retreat to their personal favourites.'

21 A: She says: 'I think a lot of writers share an appreciation of the power that literature had over them as young people and I just wanted to voice that.'

22 C: She describes her early writing as being 'par for the course', which means something that is typical of her development as a writer.

Part 4

23 B: The speakers both contribute points to support the view expressed by Alex that the researchers 'go out and look for what they want to find'.

24 A: Alex says: 'It's pretty irksome, though', whereas Mandy says: 'You have to take it with a pinch of salt' and also: 'I've always found that quietly amusing.' In other words, it doesn't bother her.

25 B: They both enjoyed confusing their teachers at school by swapping badges.

26 M: Mandy says: 'I don't think we'd get away with it now', meaning that they look less similar. Alex contradicts this: 'Oh I don't know.'

27 M: The speakers both complain that people often view twins as a 'single identity'. Alex then says: 'You're lucky your parents saw beyond that', implying that Mandy's parents, not his, were different.

28 B: Mandy says: 'I'm still trying to outdo my sister at something.' Alex supports this idea: 'It's a constant battle for one-upmanship.'

Questions 1–28   =   1 mark
Total score   =   **28 marks**

Test 2

Part 1
Debut Goal

1 B: Only noun with correct meaning of 'the centre of public attention' that collocates with 'steal'.

2 A: Correct verb in phrase 'take an unexpected turn', where 'turn' means 'a new development'.

3 D: Correct prepositions in phrase 'in with a chance', meaning 'having a chance'.

4 C: Only adjective that collocates with 'disbelief'.

5 D: Sentence adverbial 'strictly speaking' adds more precise information.

6 A: Correct verb in phrasal verb 'sign up', meaning 'to sign an agreement to take part in something'.

Dance for your Health

7 B: Correct noun that collocates with 'give' in phrase 'give something a try'.

8 C: Only correct noun in context, meaning 'the way the upper body is held'.

9 B: Correct noun in phrase 'go at your own pace'.

10 C: Correct adjective meaning 'taking all one's attention'.

11 D: Correct verb in phrase 'take your mind off something'.

12 B: Only verb meaning 'improve' that collocates with 'mood'.

Stuck on You

13 B: Verb with correct meaning of 'fixed firmly within'.

14 A: Adverb with correct meaning of 'for both equally'.

15 C: Only adjective that collocates with 'run' to mean 'to have little stock left'.

16 C: Noun with correct meaning that collocates with 'stubborn' in phrase 'stubborn streak'.

17 C: Verb with correct meaning of 'make someone aware that action is needed'.

18 D: Verb with correct meaning of 'look like'.

Part 2
A Family Affair

19 C: 'quite distinct' indicates a difference; 'lone commuter' implies forced isolation.

20 B: Silence 'binds the whole family in a web of mutual dependence', which eliminates isolation and anxiety. The meals are eaten in 'a peculiar, contented, sociable silence'.

A Species That I Wanted To Kill

21 D: 'breezily', meaning 'cheerfully, in a light-hearted manner', implies a lack of concern.

22 C: 'Bart instantly complied.'

Can't Stand the Music

23 A: Correct because it implies disrespect and is intended to make the recipient of the look feel ashamed.

24 C: The writer attends the 'evening session' when 'more upbeat music will be selected with an increase in volume to compensate for a busier gym.'

What Price Peace and Quiet?

25 D: The first paragraph describes trends. There is no reference to a proposal, or protest, so the answer is not A or B. Although blame is apportioned, the problem is recognised, so C is wrong.

26 A: 'to me smack more of affected self-indulgence'.

Part 3
A Matter of Trust

27 E: Link between first sentence of text and E; link between E and 'examine the first of these motivations' in following paragraph.

28 G: Link between the aim of the games in preceding paragraph, the format referred to in G and the 'possible outcomes' described in the following paragraph.

29 H: Link between the explanation of the outcomes in preceding paragraph and 'maintaining trust gives the best overall outcome'.

30 A: Link between 'By the tenth round …' and 'The levels of mutual distrust had racheted up in the intervening play' in the following paragraph.

31 D: Link between the two methods of refining results as described in the preceding paragraph and 'Simply raising the stakes … But in the second case …'.

32 F: Link between 'the first player received a small sum of money' in the preceding paragraph and the example in F.

33 B: Link between the effect of trusting strangers in the preceding paragraph and the additional effect of 'a previous acquaintance.'

Part 4
The New Housekeeper

34 B: Cued by 'she liked to' and the use of the 'would' to indicate habitual or repetitive behaviour.

35 A: Characteristically, Miss Hare 'would draw a curtain cunningly'.

36 C: Mrs Jolley's life: 'whose breathing would be heard'; Mrs Jolley's relationships: 'whose letters would lie upon the furniture …'.

37 A: 'they had not yet grown insincere', in other words, they can lie innocently.

38 B: 'daring' and 'more daring, if not actually reckless' are mocking in that the clothes themselves are prim and could not be described in this way.

39 C: 'it must be done' implies that Miss Hare is resigned to it.

40 D: 'Each wished she could have repudiated the connection.'

Questions 1–18	= 1 mark
Questions 19–40	= 2 marks
Total score	**= 62 marks**

PAPER 2   Writing

Part 1
Question 1

Style: Formal, structured essay with clear points, good cohesion between main ideas, and specific examples where appropriate.
Content: Essay should expand on the notes and discuss global/historical attitudes to dress at work, the desirability of a dress code at work and the wearing of uniforms.

Part 2
Question 2

Style: Semi-formal, clear recommendations possibly using section headings. Register appropriate to employer.
Content: Proposal should briefly inform reader on current situation and make suggestions about appearance of store and advertising. An awareness-raising activity should be proposed.

Model Answer

In response to your recent request, I would like to submit the following proposal, which I have divided into three sections for ease of reference.

Physical Improvements

As in many other retail outlets, people can spend a long time browsing in bookshops and need, therefore, to feel that they are in a comfortable environment. Although our bookshop is well staffed, customers do not necessarily appreciate this or directly benefit from it. Rather, I suspect that it is the décor and the general layout of the store that might appeal more to them, and encourage them to stay longer. So my first recommendation would be for a total 'facelift'. In other words, I believe that the store should be completely redecorated. Recent studies have shown that colour can have a tremendous impact on mood, and strong colours, such as yellow and terracotta would definitely enliven the general ambience. In addition, a softer floor covering, even a carpet, would improve the overall 'feel' of the shop and have a positive effect on staff and customers.

Advertising

In my view, advertising is important both within the shop and outside the premises. As far as interior advertising is concerned, I would suggest using large, colourful posters to announce recent publications and best sellers. Also, clear labelling of the different book sections would have both a functional and a marketing role. While I appreciate that newspaper and radio advertisements are relatively expensive, it would surely be worthwhile to place at least one advertisement in the local newspapers from time to time and possibly even design a radio advertisement for special occasions.

Event

Finally, I believe that we might be able to boost sales by holding a special interest event at the shop. One idea that is not original, but is certainly realistic and appropriate for a bookshop, is to invite an outside speaker to give a talk. This could be held one evening at the shop so that those who attend also have the opportunity to look around the bookshop outside normal opening hours. A well-known author or poet would certainly bring in a crowd. This may require some funding, but I am firmly convinced that the publicity that would result would more than cover any outlay that may be required.

I hope you will find my suggestions useful.

Mark: Band Score 5

Questions 3

Style: Formal (or may be semi-formal but register should reflect relationship between the writer and readers. Section headings may be used.

Content: Report should present a number of suggestions and recommend how these might operate. Reference may be made to other, less desirable facilities by way of comparison.

Question 4

Style: Formal. Moderate tone: general arguments with some personal input.

Content: Letter should indicate reasons for writing. It should discuss potential problems related to the impact of the complex on the area, and propose solutions to these. It should also ask a relevant question on the topic.

PAPER 3   Use of English

Part 1

Science Fact and Science Fiction

1 *can/may (modal)*: completes verb in passive structure.

2 *out (preposition)*: phrasal verb 'turn out', meaning 'to happen to be in the end'.

3 *did (auxiliary verb)*: used for emphasis.

4 *failed (past tense verb)*: 'fail' + infinitive, meaning 'not to succeed in doing something'.

5 *means (verb)*: + 'that'; linking phrase used to preface a consequence.

6 *is (verb)*: main verb of sentence following subject 'what strikes you most'.

7 *slow (adjective)*: from informal expression 'be slow on the uptake', meaning 'to be slow to understand /realise something'.

8 *it (pronoun)*: impersonal 'it' from expression 'when it comes to', meaning 'when … is concerned'.

9 *which (relative pronoun)*: after 'to'.

10 *very (adverb)*: forms compound adverb with 'much'.

11 *were (past tense verb)*: + 'not' + infinitive; used for emphasis, 'they were not to know' means 'they had no means of knowing'.

12 *let (verb)*: part of phrase 'let alone', used to show that the thing mentioned next is even less likely or believable than the one mentioned before.

13 *less (adverb)*: comparative + 'within the realms of possibility now' + 'than'.

14 *more (adverb)*: part of phrase 'what's more'; informal linking phrase used to indicate that a more significant point will follow.

15 *might (modal)*: used with 'just' to indicate a slim possibility.

Part 2

Meditation

16 *straightforward (adjective/adverb to compound adjective)*

17 *simplicity (adjective to noun)*

18 *undertaken (verb to past participle by adding prefix)*

19 *substantially (noun to adverb)*

20 *irritability (adjective to noun)*

21 *regularity (adjective to noun)*

22 *disposition (verb to noun)*

23 *supposedly (verb to adverb)*

24 *subsequent (noun to adjective by adding prefix)*

25 *consciousness (adjective to noun)*

Part 3

26 *capacity (noun)*: role; phrase 'filled to capacity', meaning 'completely full'; 'capacity for', meaning 'ability'.

27 *come (verb)*: phrasal verb 'come out', meaning 'to disappear, to be removed by washing'; to be; phrasal verb 'come back', meaning 'to return/happen again'.

28 *run (verb)*: from phrase 'run for', meaning 'to be or become a candidate'; to print; phrasal verb 'run through', meaning 'to read or examine quickly'.

29 *apply (verb)*: 'apply oneself', meaning 'to work hard at'; to put or spread on a surface; to relate.

30 *bearing (verb)*: to carry; phrasal verb 'bear down on', meaning 'to move towards forcefully and threateningly, especially at high speed'; phrase 'bear in mind', meaning 'to keep in mind'.

31 *deal (noun)*: share; business transaction; phrase 'a good/great deal of', meaning 'a large amount of'.

Part 4

32 *observe the company's dress code could/may/might result in*: verb 'fail' is replaced by noun 'failure'; a modal maintains the condition; 'result' is followed by 'in'.

33 *no fault of her own, Melanie*: 'through no fault of her own', meaning that it wasn't her fault.

34 *a medical examination has been successfully completed*: the condition (using a passive structure) precedes the outcome.

35 *remains to be seen whether there*: 'it remains to be seen' (meaning 'it is not yet known') + 'whether'.

36 *be (left) up to the students to decide*: 'be up to' is used to mean 'it is someone's responsibility'; this is followed by an infinitive.

37 *who suggested that the entrance fee should be*: relative clause including a passive structure; 'suggested' + 'that' + subject + 'should'.

38 *does one get the chance of*: negative adverb 'rarely' is followed by the auxiliary verb 'does'; the change from infinitive to gerund prompts 'chance of'.

39 *it that Miranda is on the verge of*: 'Rumour has it' (meaning 'according to rumour') + 'that'; 'on the verge of' means 'about to'.

Part 5

40 They should not expect immediate success.

41 A writer will not produce a good novel if it is about something they do not enjoy.

42 'what makes them tick' and 'getting inside the character's head'

43 No two people have the same personalities/characters.

44 The summary should include the following points:
  - The writer should enjoy his/her work.
  - The writer should become totally absorbed in the work.
  - An understanding of psychology can help the writer with characterisation.
  - It will help the writer to refer to other books on psychology.

Questions 1–25   = 1 mark
Questions 26–43 = 2 marks
Question 44   = 14 marks
Total score   **= 75 marks**

PAPER 4   Listening

Part 1

1 C: May says: 'I had no idea.' Peter says he thought they were 'invented in the 50s'.

2 A: His tone in 'Thanks a lot' is indignant.

3 B: The key words are 'its true distinctiveness'.

4 A: The correct answer is suggested in 'it has too many uses for its own good.' Also, 'The once thriving tree population' implies that it no longer is thriving.

5 B: 'it's my muse'.

6 C: 'My interpretation of the environment fluctuates like the places themselves.'

7 A: 'I sometimes even feel guilty … and that does … crush my credibility.'

8 C: 'him being there … brings out the best in us.'

Part 2

9 *fragile*: 'their colour is equally splendid and they are, unfortunately, just as fragile'.

10 *jellyfish*: 'I was rather taken aback to discover that the jellyfish is another member of this same family.'

11 *feeding*: 'tiny poisonous threads or "cnidae" that are fired from these cells for defence during feeding'.

12 *colony*: the cup coral 'lives alone rather than in a colony like many other types.'

13 *sunset*: 'the least common of all is the sunset coral.'

14 *white and fluffy*: 'known all around the British Isles for making underwater cliffs look white and fluffy'.

15 *red fingers*: 'On southwest coasts, a slightly smaller soft coral called "red fingers" is more common.'

16 *(tiny) trees*: 'These corals grow in a branching form rather like tiny trees.'

17 *divers*: 'they are still easily damaged by clumsy divers or badly-placed fishing gear.'

Part 3

18 C: 'It was rather sudden to imagine going from being "in the living room" nightly to having no real "persona" at all. … you do become rather like a member of the family.'

19 D: 'And sometimes there were glitches when we were on air, and we had to cover them up – I still shudder when I think of them today.'

20 B: 'these tend to be cosmetic, they don't impede the transfer of information.'

21 D: 'we do what we have time to do in the allotted space on the programme'.

22 A: 'people side-step world affairs because they're so bogged down with their own issues. … it's where they went on holiday and what supermarket they shop in. … that kind of conversation doesn't expand the mind.'

Part 4

23 J: Jack says: 'She's obviously not spending time on the things that matter.' In response, Georgia says: 'That's a bit unfair.'

24 G: Georgia says: 'I suspect she just feels outnumbered – wouldn't you?' Jack disputes this: 'But if there are cafes there are people – customers.'

25 B: Georgia says: 'You know, it sounds awful to say but I find her taste a bit, well … it's very 80s.' Jack obviously likes the 80s style but agrees that they could 'mention it to her'.

26 G: Georgia makes the suggestion and specifies the advantages. Jack says: 'it's a lot of money and time to spend finding out what you and I could tell her if we wanted to.'

27 B: Jack says: 'It may be, of course, that this is just a slack period. Most retailers will confirm that there's a lot of annual fluctuation.' Georgia doesn't disagree, and says: 'She's inevitably going to get jittery about that, though.' Both agree that the bank would have needed Amelia to take account of fluctuating profits.

28 J: Jack says: 'you certainly can't take on a business without having the will to make it succeed', implying that he believes Amelia can cope with the situation. Georgia disagrees.

Questions 1–28   = 1 mark
Total score   **= 28 marks**

Test 3

Part 1
In Praise of Face to Face Communication
1 C: Adverb that suggests some doubt regarding the truth of the statement.
2 D: Correct noun in phrase 'at someone's disposal', meaning 'able to be used freely by someone'.
3 A: Only adverb that adds emphasis.
4 A: Only verb with correct meaning that collocates with 'the message'.
5 B: Only noun that can be 'made' or 'emphasised' in the context of conversation.
6 B: Adjective with correct meaning that collocates with 'type'.

Home Security
7 C: Only correct verb that takes 'with'.
8 C: Only correct adverb meaning 'to whatever degree' that is followed by adjective + subject + verb.
9 A: Adjective with correct meaning of 'having no basis in fact'.
10 D: Only phrasal verb with correct meaning of 'to pay a visit' that does not need an object.
11 B: Noun with correct meaning in the context of crime.
12 B: Verb with correct meaning of 'give up'.

Ballet Shoes
13 B: Correct verb in phrasal verb 'wear in', meaning 'to wear new shoes to make them lose their stiffness and become comfortable'.
14 A: Verb with correct meaning that takes 'to' + -ing verb form.
15 C: Only noun that collocates with 'of pliancy'.
16 D: Adverb with correct meaning of 'mainly' in this context.
17 D: Correct noun in phrase 'in this way', meaning 'as a result of this'.
18 A: Verb with correct meaning of 'to strengthen'.

Part 2
Fanana
19 B: Fanana makes the point and the reference is forward to: 'left none of us in any doubt as to who was the boss'.
20 D: 'swaggering like a triumphant gunslinger' and 'as if taking part in some eccentric country dance' allow the reader to draw a mental picture of Fanana's behaviour.

The Ape and the Sushi Master: Cultural Reflections of a Primatologist
21 B: 'He spans divides: Europe-America, field-laboratory, monkey-ape, chimpanzee-bonobo.'
22 A: 'Targeted at the educated layperson'.

Too Much Monkey Business
23 B: The gist of the second paragraph is that humans decided when Congo had finished a painting (by removing it) and thereby influenced the appearance of the final product.
24 C: '... but consciously so ... With the monkey painter ... there is only execution.'

The Culture Club
25 C: The text explains why a certain approach was taken to the research.
26 D: The second paragraph explains what is usually omitted; the third paragraph states that 'all the behaviours' were listed.

Part 3
Happy as your genes allow
27 E: Link between 'one of life's inevitable setbacks' and 'such specific events'.
28 G: Link between 'Lykken' and 'the psychologist'. Also link between main idea of preceding paragraph and 'shed some further light on the subject'.
29 A: Link between the results cited in the preceding paragraph and 'those findings'. Also, forward link in 'he decided to ask the same subjects the same questions'.
30 F: Link between 'a futile exercise' in the preceding paragraph and 'trying to be happier might be the same as trying to be taller'. Also, forward link between the idea at the end of the paragraph and Lykken's explanation of how he tries to achieve this in his own life in the following paragraph.
31 B: Link between preceding two paragraphs and 'another regular way of boosting happiness quotients'.
32 D: Link between preceding paragraphs and 'such happiness inducing arrangements'.
33 H: Link between preceding paragraph and 'even this possibility'.

Part 4
The Sound of Silence
34 D: 'Although people are speaking, no one is saying anything.'
35 D: The people in the meeting are 'hiding' ideas; 'they do not share'.
36 A: Not sharing ideas leads to 'impoverished conversation – potentially to the detriment of good policymaking'.
37 A: 'And the danger of legally based approaches is that they will make us more guarded, not less so.'
38 B: Refers back to 'But most of the information we receive is of limited value.'
39 B: The eighth paragraph focuses on the positive effects of acknowledging the source of ideas, i.e. there is an increase in trust and therefore a greater willingness to share ideas.
40 D: 'Maybe they are storing up the best stuff for the online consultancy they run from home.'

Questions 1–18 = 1 mark
Questions 19–40 = 2 marks
Total score   = **62 marks**

PAPER 2   Writing

Part 1
Question 1
Style: Likely to be semi-formal, persuasive, and addressed directly to the reader, although a more formal style would not be inappropriate.
Content: Letter should indicate reason for writing and discuss the points raised; i.e. the fact that parents are busy, the issues of going out often and late, and the use of the computer. Answers should analyse these problems and suggest what might be done to alleviate them.

Model Answer

Dear Editor,

I read with interest and concern the letter that you printed in your magazine last week from a young reader, regarding her relationship with her parents. I am twenty-five years old, and I too experienced some communication problems with my parents when I was a teenager. Perhaps I can make some comments on the situation that might be relevant and offer a little advice.

It seems that everyone is busy these days. Not only are we constantly bombarded with a variety of leisure time activities to choose from, but also work patterns seem to have changed, so that this part of our life no longer ends when we close the office door. At the same time, both men and women have been made to feel that they should be able to perform a number of quite distinct roles successfully, and this adds further stress to personal relationships. I now realise that my parents were subject to these pressures but, being unaware of this, I was. If and when they did talk, it was usually to chastise me for something or establish boundaries for my behaviour, as seems to be the case with your reader's parents. With the benefit of hindsight, I can now see that although my parents had no time for casual conversation, they were nevertheless keen to ensure my physical safety.

I strongly believe that in any situation it is always better to discuss one's feelings in a rational manner than to bottle them up. If your reader decides that her parents are working too hard or trying to be too many things, then ultimately they may thank her for bringing this to their attention. If there is bad feeling within the home, then you can be quite sure that young people will be aware of it, though they may lack the insight to diagnose the causes or be too preoccupied to face them head on. However, by writing to the magazine your reader is already showing that she is sensitive to the issues and has a desire to do something about them.

I would now advise her to try and initiate a discussion about her problems with her parents.

Mark: Band Score 5

Part 2
Questions 2
Style: May opt for formal or semi-formal but style should be consistent throughout. Some humour would not be inappropriate.
Content: Review should briefly inform the reader about the restaurant. It should praise positive features and criticise negative ones. Some recommendations for improvement should be given.

Questions 3
Style: Formal. Objective tone: register should reflect authority of reader. Section headings may be used.
Content: Report should provide information about the course and evaluate the features listed. It should also asses the use fulness of the course.

Questions 4
Style: Likely to be formal but a semi-formal style may also be appropriate. Tone should be persuasive. Internal headings may be used.
Content: Proposal should include recommendations and justification of these. Also some analysis of benefits.

PAPER 3   Use of English

Part 1
Niagara Falls
1 *Apart (adverb)*: from phrase 'apart from', meaning 'with the exception of'.
2 *little (determiner)*: phrase 'precious little' means 'not very much'.
3 *that (determiner)*: from phrase 'that is', used to give more information or detail.
4 *In (preposition)*: 'in operation' means 'working'.
5 *often (adverb)*: from phrase 'more often than not', meaning 'usually'.
6 *with (preposition)*: used with 'supply' after object.
7 *worth (preposition)*: 'worth' + noun or -ing verb form.
8 *nothing (pronoun)/little (determiner)*: 'nothing short of'; used to add emphasis.
9 *For (preposition)*: 'For those who', meaning 'people who'.
10 *come (verb)*: part of phrasal verb 'come across', meaning 'to meet by chance'.
11 *too (adverb)*: 'only too', meaning 'very'.
12 *on/at (preposition)*: 'on the brink' is more common, meaning 'on the very edge'.
13 *can/may (modal)*: completes passive structure.
14 *As (adverb)*: from phrase 'as with', meaning 'like'.
15 *what (pronoun)*: the question is rhetorical and means 'What else would you expect in these circumstances?'

Part 2
The Invisible Profession
16 *unassuming (verb to adjective by adding negative prefix)*

17 *unknown (verb to adjective by adding negative prefix)*
18 *weariness (adjective to noun)*
19 *intellectually (noun to adverb)*
20 *commercial (noun to adjective)*
21 *assessment (verb to noun)*
22 *specialise/specialize (adjective to verb)*
23 *appraisal (verb to noun)*
24 *packages (verb to plural noun)*
25 *rarity (adjective to noun)*

Part 3

26 *snap (verb)*: to break; expression 'snap out of it', meaning 'to free oneself quickly from an unhappy or unhealthy state of mind'; to speak quickly with irritation.

27 *cast (verb)*: phrase 'cast a shadow', meaning 'to make something less enjoyable than it might have been'; to give an acting part to a person, or choose an actor for a play or film; phrase 'cast aside', meaning 'to forget about'.

28 *depth (noun)*: degree; phrase 'out of one's depth', meaning 'beyond one's ability to understand'; distance below the surface.

29 *edge (noun)*: expression 'on the edge of one's seat', meaning 'fully attentive due to excitement'; expression 'take the edge off', meaning 'to reduce'; phrase 'on edge', meaning 'nervous'.

30 *laying (verb)*: 'to make (an accusation); expression 'lay oneself open to', meaning 'to put oneself into the position of receiving blame or attack'; phrase 'lay on', meaning 'to organise or provide'.

31 *led (verb)*: phrase 'lead someone to do something', meaning 'to cause wrongly'; to conduct; phrase 'lead to', meaning 'to result in'.

Part 4

32 *but to put up with changes*: 'have no choice' + 'but' + infinitive; phrasal verb 'put up with' means 'to tolerate'.

33 *the runner as (being) too young to compete*: 'describe someone' + 'as'; adjectival phrase incorporating 'too' + adjective + infinitive.

34 *resulted in the closure/closing down of*: 'resulted in' + noun ('closure')/-ing verb form ('closing down') formed from main verb ('close').

35 *to be on the verge of announcing*: 'on the verge of' (meaning 'about to') + -ing verb form.

36 *don't hold me responsible for its*: 'hold someone responsible' (meaning 'to blame someone') + 'for' + possessive + -ing verb form.

37 *had known he was not/wasn't going to be*: third conditional indicates that the experience is over and the condition is not possible; 'going' prompts 'to be here' rather than 'wasn't here'.

38 *one by one/one at a time in her/an*: 'one by one/one at a time' means 'separately' + phrase 'in an attempt to'.

39 *would have liked her project to have been/to be*: 'would have liked' + object + perfect infinitive or infinitive; used to express wishes.

Part 5

40 Have an exclusive appeal.
41 'its cumulative character'
42 'The reach and scope of what we know, moreover, is unmatched in history.'
43 We have the knowledge to develop a new form of energy but we are uncertain about its safety.
44 The summary should include the following points:
- It affects everyone's life.
- It builds on what is already known to create higher levels of knowledge.
- It encourages a spirit of co-operation.
- It creates as many problems as it solves.
- It has become fragmented and highly specialised.

Questions 1–25 = 1 mark
Questions 26–43 = 2 marks
Question 44 = 14 marks
Total score = **75 marks**

PAPER 4   Listening

Part 1

1 A: 'it needs to rediscover itself in a way, shake off its dowdiness'.
2 B: Hilary says managers 'aren't listening to their curators who really know and love the exhibits, know how to put an idea across and are in touch with the people'.
3 C: In most of the extract the woman is comparing herself with the character.
4 B: She says: 'everyone waits for me to behave this way or that way'.
5 A: 'I shall have to wait until he comes back on Monday now before I can go ahead with this agreement' indicates an office environment.
6 C: The woman is frustrated because 'you can't go rummaging around in someone else's things'. She is not amused or anxious.
7 C: The man asks: 'It's not all exhilaration then?' The journalist replies: 'it has its moments – it isn't always like that'.
8 A: 'we're just trying to bring the news to the world'.

Part 2

9 *fire prevention*: 'Like all my male colleagues, I *am* increasingly involved in areas like fire prevention'.
10 *false alarms*: 'it's just a result of one of the many false alarms we get'.
11 *(vast) warehouse*: 'It was in a vast warehouse in a factory area in the outskirts of London.'
12 *revolving platform*: 'I ended up going up on a revolving platform'.
13 *de-briefing (session)*: 'We usually sit around afterwards and have what's called a debriefing session.'
14 *confined space*: 'I may be one of the first they approach if there was a confined space that somebody had to crawl through'.

15 *stamina*: 'they also test your aerobic fitness and your stamina'.

16 *height limit*: 'there was an unrealistic height limit imposed'.

17 *glamorous*: 'it's a demanding, but worthwhile job which isn't that glamorous actually'.

Part 3

18 C: 'although these events take place on a regular basis, … they're really not scheduled in the western sense.'

19 A: 'But the approach that Bob and I take is to adopt the pace of Africa. … we invest time in making friendships … only gradually do we start working with them.'

20 D: 'we carry rudimentary supplies'.

21 C: 'over twenty years, we've been visiting certain groups of people very regularly and eventually we felt able to ask if we could attend a closed ceremony. … these things take patience.'

22 B: 'Our project is all about explaining, in a very sympathetic and comprehensive way, extremely important traditions that have real meaning for the people involved.'

Part 4

23 B: Cathy's stress in '*just a few* other songs', indicates that a lot of her songs don't get recorded. Paul supports that with 'most bite the dust long before that'.

24 B: Both agree that they do their work 'for a living'.

25 P: Paul refers to the 'odd occasion' when he can't write, whereas Cathy says: 'I'd love to have that scale of problem. I can be prolific for six months, nine months, and then … I'm into a creative void.'

26 P: Paul says he allows a couple of hours, then he says: 'After that I can't see the point.' Cathy, on the other hand, refers to several songs which wouldn't exist 'if I'd stuck by that principle'.

27 B: Cathy was surprised by the success of 'Hug me'. Paul says he had a similar experience with 'Catch me falling'.

28 C: Paul says that he can 'just pick up a guitar and do it'. Cathy says: 'I'll have to try that', indicating that she needs to have an idea first.

Questions 1–28　　=　1 mark
Total score　　=　**28 marks**

Test 4

PAPER 1　Reading

Part 1
Happy Landings

1 A: Correct verb in phrasal verb 'touch down' meaning 'to land'.

2 C: Only noun that forms compound noun with 'flight' to indicate direction.

3 C: Correct noun that takes 'to'.

4 B: Correct conjunction + -ing verb form.

5 D: Correct noun in phrase 'field of vision'.

6 B: Correct verb with 'close to'.

The Death of Languages

7 D: Correct verb in phrase 'play a part'.

8 B: Verb with correct meaning of 'to speed up' followed by direct object.

9 A: Correct noun in phrase 'in favour of'.

10 D: Only adjective that collocates with 'culture'.

11 B: Adjective with correct meaning of 'that cannot be regained once lost'.

12 C: Verb with correct meaning of 'to maintain'.

Old Friends

13 B: Correct verb that takes object + 'in' + -ing verb form.

14 D: Correct adverb in phrase 'regardless of' meaning 'despite'.

15 A: Adverb with correct meaning of 'carefully, with attention to detail'.

16 C: Correct verb in phrasal verb 'go through', meaning 'to experience'.

17 B: Only verb with correct meaning in this context.

18 D: Verb meaning 'to be important'.

Part 2
The Thinking Person's Hotel

19 A: The writer has specific 'personal experience' of philosophers but the implication is that Ida Jongsma is different: 'cutting across type'.

20 C: 'I'd certainly rebook on the strength of the late-night conversation alone'.

Extract from an autobiography

21 D: He refers to flats in London as 'the drawers in the human filing cabinets that stand in blank rows'.

22 C: He is hypocritical because he has a negative attitude toward London and yet continues to live there.

Hitching a Ride

23 B: 'They do not sit there slumped and morose … They tell me all about themselves, they learn all about me'.

24 B: 'kindly' refers to the attitude of those who are correcting the writer but does not indicate the writer's view of being corrected.

Steak and Chips

25 C: 'But I might have been forgiven for thinking … that I stood some chance of sampling the same delights as its reviewer.'

26 A: The narrative style is ironic and the sentence 'I managed not to ask him how one took stock when one had run out of ingredients' is particularly ironic.

Part 3
Give Pennies a Chance
27 F: Link between the anecdote in the first paragraph and 'The tale was reported'.

28 H: Link between the writer's collection as described in the preceding paragraphs and 'Hence I began to display…'.

29 C: Link between 'a grand total of £78' in preceding paragraph and 'such a miserable yield'.

30 G: Link between 'The conundrum remains, however, of what people should do' with their small change in preceding paragraph and 'Putting the most minuscule of small change in charity collecting boxes is one way out'.

31 A: Link between the 'a new machine' in preceding paragraph and 'it sorts out your change'.

32 E: Link between 'one man lugged in a suitcase of change containing $8,000' and 'Other equally mind-boggling stories abound' in following paragraph.

33 B: Link between 'throwing them away is vulgar and wasteful' and 'the rich, and more so, the famous, might not see things in quite the same light'.

Part 4
The Other Side of Eden
34 A: 'Reading such a claim at the beginning of a book, you tend to think 'uh-huh' – and wait for it to fall short. But it does not.'

35 B: 'expeditions of genuine hardship'.

36 A: 'If his portrait of them appears at times a little rosy'.

37 D: 'calm self-confidence' and 'they are 'largely immune to the kind of mental anguish that arises from half-truths'.

38 A: The phrase means something is done without sensitivity and in a way that is hurtful.'

39 C: 'Those who do survive may not be typical.'

40 D: 'Brody breaks the rules by writing well and saying what he thinks.'

Questions 1–18   =   1 mark
Questions 19–40   =   2 marks
Total score   =   **62 marks**

PAPER 2   Writing

Part 1
Question 1
Style: Formal style and register with clear organisation of points. Headings may be appropriate. Tone may be covertly persuasive.
Content: Proposal should relate directly to the advertisement and address each of the requirements. It should give a well-reasoned analysis of the individual contribution that the person concerned could make to the scheme.

Part 2
Question 2
Style: Formal letter with good paragraphing and well-structured arguments. Some personal input may be relevant
Content: Letter should describe and evaluate methods of protecting the environment. It should also compare government and individual roles and suggest how they can cooperate.

Question 3
Style: Consistently semi-formal or formal as befits a newspaper article. Tone likely to be objective rather than personal.
Content: Article should include discussion of key issues with some prioritisation. Also a clear recommendation should be made for something that school leavers can do to help them in their decisions.

Model Answer

At some point in their life, every young person has to make important decisions that relate to their future. These may include the selection of a university or college course, the decision as to whether or not to take time off between school and study or, possibly, the question of residence: is it best to stay at home or should an independent lifestyle be sought, in the home country or abroad? None of these decisions is easy.

Some youngsters know exactly what career path they want to follow. People who fall into this category should follow their instincts. For them, the decisions are 'made' and unless there are obstacles that cannot reasonably be overcome, they simply need to find a good course in their chosen field of study. They are intrinsically motivated to succeed in their ambitions, and often do.

For others, the career path is much less clearly defined, but there are a number of considerations that can be helpful. First, it is worth asking questions that pertain to the area of study, questions such as 'Which subjects am I good at?' or 'Which subjects do I enjoy?' The answers may vary in each case, but if they do not, then that will be a good starting point.

From here, it is worth considering other personal preferences that might offer some insight. For example, those who prefer to be active are ill advised to go into a sedentary job. Similarly people who are stimulated by the company of others should avoid solitary occupations. Such considerations seem very obvious, but it is surprising how many people ignore their own personality and then wonder why they are unhappy at work.

Last, but certainly not least, it is worth consulting others who know us well. Older people such as parents and teachers have considerable life experience and may be able to use this to gently counsel a younger friend or relative.

As many people would admit to ending up in the 'wrong' field of work or the 'wrong' type of employment, it is obviously worth giving serious consideration to the choices that have to be made as a school leaver. The decisions *are* difficult, but there are good reasons for this.

Mark: Band Score 5

Question 4
Style: May range from informal to formal but should be consistent.
Content: Review should briefly inform reader of the type of documentary and its content. Reasons should be given for the selection and recommendations made as to how it might be incorporated into the group's discussions.

PAPER 3   Use of English

Part 1
The Sensual Shopper
1 *it (pronoun)*: refers back to idea in first sentence.
2 *when/as (adverb)*: used with 'just' to denote that the events were happening at the same time.
3 *over (preposition)*: phrasal verb 'look over', meaning 'to examine quickly'.
4 *without (preposition)*: phrase 'without exception'.
5 *What (adverb)*: phrase 'what else?' used to emphasise the fact that there is no other course of action.
6 *by (preposition)*: used to denote method; 'by' + -ing verb form.
7 *against (preposition)*: used to mean 'touching'.
8 *of (preposition)*: phrase 'the principle of' + noun.
9 *would/could (auxiliary verb)*: reported future time, so 'will/can' not possible; + passive infinitive.
10 *was (auxiliary verb)*: in passive structure.
11 *with (preposition)*: adjectival phrase 'alive with' meaning 'full of'.
12 *a (article)*: phrase '(for) a moment'.
13 *which (relative pronoun)*: refers back to previous sentence, so relative pronoun 'that' is not possible.
14 *for (preposition)*: follows noun 'basis'.
15 *be (auxiliary verb)*: in passive structure with modal.

Part 2
Ventriloquism
16 *derivative (verb to noun)*
17 *misleading (verb to adjective by adding negative prefix)*
18 *utilises/utilizes (noun to verb)*
19 *application (verb to noun)*
20 *inability (adjective to noun by adding negative prefix)*
21 *reference (verb to noun)*
22 *association (verb to noun by adding negative prefix)*
23 *comparatively (verb to adverb)*
24 *focal (noun to adjective)*
25 *practitioners (verb to plural noun)*

Part 3
26 *sense (noun)*: awareness; phrase 'no sense in', meaning 'no point in'; impression/feeling.
27 *scraping (verb)*: phrasal verb 'scrape together', meaning 'to gather with difficulty'; to remove (unwanted material) from a surface by pulling or pushing an edge firmly across it repeatedly; phrase 'scrape by', meaning 'to live with no more than the necessary money'.
28 *switch (verb)*: to change; phrasal verb 'switch off', meaning 'to turn off by means of a switch'; to change (in terms of attention or mental effort).
29 *stream (noun)*: a continuous flow; phrase 'come on stream', meaning 'to become available'; (in schools) a group of pupils of the same level of ability.
30 *maintain (verb)*: to declare to be true; to preserve; to continue to have.
31 *wide (adverb)*: phrase 'wide open to', meaning 'vulnerable to'; phrase 'wide of the mark', meaning 'inaccurate'; in this context 'wide' means 'fully'.

Part 4
32 *one of the more/most rewarding ways of*: 'one of' + comparative/superlative noun phrase.
33 *able to tell the difference between*: 'tell the difference' (meaning 'to distinguish') + 'between'.
34 *seafood brings me out in*: phrasal verb 'bring out in', means 'to cause to suffer the stated skin condition', in this case, 'a rash'.
35 *less able to identify their own faults than*: comparative + 'able' + infinitive + object + 'than'.
36 *had undergone extensive repair(s)/repair work*: 'undergo' + noun phrase.
37 *despite the fact that it cost him £11*: linker 'despite the fact that' is used for contrast; the pronoun ('it') precedes the noun phrase ('the swimming lesson').
38 *was little likelihood/chance of her going*: 'likelihood/chance' + 'of' + -ing verb form.
39 *didn't/did not do something about (improving) his appearance*: direct to reported speech; 'do something about' means 'to improve'.

Part 5
40 'a lifetime spent being paid to say other people's lines'
41 'quenches'
42 'losing any more face'
43 Empty words do not improve communication; they damage it further.
44 The summary should include the following points:
- The listener should feel involved.
- The speaker's points should be relevant and succinct.
- Preparation helps the speaker to say what they really mean.
- Keeping calm prevents misunderstanding.

Questions 1–25	=	1 mark
Questions 26–43	=	2 marks
Question 44	=	14 marks
Total score	**=**	**75 marks**

PAPER 4　Listening

Part 1

1 C: The presenter says: 'although they'd released five fine albums in seven years, gaining an enthusiastic niche audience in the process'. This suggests that he feels they should have been widely admired.

2 A: 'A pair of handcuffs dangled from the microphone stand – symbol, claimed singer MM, of what it was like to be in a band.'

3 B: 'they'll get put through to someone else when they do', indicates that they work on the telephone in a call centre.

4 C: The comments 'get rid of them' and 'Yeah, me probably' underline the workers' lack of genuine concern for the callers' problems, which is gradually revealed as they speak .

5 B: 'sinister' and a reference to children's 'vulnerability' indicate the correct answer.

6 A: The presenter says: 'For me, this really says a lot about just how far consumer culture has come, a topic we'll be investigating with my guest today' and also that Amanda has written a book on 'marketing history'.

7 C: 'It was done in the last session before Christmas. The model was ... The studio was ... I worked quickly ... the result took my breath away.'

8 A: 'one of the things I've learnt is that when I am brave, I get the best results. So I persevere.'

Part 2

9 *deeply moved*: 'I could see that he had been deeply moved by the experience.'

10 *endangered*: 'they now feature on the official list of endangered species.'

11 *20,000/twenty thousand*: 'And an estimated 20,000 of those are thought to have been lucky enough to get a sighting since the wolf reintroduction programme began.'

12 *park warden*: 'my visit began with an evening lecture given by a park warden.'

13 *paler:* 'The coyote is smaller, with longer ears and a paler coat.'

14 *biologist:* 'he'd studied to be a biologist before retraining as a professional guide.'

15 *tracking collars:* 'about 50 per cent of the wolves have been fitted with devices known as tracking collars'.

16 *grey rocks*: 'I should keep my eyes peeled for grey rocks sticking up out of the snow.'

17 *telescope:* 'clearly visible through the excellent telescope Ken thrust into my hand.'

Part 3

18 D: The gist of Tansy's first speech is that she had a natural inclination for selling her products.

19 B: 'Once I'd found the right backers'.

20 D: Tansy says: 'Well, it's partly seeing the way the market's going and responding to that.' She then expands on this idea.

21 C: 'They have to energise and tranquillise, deal with depression and jealousy, they need to uplift and to inspire.'

22 A: 'People these days want versatile fragrances, ... many people now have a wardrobe of perfumes for different purposes.'

Part 4

23 B: In discussing the theme, Mathew says: 'nothing unusual there. But the treatment is far less run-of-the-mill. Daniella agrees: 'we've only to think of a couple of famous children's novels to recognise what's going on.'

24 M: Mathew says that it 'added atmosphere to the story'. However, Daniella says: 'Johnson's faceless running commentary struck me as rather odd. In the end, it interfered for me, became almost tedious.'

25 D: Mathew thinks the film should have centred on him. Daniella differs in her view: 'the focus should really have been on the island community'.

26 B: Mathew says: 'there are all the typical personalities for this genre of film. Daniella agrees: 'then there are all the classic stereotypes'.

27 B: Daniella says: 'It's a potentially explosive situation and I think that's what does it, makes it work, even though that situation never really detonates with the power that you'd hope for.' Mathew agrees: 'It promises a great deal but, to be honest, it never quite delivers in the end.'

28 D: Mathew defies 'anyone who's seen the film to say that they weren't gripped by it.' But only Daniella refers to the target audience: 'it's clearly the gap year student who's supposed to identify most with it.'

Questions 1–28　=　1 mark
Total score　**=　28 marks**

Test 5

PAPER 1　Reading

Part 1
Beauty from the Beast

1 D: Adverb with correct meaning of 'entirely'.

2 A: Only verb that is appropriate in context.

3 C: Only adjective that collocates with 'grazing'.

4 C: Correct noun in phrase 'with the result that'.

5 B: Adjective with correct meaning of 'valued'.

6 B: Correct conjunction meaning 'despite the fact that' or 'although'.

'Chasing Science: Science as Spectator Sport'

7 B: Only correct noun meaning 'a method of doing something' in this context.

8 A: Only verb that takes 'into'.

9 D: Only adjective that collocates with 'deceptively'.

10 A: Only adverbial phrase indicating that comparison showing similarity follows.

11 B: Verb with correct meaning of 'to recognise and enjoy the worth of; to value'.

12 C: Only adjective that is an appropriate contrast to being 'everywhere', commonplace.

Television

13 B: Adverb with correct meaning of 'for the reason just stated' and that is followed by a noun phrase.

14 C: Verb with correct meaning that takes 'up'.

15 A: Conjunction with correct meaning of 'but even so' that indicates a contrast with previous sentence.

16 D: Correct verb in phrase 'keep one's eyes on', meaning 'to observe regularly'.

17 B: Verb with correct meaning of 'to see'; used informally.

18 D: Adjective with correct meaning of 'very surprising'.

Part 2
Futurology

19 B: 'the futurologist must always take account of the resources which we already have before he begins to factor in his range of variables'.

20 C: Final sentence of text indicates that TV producers welcome innovation regardless of how successful it might prove to be.

Hypermobility

21 C: The second paragraph highlights the drawbacks to the hypothetical advances listed in the first paragraph with the sentence: 'But if successful, these will lead to further increases in physical mobility.'

22 B: The use of 'fix' implies a temporary solution.

Extract from a novel

23 C: 'the destination which was his aim' indicates a desire for control; 'life can throw obstacles' shows a loss of control.

24 C: 'monotonous existence' contrasted with 'desperately seeking someone who would rescue her' show that she is frustrated.

Memo to the Future

25 A: 'and the process is accelerating'.

26 C: 'But surely there are things …' and the idea expressed in the last sentence. There is no indication of A, B and D.

Part 3
Pain and Pleasure under the Big Top

27 D: Link between the information about circuses in other countries, the information about circuses in Britain and 'It was an entrepreneurial cyclist', which introduces the person responsible for rectifying the situation in the following paragraph.

28 H: Link between references to Circus Space and what it provides. Also 'whistle-stop tour of basic circus skills' leads to next paragraph.

29 C: Link between 'Hours of practice, it seemed, were needed to achieve better flight control' in preceding paragraph and 'Here the problem is reversed – progress is heavily front-loaded.'

30 A: Link between preceding and following paragraph and the idea of turn-taking on the equipment. Lexical links include 'up there' and 'the bar'.

31 E: Link between the accident described in E and the reference to pain in following paragraph. The notion of turn-taking continues. (Note: C does not fit here because of the reference to 'progress'.)

32 G: Link between 'strikingly easy to achieve' and 'got it off to a fine art' in following paragraph.

33 F: Link between 'The laborious *corde lisse* … presented us with a further challenge', which suggests it will be difficult, and 'balance stylessly' and 'lacklustre performance', in the following paragraph, which confirm this.

Part 4

34 B: 'I content myself with contributing research papers, encouraging my students to take the podium in my stead'.

35 B: 'There was also the matter of a couple of first class return air tickets, which swung the balance.'

36 A: The main idea expressed in: 'But it turned out to be an enormous international gathering of many disciplines, and I found myself more involved and excited than I'd expected.'

37 D: 'alas' indicates that there was an unfortunate or momentous consequence to leaving.

38 A: Only 'stooped' can be used to describe posture. The other options describe behaviour.

39 C: 'I gingerly edged past the plethora of wires and cables … As I struggled with the armrest, … Thus I missed the speaker's opening remarks.' A, B and D express attitudes which are not described in the text.

40 C: 'juxtaposition' here refers to the superimposing of images.

Questions 1–18　　=　1 mark
Questions 19-40　　=　2 marks
Total score　　　　**=　62 marks**

PAPER 2　Writing

Part 1
Question 1

Style: May be semi-formal or formal but must be consistent. Tone is likely to be personal and may also be philosophical or speculative.

Content: Article should discuss the points raised; i.e. that reunions force people to consider how they have changed as individuals, what their aspirations are at the time of the reunion and how they get on with other people present. Opinions (positive or negative) should be justified and the purpose and value of reunions should be assessed.

Part 2
Question 2
Style: Formal (or neutral) bearing in mind the topic and the competition. Review should both describe and evaluate. Headings would be appropriate, though not essential.
Content: Review should inform the reader about the content, approach and style of the book and offer opinions on these. It may be wholly positive or there may be a mix of positive and negative views.

Question 3
Style: Semi-formal or formal, as the letter is not to be published.
Content: Letter should assess particular features of the magazine and draw comparisons with other publications. A clear recommendation should be made for future editions.

Question 4
Style: Formal, clearly addressing the requirements of the task. Section headings may be used.
Content: Report should inform the reader about a news story that is familiar to the writer. It should give the writer's opinion and raise issues that might reasonably lead to some kind of informal discussion.

Is Motherhood a Right?
Last month, a fifty-five-year-old woman announced to the British press that she had become pregnant. This will not be her first child; she already has a thirty-year-old daughter and a two-year-old grandson, but the woman described herself as being 'desperate' to have another child, and is said to be delighted with the recent news.

When the child is born, it will not be the first time that someone of this age has become a mother, and it will certainly not be the last. Scientists are making rapid progress in the area of assisted fertilisation. It will almost certainly be possible, in the next decade or so, for many more women, who would otherwise be unable to bear children, to take advantage of these techniques. This, coupled with the fact that many young women are delaying having a family until they have established themselves in a career, means that we are likely to see many more 'older' parents.

For those of us who grew up with young, active parents, this doesn't seem quite right. Bringing up a child takes years and during that time, a parent needs to be able to endure sleepless nights, teach the infant certain skills, mix with other parents and, as time goes by, be able to remember how it feels to be a teenager, and thus help someone through what may be a difficult period. It is a demanding role at the best of times; how is a sixty-year-old going to cope?

Regrettably, these are just the practical concerns. On a more fundamental level, does every woman or couple have a 'right' to have a child, whenever it suits them? And what about the child? Surely they have rights too, some of which include the right to 'good' parenting.

Finally, there is another viewpoint that needs to be considered, and that is the young couple who really do have fertility problems and for whom these techniques were developed in the first place. In the battle to be first in the queue, are the genuine cases going to lose out? Or is money going to be the critical factor in deciding whether or not a woman receives fertility treatment? It seems there are a number of issues here that need to be addressed.

Mark: Band Score 5

PAPER 3   Use of English

Part 1
The Science of Cooking
1 little (determiner): used with indefinite article ('a') to mean 'some'.
2 go (verb): collocates with 'awry' to mean 'go wrong'.
3 behind (preposition): used to denote the reason for something being done.
4 with (preposition): used with 'combine'.
5 a (article): introduces noun phrase.
6 like (conjunction): used to introduce example.
7 of (preposition): part of phrase 'a sprinkling of', meaning 'a small scattered amount or number'.
8 out (preposition): phrasal verb 'work out', meaning 'to find out' or 'to estimate'.
9 that (pronoun): part of phrase 'that said'; used to refer back to previous statement and to indicate that a contrasting statement will be made.
10 not (adverb): a negative is needed to make sense in context.
11 one (pronoun): refers back to 'experiments'.
12 over (preposition): used with 'placing' to indicate position.
13 were (verb): used in conditional structure to emphasise that a possibility is very unlikely.
14 up (preposition): phrasal verb 'rustle up', meaning 'to provide or find quickly'; often used in the context of food.
15 should (modal): used in conditional structure to talk about what might happen.

Part 2
Preface to 'Guide to Handwriting Styles'
16 (re)awakening (adjective to noun, alternative formed by adding prefix)
17 impersonality (noun to noun by adding negative prefix)
18 fingerprints (noun to compound noun)

19 *unreasonable (noun to adjective by adding negative prefix)*
20 *sought (verb to past participle)*
21 *expertise (noun to noun)*
22 *recognition (verb to noun)*
23 *definitive (verb to adjective)*
24 *guidelines (noun/verb to compound noun)*
25 *attractively (verb to adverb)*

Part 3

26 *go (verb)*: phrasal verb 'go for', meaning 'to try to win'; phrase 'have a long way to go', meaning 'a great deal of experience needs to be gained/a great deal of improvement needs to be made'; with 'against', meaning 'to be opposed to, to disagree with'.

27 *stage (noun)*: a state reached at a particular time; a particular point or period in the course of a process or set of events; as for previous sentence, but in different context.

28 *finely (adverb)*: so as to be very thin or small; closely and delicately; to a high degree of precision.

29 *completion (noun)*: phrase 'on completion', meaning 'when they have finished'; the state of having all the necessary or usual parts; having fulfilled requirements (of a course).

30 *points (verb)*: phrasal verb 'point to', meaning 'to suggest a strong possibility of'; to show where something is; phrasal verb 'point out', meaning 'to draw attention to the fact'.

31 *slow (adjective)*: 'business is slow' means that customer numbers have fallen; not good or quick in understanding; showing a time earlier than the true time.

Part 4

32 *has an/its effect on*: 'play a role' is replaced by 'have an effect', which is followed by 'on'.

33 *how/where to draw the line*: idiomatic expression 'draw the line' means 'to tell the difference, to distinguish'.

34 *hard/difficult to get their business going* **or** *hard/difficult to get going with their business*: phrase 'get going' means 'to start operating, to cause to start operating'.

35 *it meant (her) being able to*: conditional; 'meant' is followed by -ing verb form.

36 *understand a single word/thing (that) she*: 'not to understand a single word' means 'not to understand anything at all'.

37 *that can prove/to prove the existence*: 'that' clause or infinitive; 'of' prompts noun phrase 'the existence of'.

38 *to be (more) prone to (catch(ing)/get(ting))*: 'tend' + infinitive; 'easily' prompts 'more'; 'prone to' + -ing verb form.

39 *was in no way/wasn't in any way bothered by*: adverbial phrase 'in no way' means 'not at all'; passive construction prompts 'by'.

Part 5

40 It impresses/appeals to customers because it makes them appear up-to-date.
41 'this lengthy tussle'
42 'has not lived up to its early promise'
43 'vet' and 'deemed'
44 The summary should include the following points:
  - Websites are badly-organised/slow/complicated to use.
  - It can be expensive (hardware/phone bills).
  - Somebody has to be at home when goods arrive.
  - The technology is complicated.

Questions 1–25 = 1 mark
Questions 26–43 = 2 marks
Question 44 = 14 marks
Total score = 75 marks

PAPER 4   Listening

Part 1

1 B: He says it is 'not a book that an urbanite like myself would normally choose'.

2 B: He refers to the book's 'exquisite style'.

3 A: He begins by referring to his friend's argument that 'more should be done to encourage cycling in London'. He then says: 'I beg to differ.'

4 C: He says cyclists have 'scant regard for anyone else's rights'.

5 C: She says: 'If you're like me, you'll have at least one dilapidated pair of shoes', indicating that the shoes are old and worn, not in 'pristine' condition. Then she says: 'shoes seem to grow on us, become friendlier with the years, as we wear them in'.

6 A: She expresses regret in her reference to a 'time-honoured custom'. This contrasts with her description of today's throw-away culture and the use of 'shoddy' that follows.

7 B: 'When people like Bill start wittering on in business meetings in this kind of impenetrable jargon, it's usually because they've got nothing particular to contribute but urgently need to sound important.'

8 C: 'whatever rubbish you spout, you can be sure that your words will meet with a lot of sage nodding because nobody in that sector would dare admit they weren't up to date with the latest buzzwords. You could make them up and nobody would ever know the difference.'

Part 2

9 *1905*: 'the idea really took off nationally after 1905'.

10 *cash box*: 'some fingerprints were found on a cash box within the premises'.

11 *burglary*: 'it is in the solving of cases such as burglary and car crime that they are a particularly effective.'

12 *light switches*: 'surfaces which have been highly polished and light switches, two places which it is in general very difficult to retrieve fingerprints from'.

13 *brush*: 'Police officers still dust with a brush, but they've progressed from the simple black powders of years ago to aluminium powders and gels.'

14 *database*: 'the prints are immediately scanned on to a database known as the National Automated Finger Identification System, or NAFIS for short.'

15 *spot the difference*: 'The job itself is rather like the children's game called "spot the difference"'.

16 *spirals*: 'they are either arched, arranged in spirals or they have a series of loops'.

17 *identical twins*: 'Even identical twins have different fingerprints'.

Part 3

18 A: 'I was born with the bug, had the right instincts from the start'.

19 B: 'It's easy to run them down, but I try to avoid that because, you know, that's how you cut your teeth in the business, learn the ropes.'

20 B: 'if they respect your work and providing you're mature enough to cope with the situation, then actors treat one another like equals and that's mostly what I've experienced.'

21 D: He says: 'I concentrate on the job' and then goes on to say he 'tried not to worry about what other people on the set were up to.'

22 C: He says: 'my parents really had their heads screwed on. 'He also says: 'they managed to keep me pretty much on track as far as friends, schoolwork and all that was concerned.'

Part 4

23 K: Adam says: 'most of us take it in our stride'. Kayleigh disagrees: 'the majority don't, if you ask me. … it's bewildering for the average person.'

24 K: Kayleigh says: 'I'm not convinced it's the answer anyway.' Adam disagrees: 'Oh, I wouldn't be so sure about that.'

25 B: Kayleigh says: 'I remember a time when new technology in the home really meant something to people.' Adam adds to this: 'Like if somebody got a new car or washing machine it was something to shout about'.

26 A: Adam says: 'Well, they've got more and more similar … if you see a new model, you hardly notice because they all look much the same.'

27 B: Kayleigh says: 'they haven't got their heads around exactly what it *can* do, and don't want to advertise the fact.' Adam agrees: 'no doubt there *is* something in that.'

28 K: Kayleigh says: 'The voice of the end user's being neglected'. Adam does not agree entirely with her: 'But the customer's opinion's not always that helpful, is it?'

Questions 1–28   =   1 mark
Total score   =   **28 marks**

Test 6

PAPER 1   Reading

Part 1
The Elephant Orchestra

1 A: Only verb with correct meaning that does not take a preposition.

2 B: Phrasal verb with correct meaning of 'to comprise'.

3 C: Noun with correct meaning of 'a different form of something'.

4 C: Only correct noun in context, meaning 'signal'.

5 D: Only adjective that collocates with 'sense of rhythm'.

6 A: Verb with correct meaning of 'to suppose'.

The Pencil

7 B: Correct verb meaning 'to belong to a certain group' in phrase 'fall into a category'.

8 A: Only noun that takes 'to'.

9 D: Noun with correct meaning of 'manner' in context.

10 D: Only linking phrase that indicates that a contrast follows.

11 C: Only noun that collocates with 'roll into'.

12 A: Verb with correct meaning of 'to uncover or show something that was hidden'.

New Adventure

13 D: Verb with correct meaning of 'to begin' that takes 'on'.

14 C: Correct noun in expression 'into the bargain', meaning 'in addition to everything else'.

15 C: Correct verb in phrase 'throw off course'; only verb possible in context.

16 A: Correct verb in phrase 'set/put things right'; 'put things right' is more usual.

17 D: Verb with correct meaning of 'to be the means of reaching a place, point or state'.

18 B: Correct noun in phrase 'for that matter', which indicates that the previous statement will be true in another situation.

Part 2
Extract from a novel

19 A: 'it does not offer you at one delightful glance all it has to give'.

20 C: Attitude can be inferred from phrases like: 'doubtless achieve the satisfaction that rewards honest industry', 'in a fine frenzy attack their canvas with a pallet knife charged with a wad of paint', and 'These for the most part are strong silent men who waste no words'.

On Art

21 A: 'I am profoundly impressed by the imaginative scope and able hands of the first artists'.

22 B: 'Even if its results are tangible and intentional, we tend to think of the artistic process as something arcane and mysterious.'

Pay More and You Can't See the Point!
23 D: 'in the traditional belief that nothing matches a brush made of pure sable'.
24 D: 'In *Connoisseur* you have a whole range of effects at your fingertips without swapping brush sizes.'

Evening Stroll
25 C: 'the level of the beach should not rise above the horizon. Here it appears to be higher'.
26 A: There is no indication at all of B, C and D; throughout, reference is to an individual work.

Part 3
Bombay's pedalling waiters
27 C: Link between end of first paragraph and 'But despite this growing ricketiness, Baba and his 1968 touring bicycle have together clocked up more than 150,000 miles'.
28 F: Link between 'the biggest food delivery relay system in the world' and the explanation in the following paragraph. These paragraphs together explain the system and what it involves.
29 A: Link between Baba's explanation of what his job entails in a previous paragraph and 'Baba adds, "We are the oldest meals-on-wheels service in India …"'.
30 H: Link between 'In those days' in preceding paragraph and 'Today'. Also, 'Both' in the following paragraph refers back to Baba and Kohindkar.
31 D: Link between 'demand for the service is growing' and 'To account for this, Baba points to the obvious advantages of the system.'
32 G: Link between the activity described in G and the description of the routes and rendezvous in following paragraph.
33 E: Link between the reference to Grant Road and 'On arrival here'.

Part 4
Turn up the light and you, too, can grow your mind
34 D: 'Until recently, this aversion to a phenomenology that could not be measured or shared was enough to focus most scientists on the smaller, but still awesome, problems of brain function'.
35 A: 'The problem has been that in our enthusiasm to be objective we have thrown the baby out with the bath water, and turned our backs on the very quality that perplexes the non-biologist'.
36 B: 'Perhaps the mistake has been to liken consciousness to some kind of monolithic property that cannot be deconstructed.'

37 D: Like the light, 'our consciousness varies in degree from one moment to the next', whereas the brain, like the dimmer switch, operates the light.
38 B: 'Imagine some kind of trigger … that acted like a stone thrown onto a smooth surface of water …' and 'in the middle of a bungee jump, where the inputs come fast and furious, … the next set of ripples'.
39 C: 'most marvellously of all, reflect individual experience'.
40 C: The phrase means 'seeming not to be related to real facts'.

Questions 1–18   = 1 mark
Questions 19–40   = 2 marks
Total score   = **62 marks**

PAPER 2   Writing

Part 1
Question 1
Style: Formal, structured essay with clear points addressing the issues raised. Good cohesion between main ideas, and specific examples where appropriate. A clear position may be taken.
Content: Essay should discuss the questions posed at the end of the paragraph; i.e. the desirability of courses and the demands that can be reasonably placed on rescue teams. Candidates should then address the final question that relates more generally to dangerous sporting activities.

Model Answer

The term 'sport' encompasses a wide range of activities that offer varying degrees of challenge. For some, sport is something they watch rather than actively do, something that provides them with relaxation after a hard day's work. For others, it is an important means of keeping fit and healthy, often within a pleasant social environment. However, there is a growing sector of the population who seek more than comfort or exercise from sport. These people see sport as a physical test of strength and endurance.

Sports such as rock climbing and potholing offer the individual the opportunity to experience intense emotions, while developing the strength and expertise required to excel. Yet these sports cannot be undertaken without training, and for this reason, courses are essential. Without structured courses, there would be even more accidents. What the article highlights is the need for very close scrutiny of such courses in the form of regular inspections, the appointment of fully-certificated tutors and adherence to a national or international code of practice. If such standards are not maintained, the consequences may be fatal.

Members of rescue teams are specially trained to deal with situations in which people get into danger, but it is important to remember that the rescuers have their own lives and families to consider. They expect to deal with incidents that have resulted from things like unexpected environmental change. Like the ambulance service, they respond to alarm calls first and ask questions later. If they subsequently discover that an incident occurred through negligence or a lack of preparation, how do you think they might feel?

It is true that people are free to choose to put their own lives at risk. We certainly should not ban certain sports because they are dangerous. People have always been attracted by dangerous activities and will continue to be so. But those who take up dangerous sports have a responsibility to themselves and to others to ensure that they have the necessary skills and take adequate safety precautions. Otherwise they should not expect rescue teams to take unnecessary risks on their behalf.

Mark: Band Score 5

Part 2
Question 2
Style: Likely to be formal bearing in mind the status of the reader and the purpose of the proposal. Tone should be neutral.
Content: Proposal should identify and discuss a number of key areas to which the money should be allocated. (Brief reference to existing facilities may be included as support.) All suggestions should be justified.

Question 3
Style: Consistently formal or semiformal. Tone will reflect the standpoint taken.
Content: Article should clearly assert the position taken on the topic. (In doing this, reference may be made to the television programme.) Arguments should relate to the points made in the task that aim to justify the existence of this sector of society. Exemplification may include reference to certain individuals.

Question 4
Style: Consistently semi-formal or formal. Tone may be personal or a more objective approach may be taken. Some speculation may be appropriate.
Content: Letter should offer a number of well-reasoned arguments as to why people might prefer not to travel during their holidays. In suggesting a preferred type of holiday, a number of options may be evaluated.

PAPER 3   Use of English

Part 1
Growing or Going?
1 *any (determiner)*: meaning 'all, it doesn't matter which'.

2 *for (preposition)*: phrase 'bad news' (meaning 'not good') + 'for' + someone/something.
3 *from (preposition)*: used with 'emerge'.
4 *less (adverb)*: negative needed to make sense in context.
5 *was (auxiliary)*: completes passive structure.
6 *being (present participle)*: completes phrase 'the reason being', meaning 'the reason (for this) is'.
7 *of (preposition)*: completes phrase 'loss of something'.
8 *even (adverb)*: from phrase 'even so', meaning 'in spite of this fact'.
9 *that (pronoun)*: refers back to 'loss'.
10 *much (determiner)*: meaning 'a lot'.
11 *as (preposition)*: structure 'as … as' used for comparison.
12 *once/previously (adverb)*: referring to an earlier time.
13 *together (adverb)*: phrase 'draw together', meaning 'to gather'. (Note: phrasal verb 'draw up' has a different meaning.)
14 *the (article)*: completes phrase 'on the increase', meaning 'becoming more frequent'.
15 *deal (verb)*: phrasal verb 'deal with', meaning 'to take action about; to tackle'.

Part 2
Life on Mars
16 *exceed (noun to verb)*
17 *unaided (verb/noun to past participle by adding negative prefix)*
18 *engineer (noun to noun)*
19 *unperturbed (verb to adjective by adding negative prefix)*
20 *civilisations/civilizations (adjective to plural noun)*
21 *pioneering (verb/noun to adjective)*
22 *highlights (verb/noun to compound verb)*
23 *freedom (adjective to noun)*
24 *democracy (adjective to noun)*
25 *legislation (verb to noun)*

Part 3
26 *gain (verb)*: to obtain; phrase 'gain insight into' meaning 'learn a lot about'; 'have nothing to gain', meaning 'to be unable to profit from'.
27 *dry (adjective)*: 'amusing without appearing to be' in phrase 'dry (sense of) humour'; without phlegm; phrase 'on dry land', meaning 'on shore'.
28 *doubt (noun)*: uncertainty; lack of confidence or trust; phrase 'have no doubt' expresses confidence.
29 *wiped (verb)*: phrasal verb 'wipe out', meaning 'to destroy completely'; to rub with a cloth in order to remove dirt, etc.; to remove by rubbing.
30 *swing (noun)*: expression 'in full swing', meaning 'having reached a very active stage'; a change from one opinion to another; a seat for children, fixed by ropes or chains and on which one can swing backwards and forwards.
31 *draw (verb)*: to form by the use of reason or information; to involve someone; phrasal verb 'draw on', meaning 'to make use of'.

Part 4

32 *no point did the inventor actually claim*: negative adverbial phrase 'at no point' with inversion of subject and verb prompts auxiliary verb 'did'; used for emphasis.

33 *resignation took her colleagues by*: noun 'resignation' formed from verb 'resign', + expression 'take somebody by surprise'.

34 *to the stadium is restricted to those/people in*: noun phrase 'entrance to the stadium' is followed by passive construction + 'by'; 'possession' prompts phrase 'in possession of'.

35 *reason for going to Africa was*: 'reason for' + -ing verb form.

36 *in succession, the basketball championship has been won*: phrase 'in succession' (meaning 'following one after the other') + passive construction.

37 *was not alone in noticing*: phrase 'not alone in' + -ing verb form, meaning there were other witnesses.

38 *asked to refrain from using*: passive construction + 'refrain from' + -ing verb form.

39 *choice of holiday resort was influenced by a*: noun phrase + passive structure.

Part 5

40 'to cross trackless moorland'

41 Neither is compatible with working in an office.

42 Both would prefer open countryside to city streets.

43 the need to make other people respect/admire us

44 The summary should include the following points: Four-by-four vehicles are used by their urban owners:
- for getting to work/city commuting
- for local trips/like a normal car
- for weekend trips to the countryside
- as a status symbol/to impress others

Questions 1–25	=	1 mark
Questions 26–43	=	2 marks
Question 44	=	14 marks
Total score	**=**	**75 marks**

PAPER 4 Listening

Part 1

1 B: 'most of us mere mortals are bent on finding a mirror that somehow deceives us by creating a benevolent illusion.'

2 A: 'People are attracted to patterns in the frame, because these draw the eye away from the mirror glass at the centre, so they become less obsessed with flaws in their own image.'

3 C: 'some needle-sharp tactical racing around a challenging 50-mile course.'

4 A: 'They take it seriously enough, but it might be the only racing they do all year, because most events hike up the fees to keep out amateurs. But here …'.

5 B: 'Imagine … that traditional men's evening dress … didn't exist and that some hot new designer was trying to launch it as a brand new apparel category.'

6 C: 'failure to invest sufficient funds and a certain amount of sartorial elegance in the garment will result in your being mistaken for a waiter.' In other words, the wearer must take the outfit seriously.

7 A: References are made to a 'domestic situation' and 'you or your partner'.

8 C: She says: 'it's usually best to leave them to sort conflicts out for themselves'. He agrees: 'Yes, if you *can* stay out of the way, fine, then do.'

Part 2

9 *cattle*: 'It's actually a working ranch, where cattle are reared'.

10 *social*: She says she 'could find little about their social habits'.

11 *smell and sounds*: 'the rhino understands the world around it through smells and sounds'.

12 *intelligent*: 'When a female rhino has a calf, she keeps it with her for up to four years … the longer the period of mother-child interdependence, the more intelligent the animal … So I don't go along with the idea that they are stupid.'

13 *tail*: 'tail up or curled means it's alarmed'.

14 *(electric) fence*: 'The installation of an electric boundary fence … has helped local people a great deal. Before this, a single elephant could … wreck an entire crop on any of the adjacent smallholdings.'

15 *handicrafts/(handy) crafts*: 'providing a potential market for locally produced handicrafts'.

16 *donations*: She says the centre hopes to 'no longer have to depend on donations for the huge expenditure needed to keep our rhinos safe.'

17 *tourist lodge*: 'we have to raise the capital to build a small tourist lodge'.

Part 3

18 C: He says the audience should 'relax about the actors and feel terribly worried about the characters.'

19 D: 'Only actors already trained in sword fighting were invited, even if they'd not used those skills on stage.'

20 B: The presenter says: 'So, no room for inspired moments of improvisation?' Simon replies: 'Indeed. Every move is tightly choreographed.'

21 A: He says that the fighting has to 'convince', and be 'creative'. He also says that they have to 'avoid it getting tedious'.

22 B: 'it has to be truthful. It mustn't become slick. It has to look spontaneous every night.'

Part 4

23 C: Clarissa says: 'it always makes me think of a factory, it's like some great mechanised production line'. Andrew is 'less than wholly convinced by the industrial analogy.'

24 C: Clarissa says: 'It's a wonder really that people are willing to meekly go along with it all.' But Andrew finds the check-in procedures 'reassuring'.

25 A: Andrew says: 'Anyway, it's such a relief to get that bit over and done with. You know, when you put yourself in someone else's hands. It's liberating, isn't it? Clarissa replies with 'hardly', which shows that she does not agree.

26 A: Clarissa's references to 'people in uniform', a 'blind alley' and the 'close-circuit video trained on you' show that she is unnerved. Andrew disagrees: 'To my mind all that waiting is just boring. I'm afraid the sinister aspects of it all are lost on me.'

27 B: Andrew says: 'It's as if they want to protect you for as long as possible from the fact that you're about to go up in a little tube of metal.' Clarissa adds to his point: 'And there's no turning back', showing that she agrees.

28 C: Clarissa says: 'there's a sort of futuristic side to them, like something out of a science fiction novel.' She then adds that they reflect what 'the whole of society' will be like in the future. Andrew finds this idea 'far-fetched'.

Questions 1–28 = 1 mark
Total score = **28 marks**

Tapescripts

Test 1

Part 1

You will hear four different extracts, For questions 1–8, choose the answer (A, B or C) which fits best according to what you hear. There are two questions for each extract.

Extract One

Woman: The thing is, I can really relate to Rosie Pearson because she seems so normal. You know, you read her books and you think, 'What on earth am *I* worrying about?' She makes you believe that, at your blackest moments, something will turn up if you can just keep plugging away at it all and you end up thinking, 'What's the worst thing that can happen?' If you lose some of your hard-earned clients, for example, you can always get more. She makes you believe that you really can build a business. It won't all be a waste of money and effort if, like me, that's what you want. I guess it's the notion of the indomitable spirit overcoming adversity. It's a pretty common idea but she puts it all across in such a down-to-earth way.

Extract Two

I formed a production company and we didn't have any work, so when I was asked to make a puppet film I said 'yes'. Gradually we were able to make the puppets more like actors but the only thing we couldn't do was make them walk. It sounds quite ridiculous now but this was over 40 years ago. So I came up with the idea for a *Supercar* that they could whiz around in and seemingly move very fast. So then, once the show was completed, people would come up to me and say, 'Dave, I see you're into science fiction now', and I'd say. 'Am I?' Of course the car didn't last five minutes. If it appeared in one episode, then you knew damn well that it would get pulverised before the end credits and you'd need another model for next time, so you couldn't get too protective about it.

Extract Three

A: From what I've read about you, you seem to be saying that a love of nature is something ingrained within us. Might that be why the idea of extinction, for example, bothers people so much?

B: Yes. I've never said that the reason we've got to preserve the tiger or the seahorse or whatever, is because if we don't, there will be some eco-disaster. Neither have I said that we've got to do this because of some pharmaceutical advantage there may or may not be.

The fundamental issue is the moral issue, and I've always said that. Take, for example, the 'we must preserve the rainforest because the cure for serious illness might be in there somewhere' school of thought; I mean it's not really the point is it?

There might be a cure there, but the overwhelming reason for preserving it is our imaginative health. It would be a grave impoverishment of our world.

Extract Four

Man: So how was Steve's birthday party? Did it live up to your expectations?

Woman: More than that. I've got it all on video so you can have a look sometime.

Man: No squirming in your seat then?

Woman: Mm. I can't believe I said that. There I was imagining all these titters of nervous laughter as the poor wretches read out their 'poem for Steve', but it was nothing of the sort.

Man: I think his wife had a really good idea asking people to write a poem about him for his birthday.

Woman: I thought there'd be all sorts of excuses but everyone was really keen to get up and do it. It was like wedding speeches only much better. Each poem added to the next. They sort of pieced together his life and yet no two were the same.

Man: Mm. You realise that we can all do it, if we put our minds to it.

Woman: Yeah, it almost inspired me.

Part 2

You will hear a talk about Phyllis Pearsall, the creator of the London map-book known as the A–Z. For questions 9–17, complete the sentences with a word or short phrase.

The London A–Z is a little book containing page after page of street maps. By referring to the alphabetical list in the back, you can find your way to any address in the city. Many people living and working in London use it on a daily basis and would literally be lost without it.

But what few people realise is that the little book has only existed since 1936 and it was the work of one woman named Phyllis Pearsall. Phyllis was not a cartographer by profession; in fact she was a portrait artist and the project grew out of her frustration at never being able to find the houses of her clients. There were very few maps of London at that time and those there were, although they included roads, tended to focus on geographical features. They were not really intended for the general public and certainly didn't include street names. So Phyllis, seeing a gap in the market, started her mapping project. It was a huge undertaking. She got up at five every morning and she would walk and walk, systematically sketching streets as she saw them, and ended up walking three thousand miles along twenty-three thousand streets in a single year.

She became very obsessed with completing this task, maybe because her father had been a map-maker with his own company in London, but he'd gone bankrupt. That had affected her greatly, and when she started this project, he was unsupportive saying: 'You'll never do it. I'll give you a week.' So she really wanted to prove that she could run a business, that she could outdo him.

Now, the maps themselves are different from most other kinds of map in that they don't have their basis in mathematical calculations. When you look at an A–Z map, the emphasis is on the streets, so you'll see where you want to go. Now, if you want to buy a house, don't look at the A–Z, because it won't show you the actual space that surrounds the roads, because it distorts reality for the convenience of the pedestrian and driver. Now that is why, for the most part, Phyllis was disregarded by a lot of the academics of the map world. She had no qualifications in cartography at all, just lots of determination. As an artist she was very, very efficient, though, probably sketching about five roads an hour, and she was also extremely observant, with a great eye for colour, and that was the other striking thing about the A–Z maps when they first came in.

But right at the end of the project, she almost had a disaster. She was cataloguing all the streets she'd sketched on index cards, arranged in shoe boxes around her tiny bedsit, and she'd got as far as the Ts. One hot summer night, she left the T box on her desk, next to an open window. She was woken up by a storm. A big gust of wind had taken hold of the T box and blown it out of the window. She ran to the window, looked out, and she could see a whole fluttering of white index cards on the street and one white card on top of a red bus. She ran down, scooped all these cards up and ran in front of the bus waving, but it didn't stop. Later, she and her editor went through all the cards, but couldn't find which street was missing. Fortunately, when the book got to the printers, somebody there spotted it and said, 'Excuse me Mrs Pearsall, but is there any reason why you've left out Trafalgar Square?' and it was one of the most famous addresses in the whole city!

Initially, she found the books very difficult to sell. She tried to interest all the large department stores, but at first no-one saw the potential. Then finally, a large chain of newsagents agreed to stock them on a strictly 'sale or return' basis. And they took off immediately. Today, bookshops stock A–Z maps of most British cities and they have been imitated all over the world.

You will hear an interview with an author called Rachel White. For questions 18–22, choose the answer (A, B, C or D) which fits best according to what you hear.

Interviewer: Rachel White shot to fame in the 1990s with the publication of her first novel *Crying Wolf*. She has since become a well-established author and critic and I have her in the studio with me today to talk about her work and her inspiration as a writer. Welcome to the programme, Rachel.
Rachel: Thank you.
Interviewer: Rachel, if we can talk about inspiration first. You always say that you were inspired to write novels by other famous novelists but was there a particular moment when true inspiration occurred and writing, as such, fell into place for you?
Rachel: Oh yes. I was a fairly academic girl at school, which, well, it sort of went against the grain. I was in my fifth year and, um, I was really keen to shake off this reputation I was getting for being a model pupil, particularly in the literature classes, when one day the teacher started the lesson by reeling off all these compliments about an essay I'd done on the author Lawrence Durrell – one of my personal favourites. This resulted in titters all round and all the efforts I'd been making to keep a low profile were completely dashed. Then, to cap it all, he got me to read it aloud.
Interviewer: Never a happy experience. But deep down, was it an essay you were particularly proud of?
Rachel: No, and what's more, it went on for ten pages but most of it I'd pinched from a couple of books on literary criticism that I had at home. I'd tried reading Durrell but I hadn't succeeded, although I must say, it was unusual for someone my age to be reading criticism at all. So, I stood there spouting this stuff about a book and a writer I didn't know. And then suddenly I came to a quote and I was stunned – it was sheer poetry and I thought 'I must read this'.
Interviewer: And you couldn't help voicing this observation.
Rachel: Mm. I think I was loathed from that moment on but it didn't matter then. I'd fallen in love with literature.
Interviewer: You're also quoted as saying that the classics – and I'm thinking particularly of Jane Austen – were terribly important to you. You say you were 'struck by the timelessness of Austen'.
Rachel: Yeah. I think Jane Austen is one of those writers that people like to 'tick off' on their personal book list, so they flick through, say, *Pride and Prejudice* on a quiet day and then they make a quick retreat to their personal favourites. I felt fortunate in some way that, at 16, I could appreciate the insights that she'd had.
Interviewer: You're well known in literary circles for your essay 'Literature and the Young Mind'. Tell us more about that.

Rachel: I think literature has really made an impact when you look back and realise that aspects of your own philosophy of life have evolved in response to things that you read – obviously experience plays a large part, too, but that comes later and is often a reinforcement. I think a lot of writers share an appreciation of the power that literature had over them as young people and I just wanted to voice that. I owe a debt to Austen, for example, because I refrain from forming judgements about people on the basis of first impressions.

Interviewer: So once you were bitten by the literature bug if you like, how long did it take? Did you start writing at an early age or did that come later?

Rachel: No, after the Durrell essay there was no turning back. Of course, it was all self-conscious, self-indulgent stuff about family and boyfriends and a little striving for a better self, but not much. All par for the course, I think.

Interviewer: Something you have to get out of your system.

Rachel: That's what they say. Anyway, I think I've done that now and I can turn my mind to some of the more deeply held ideas that I have and bring those to the surface.

Interviewer: Would you like to see your own books described as inspirational?

Rachel: I don't think any writer sets out to stir other writers into action. It's much more a question of art, of creating something that works, that has resonance and that provides fulfilment for the writer and reader. Anything more than that is a bonus.

Interviewer: Thank you very much, Rachel White.

Part 4

You will hear two people, Alex and Mandy, talking about the experience of having an identical twin brother or sister. For questions 23–28, decide whether the opinions are expressed by only one of the speakers, or whether the speakers agree. Write for M for Mandy, A for Alex or B for Both, when they agree.

Presenter: Today we're continuing our series on family relationships by looking at identical twins, and the issues that arise from being born *with* a sibling and growing up to look *very* like them. In the studio, I have Alex Dunn, whose twin brother now lives in Canada and Mandy Bolton, who has a twin sister in the Royal Air Force. Both sets of twins were born in the sixties and all share a keen interest in sport. Welcome to the programme.

Alex and Mandy: Hello.

Interviewer: Now, identical twins have received a lot of media coverage recently; we've seen a couple of documentaries on the popular television channels, amongst other things. What do you think about this surge of interest?

Mandy: I guess there's been quite a bit of research going on, and people are beginning to come up with the results of their investigations into, well, particularly the area of health, and the role that genes can play in carrying or fighting off certain diseases.

Alex: That's all really useful, but then there's all the other claims; things about identical twins getting married on the same day, even though they haven't seen each other for over 30 years …

Mandy: … and live on opposite sides of the world.

Alex: All the researchers have done is to go out and look for what they *want* to find.

Mandy: They say we marry 'identical' people! My sister's husband is nothing like mine. They're, well, chalk and cheese really.

Alex: It's pretty irksome, though, because all that hype just reinforces all the, sort of, weird perceptions that people have about identical twins and what they're like.

Mandy: You have to take it with a pinch of salt. The thing about being an identical twin is, well, it really *bothers* people and I've always found that quietly amusing.

Alex: It's a kind of fascination, isn't it?

Mandy: Mm. Because however much other people might resemble each other, you just don't get *identical* siblings or strangers.

Alex: And that's something, that … Well, when my brother and I were at school, we had to wear badges on our sweaters so that the teachers could tell us apart when we were sitting at our desks. And we used to swap them over.

Mandy: Yeah!

Alex: I miss doing that!

Mandy: I don't think we'd get away with it now.

Alex: Oh I don't know. A lot of identical twins grow dissimilar as they get older; you know, certain features change. When we're together, *we* still confuse people. With us it's, well, our voices are different now. My brother has a Canadian accent. But that's not a visible change.

Mandy: It's interesting. My sister thinks we're still the image of each other but I'd beg to differ – our personalities are quite different, too. We certainly never shared the same ambitions.

Alex: Did your parents recognise that?

Mandy: Thank goodness, they did. Our teachers, when they could tell us apart, well, I think they assumed that we wanted to be together all the time.

Alex: There's that assumption that you must be indistinguishable in every way.

Mandy: It's like they treat you as a single identity.

Alex: You're lucky your parents saw beyond that.

Mandy: Well, we needed to carve out our own little piece of the world so that we weren't always in each other's pockets.

Alex: Even though you still do a lot of things together. We were both very involved in sport at school. Well, we still are now. In fact, although my brother was the keener runner of the two, I think I do more running now, which ruffles his feathers a bit.

Mandy: I'm still trying to outdo my sister at something. I tend to have a burst of enthusiasm for one sport and that lasts about five years, and then she gets better than I am at it so I move on to something else, and try to assert myself at that.

Alex: Yeah, it's a constant battle for one-upmanship. Goes with the territory, I think.

Mandy: I guess it's got something to do with …

Test 2

You will hear four different extracts. For questions 1–8, choose the answer (A, B or C) which fits best according to what you hear. There are two questions for each extract.

Extract One

Peter: Look at this, May. They've found a really ancient pair of Levi jeans.
May: What! Still in one piece?
Peter: Yeah. They dug them up in the States – in Nevada.
May: Let's have a look, Peter.
Peter: Apparently they were manufactured between 1880 and 1885. They think they're the oldest in the world.
May: I had no idea. I mean you put them on without a second thought, don't you?
Peter: I know what you mean. In fact, I thought they were just 'invented' in the 50s or sometime around then, you know, when rock music became famous.
May: Why Nevada I wonder?
Peter: Well, it's famous for precious metals, mining, I guess. Look it says, 'They do have some holes and a rip and they're faded.'
May: You've got a pair that look a lot worse than that.
Peter: Well, thanks a lot. I bought mine like that. There's a big difference, you know.
May: Only joking!

Extract Two

Love it or loathe it, the monkey-puzzle tree has an undeniable if outlandish presence. Native to Chile in South America, the tree grows to between 17 and 28 metres in height, although it has been known to reach up to 50 metres in volcanic regions. The tree has a bark, rather like elephant hide – that's strange enough – but its true distinctiveness is in its branches, which are entirely surrounded by tightly-knit, dark green leaves, rather leathery in texture. As a result, the tree is not only an enigma to primates, but most non-flying creatures find it insurmountable because the rigid pointed leaves, spirally arranged on stiff branches, form a tangled prickly network that defeats climbing animals. So the monkey-puzzle tends to *look* purely decorative, but on the slopes of the Andes it has too many uses for its own good. It produces valuable wood, its seeds are eaten, roasted, ground for flour and used as animal feed. The once thriving tree population is now beginning to …

Extract Three

I always seem to be drawn back to the river – it's my muse. I feel safe by the river. It represents freedom to me and provides an escape. It's a huge, living, breathing thing whose movement – it's tidal here, of course – and very being is governed by the elements. In a huge city, it is the one thing that is free from human control.

My interpretation of the environment fluctuates like the places themselves; moving between works of dramatised realism – where alongside the actual, there is always the anticipation of the possible – and works which reduce the details to bands of oscillating colour, where I am trying to engage with something more elemental. I'm interested in the levels of visual activity that exist in nature and I like to hint at undercurrents; the things that hover beneath the surface of what you're looking at and, eventually, alter it quite radically, like the tide coming in or dusk falling.

Extract Four

Because my mum's a manager and my dad's a famous musician, I guess I could have rebelled and become an architect, but I think the music industry was in my blood. Despite that, I know I've got a lot to prove. I mean Dad came from literally nothing, worked really hard and created a whole amazing genre of music. So I want him to feel we're not riding on his coat-tails, you know. I sometimes even feel guilty when we get a place on a tour, because a lot of my friends are in bands that have to slog it out in small clubs whereas I was, sort of, born into this world and that does kind of crush my credibility. But I'm not going to sign a disinheritance form! Dad always looks awkward at our shows, but I get nervous too, because I want him to know we're not a bunch of slackers. All the band like him and get on with him, so I guess him being there makes us … brings out the best in us. And it's cool because when he's around the other bands are a lot nicer to us.

You will hear a radio report about coral, a type of a marine creature. For questions 9–17, complete the sentences with a word or short phrase.

Good evening. Tonight the subject of my talk is coral. Now, when we think of coral, we generally imagine tropical islands, especially the type that are ringed by coral reefs, those hard stony barriers lying just offshore which are built up of deposits left by these amazing marine creatures. But coral in various forms is actually to be found all over the world and the waters of the British Isles are home to at least twelve different species.

Now, these species of coral may not be as large as their tropical counterparts, but their colour is equally splendid and they are, unfortunately, just as fragile. Up until fairly recently, coral was collected in order to make souvenirs for the tourist trade, a practice which was threatening the existence of some of the rarer varieties. But in Britain at least, coral has now been afforded protection and recent changes in legislation have put a stop to the trade in artefacts made from the material.

So what are corals and what types do we have in Britain? Well, corals actually belong to a group of animals called Cnidaria and because we often think of coral as being spiky or barbed, I was rather taken aback to discover that the jellyfish is another member of this same family. In fact, the group contains many different kinds of marine creatures which are linked by one common physical characteristic, and that is that they all have a mouth surrounded by tentacles. As well as this, all corals possess a powerful battery of stinging cells, and their name comes from the tiny poisonous threads or 'cnidae' that are fired from these cells for defence during feeding.

Like their tropical cousins, British corals can be split into three groups. There are hard corals, soft corals and what are called sea fans. What's the basic difference? Well, hard corals, as their name suggests, have a stony skeleton which is made almost completely of calcium carbonate. One type of hard coral, known as the cup coral, lives alone rather than in a colony like many other types. The most common of these solitary corals in Britain is called the Devonshire cup which comes in a variety of quite exquisite, jewel-like colours. Less common is the scarlet-and-gold cup and the least common of all is the sunset coral, which, like its name suggests, is a striking colour but found only in the extreme south-west of the country.

Then we have the soft corals. The largest of these can grow up to 25 centimetres long and are well known all around the British Isles for making underwater cliffs look white and fluffy. They look and feel much like a mass of jelly, although this is, in fact, supported by tiny hard threads. They have eight tentacles that grow from the body and these collect particles of food. On southwest coasts, a slightly smaller soft coral called 'red fingers' is more common. This one prefers vertical rock faces and more sheltered conditions than its larger relative.

And finally, we have the sea fans. They are formed from a substance called gorgonin which gives them their more scientific title of gorgonians and there are two species growing in British waters. These corals grow in a branching form rather like tiny trees. There is the northern sea fan, which grows to 20 centimetres tall and the larger pink sea fan found in the south-west coasts of England, which can grow up to 40 centimetres tall. Both types favour areas of strong currents where they can gather food from the passing water. To survive in such areas, they are fairly flexible but, like any coral, they are still easily damaged by clumsy divers or badly-placed fishing gear. So they are still vulnerable to human activity even though the immediate risk from souvenir hunters has been dealt with.

So next time …

Part 3

You will hear an interview with a man who for many years worked as a television newsreader. For questions 18–22, choose the answer (A, B, C or D) which fits best according to what you hear.

Interviewer: Society today places an ever-greater dependence on radio and television, as the media through which they keep up to date with national and international events. In Britain we have a host of newsreaders who assist us in achieving this and John White, who is sitting beside me today, was one such newsreader until his retirement three weeks ago. John, how long were you actually on our screens for?

John: Well I did attempt to retire five years ago, and CBT, the channel I worked for, they lined up Jeremy Harper, if you remember, to take over from me – a fresh young face. And he's doing quite well now, on a satellite channel. But at the time there was all that controversy over news times, and competition between channels and so they offered me an extension to my contract and I couldn't turn it down. Primarily I think because I needed a longer signing off period. It was rather sudden to imagine going from being 'in the living room' nightly to having no real persona at all. Jeremy was competent but unknown and you do become rather like a member of the family.

Interviewer: It's now a shock for audiences to suddenly find an imposter there. So overall it must have been something like forty years?

John: Mm. Yes.

Interviewer: What was it like in the early days?

John: Well, obviously, audiences were smaller and the technology was a lot simpler – that goes without saying. In fact. it was often touch-and-go as to whether some reports would actually get transmitted at all. And sometimes there were glitches when we were on air, and we had to cover them up – I still shudder when I think of them today – but overall the approach to the business of giving people information was, dare I say, more professional than it is nowadays. And that's rather a paradox when you consider all the help that we have in the twenty-first century.

Interviewer: That's a comment I've heard before and it intrigues me. This sort of 'dumming down' idea.

John: Well, it seems commercialism gets into every walk of life and it's certainly made its way into newsrooms and in many ways it's inevitable. Whereas viewers had two channels to choose from when I started, they now have many more – which causes some consternation in my family – and broadcasting companies have, in turn, to do something to hold their audiences and boost ratings. So they tend to go for a more sensational approach. Overall, it's fine as long as the facts aren't being distorted. Newsreading has evolved over time and viewers are often unaware of the slants that can be put on things in order to make them more watchable. But, again, these tend to be cosmetic, they don't impede the transfer of information.

Interviewer: Because the flip side of this coin is that we get to see many scenes from around the world, scenes that we just had to imagine once. But when you mention distortion, I wonder is it more a question of what's left unsaid? Do we get all the information, as viewers, that we need?

John: To have informed opinions, you mean? Hm. It's a bit of a double-edged sword really. If we didn't have any news, or if we had the kind of basic factual news that used to be the case, then you could argue that we don't know enough to have views on an uprising, say, that's going on in another country. Now we have the luxury of seeing that situation in our living rooms, plus the insight of reporters, and the question you're really asking is, do we lose sight of the facts? I think the answer is that we do what we have time to do in the allotted space on the programme. I have to agree that we don't always provide sufficient background information, present all sides. But then it's up to the public to find that out for themselves.

Interviewer: Yes. In reality, the unfortunate situation is that people don't have that extra time for research and so they have a lot of half-baked ideas that they can get quite animated about.

John: I don't know. I'd been thinking the opposite recently, that people side-step world affairs because they're so bogged down with their own issues. I've got quite used to it now. If there's a hot news topic, I don't expect to walk into a restaurant and hear people talking about it. Rather, it's where they went on holiday and what supermarket they shop in. Important things, and in one way amusing but that kind of conversation doesn't expand the mind.

Part 4

You will hear two people, Georgina and Jack, talking about a business which their friend Amelia runs. For questions 23–28, decide whether the opinions are expressed by only one of the speakers, or whether the speakers agree. Write G for Georgina, J for Jack or B for Both, where they agree.

Georgina: Have you heard, Jack? I went to Amelia's café this morning for coffee and it isn't doing very well. She's had six customers so far this week. She's thinking about closing it down.

Jack: Oh, that would be a pity, especially after all the work she's put into it.

Georgina: Well that's the point. She does extremely long hours and is getting really stressed out now, but it doesn't seem to be making the remotest bit of difference. She's constantly making a loss.

Jack: She's obviously not spending time on the things that matter. I think too many people think that businesses run themselves.

Georgina: That's a bit unfair. She says she's tried all sorts of approaches and come to the conclusion that it just isn't the right thing for that area of town. Maybe people are too preoccupied with other things these days to find time for cafés. And then when they do, well, which way do you turn?

Jack: Has she looked into the competition?

Georgina: I suspect she just feels outnumbered – wouldn't you?

Jack: But if there are cafes there are people – customers. She just needs to find herself a niche market, go for something that marks her out from the others.

Georgina: That's easier said than done. If you remember when that restaurant in Melbourne Street decided to put all its waiters in fancy dress.

Jack: We all went along to have a look.

Georgina: Yeah, once.

Jack: What about décor? That's important.

Georgina: I know, she's been working on that. You know, it sounds awful to say but I find her taste a bit, well … it's very 80s.

Jack: I find that quite reassuring.

Georgina: Mm. But she's trying to attract young people and it might be putting them off.

Jack: You could mention it to her. Has she talked to many people about things, you know, canvassed opinions? It's fine recognising that a certain style isn't as up-to-the-minute as it used to be, but it can be hard to know what to replace it with.

Georgina: Get ideas from her own customers, you mean?

Jack: It's a good way of mulling things over too.

Georgina: She could get one of those business consultants in to have a look at things.

Jack: They might be able to pinpoint the problems but it's a lot of money and time to spend finding out what you and I could tell her if we wanted to.

Georgina: I know they don't *use* the facilities, they don't have a feel for the atmosphere, but you can't deny that they are experts in their field. If we know how to turn her business around, how come we haven't done so already?

Jack: It may be, of course, that this is just a slack period. Most retailers will confirm that there's a lot of annual fluctuation. Perhaps it's just a case of seeing it through.

Georgina: She's inevitably going to get jittery about that, though. How long do you wait? How much money do you put in before you say: 'OK, time to give in'?

Jack: That should be something that was accounted for in her business plans. The bank would have insisted on it, I would have thought.

Georgina: Indeed, but can you imagine the sleepless nights? I wouldn't want to be in her shoes.

Jack: Some people thrive on it. I'm sure there's a basic personality difference that explains why *we*, for example, prefer to be secure in the knowledge that the salary will go in the bank every month.

Georgina: You mean you think Amelia's secretly enjoying all this?

Jack: Well, I wouldn't go so far as to say that, but you certainly can't take on a business without having the will to make it succeed.

Georgina: Oh I think that's different.

Jack: Do you? I don't.

Test 3

Part 1

You will hear four different extracts. For questions 1–8, choose the answer (A, B or C) which fits best according to what you hear. There are two questions for each extract.

Extract One

Presenter: And it's hello to our next caller. Hilary, what suggestions do you have to get more people through the museum doors again?

Hilary: Well, I think the museum's lost its way. It's resting too much on its laurels and, er, it needs to rediscover itself in a way, shake off its dowdiness. I don't think it's a question of cost – people will pay if it's worth going – but it needs to signal to us, to the general public, that it's got some kind of future.

Presenter: Do you think that means going out onto the street and canvassing opinion?

Hilary: I think it needs to be more proactive than that. I think the museum managers should be setting the tone for public taste.

Presenter: Be ahead of the times?

Hilary: Yes, not 'dumming down'. They realise something has to be done but aren't listening to their curators who *really* know and love the exhibits, know how to put an idea across and are in touch with the people.

Presenter: It's a question of artistic vision, isn't it?

Hilary: That's right.

Extract Two

Well, as you know my connection with the character, Elsha, goes deeper than the film, you know, because I'm a friend of Jenny, the author of the book it's based on. And the character in the book, Elsha – that's really me, I'm the inspiration behind her – though I'm not quite as wild and I don't get obsessive about things in quite the same way that the fictional version of myself does! That's not to say I'm at all disappointed with the way I come out in the book – quite the opposite. I mean, who wouldn't want to be immortalised in fiction? And then to get chosen to play her in the film as well! No, I mean it's just that, well, when I go out to parties now, everyone waits for me to behave this way or that way, and of course, the film character is so much wittier than me, and they stand there, all anticipation, but I don't always have a joke, and then they feel let down – and in a way, so do I.

Extract Three

Woman: He said it was here, but I can't find it. It's typical! I know they say that it's good to *personalise* your space, it leads to a greater sense of well-being and all that but …

Man: … a way of marking out your territory …

Woman: I know, but it's a bit much when you can't locate a single thing you need and you can't go rummaging around in someone else's things. I mean, surely it's a sign of disorganisation. I shall have to wait until he comes back on Monday now before I can go ahead with this agreement.

Man: It's all those squash and tennis trophies that get me – are they really necessary? I mean, they're a bit out of place here, aren't they?

Woman: It's like he's saying: 'I'm not just good at sports, I am successful too.'

Man: Quite contrived. And what about the other areas of his life?

Woman: What a joke!

Extract Four

Man: The life of a journalist is often seen as a glamorous one – well, I'm thinking now of a number of films I've seen.

Woman: Where it's all action and drama.

Man: Yes.

Woman: Mm, if only. Let me see … Now the last project I did involved standing in a blizzard while I waited for the opportunity to catch a few words with a very, how shall I say, 'off-hand personality', whose identity I won't divulge at the moment.

Man: Mm, it's not all exhilaration then.

Woman: Oh it has its moments – it isn't always like that. And I suppose journalists do their share of … well, we do intrude into other people's lives.

Man: Yes, that must be hard.

Woman: Well, I think people sometimes forget that we're just trying to bring the news to the world, you know, that without us they wouldn't be in the public eye at all, for better or worse, and the public themselves wouldn't know what's going on.

Part 2

You will hear someone giving a talk about careers in the fire service. For questions 9–17, complete the sentences with a word or short phrase.

Good evening. I'm Debbie Barnes and I've come to talk to you this evening about careers in the fire service. Now I heard a few gasps as I walked into the room in my uniform – a few people said, 'But, it's a woman!' a bit surprised like. So let me reassure you that yes, I am a professional fire fighter and, yes, I am a woman. And don't imagine that I'm only employed to do the light work. Like all my male colleagues, I *am* increasingly involved in areas like fire prevention, but just like them I go out on emergencies too – running the same risks, doing the same kind of tasks – when there's a fire or an accident.

And even after three years in the job, I still get a big adrenalin rush when that emergency call comes. Because although very often there *is* no fire – someone's dealt with it by the time you arrive or, likeliest of all, it's just a result of one of the many false alarms we get – you don't actually know that till you're there.

I well remember the first major fire that I ever attended. It was in a vast warehouse in a factory area in the outskirts of London. Fortunately, it was empty but it was well alight when we got there. It was a bit of a shock to the system seeing everybody running around, looking as if they knew what they were doing, and I felt like a bit of a spare part initially. But then I got sent up on a revolving platform, high above the action, spraying foam down into the flames. It was quite an experience, very hands on, you might say, for a first timer.

People ask me what it feels like. Well, when you're there, you do what you've got to do, you do your job. Maybe it sounds a bit callous, but you switch off and you concentrate on what you're doing. It's only afterwards you think about it. We usually sit around afterwards and have what's called a debriefing session. That's our way of getting things off our chests. It's, sort of, self-counselling really, for want of a better way of explaining it.

Now the fire service is very keen to recruit more women like me, and people often ask me how I cope. I do struggle sometimes with the heavier pieces of equipment, I'm not frightened to admit that. But there again, in an emergency, everyone has their uses. I would probably be one of the last people that they'd ask to kick doors in but I may be one of the first they approach if there was a confined space that somebody had to crawl through.

But the work's very demanding physically and I did do a lot of training before I joined: I went to the gym and swimming pool pretty much every day for about six months, because it's a job that you've got to be very, very fit for. And I went through exactly the same tests as all the lads on my recruits' course, and I passed them all or I wouldn't be here. And they're not just tests of pure strength either, they also test your aerobic fitness and your stamina. I know I'm not as strong as some of the men but I'm just as fit. So I know that I'm in this job because I'm good enough to be in it.

Until 1997 lots of women were excluded from the service because there was an unrealistic height limit imposed, which cut out 90% of female applicants. That's the only thing which has changed, though. There are no allowances made for women and indeed, the selection board doesn't know the sex of the people it chooses for the shortlist until the day of the final interview. It's all down to merit, to your performance in the tests.

So if you think you might be interested, remember, it's a demanding but worthwhile job which isn't that glamorous actually; it isn't like something off the TV. You don't see very nice things, but if you're prepared to put the work in, it's a job that anybody could do, whether you're male or female.

Thank you. Now if anyone has …

Part 3

You will hear an interview with a couple who work as photographers in Africa. For questions 18–22, choose the answer (A, B, C or D) which fits best according to what you hear.

Presenter: My guests today are Bob and Hilary Brannon, eminent photographers who've worked in Africa, recording disappearing traditions and lifestyles, for over twenty years.
Their latest collection of photographs, published this week, represents an important record of traditional African ceremonies. Bob, a lot of the ceremonies you've photographed take place annually, they're in very remote areas; how did you arrange always to be in the right place at the right time?
Bob: It's extremely challenging because although these events take place on a regular basis, whether it's annually, every ten years or whatever, they're not really scheduled in the western sense. They happen when the time is right, when the people feel ready, when various

factors come together. So often, it's a matter of keeping your ears to the ground. We've built up a network of contacts over the years and messages generally manage to reach us one way or another.

Occasionally, as with the Meda festival, held once every twelve years, we got there six weeks early just in case and, of course, we waited very patiently and filled the time very creatively. It was better than not making it in time!
Presenter: But Hilary, how do you approach a community as complete outsiders to get permission to photograph these ceremonies?
Hilary: It's true that it's odd for them having outsiders coming in and they often ask us where our families are, you know, who's looking after our children. To explain that we are doing a project, that this work is our life – very alien concepts usually – takes patience, and often we're never fully understood. But the approach that Bob and I take is to adopt the pace of Africa. So instead of entering a community and trying to take photographs straightaway, we invest time in making friendships with ordinary people and only gradually do we start working with them.
Presenter: But what about things like language, food and clothing?
Bob: In several cases, where we've spent months with people, we've actually tried to learn their language, which makes a huge difference in creating trust. But that's not always possible and we depend on translators. We often travel to remote areas with nothing but what can be carried on mules, and so we tend to have very simple clothing. Occasionally the local people say to us, you know, 'Please dress like us if you live with us and attend our ceremonies, we want you to look wonderful,' which is lovely. And of course, we carry rudimentary supplies because we don't expect to be fed by our hosts, although we never refuse hospitality where it's offered.
Presenter: Now, I know you've photographed a number of ceremonies to which outsiders wouldn't normally be admitted. How did you persuade people to let you in?
Hilary: Well, over twenty years, we've been visiting certain groups of people very regularly and eventually we felt able to ask if we could attend a closed ceremony. Some refused, others said, 'Yes, we'll honour that friendship and request.' Like everything in Africa, these things take patience and determination to achieve. We've become so very close to some groups that we're really almost invisible in the ceremonies themselves, and we do try to be unobtrusive, of course. Africa is changing, but I don't feel that's why we've been allowed to see certain things. And although we are great spokespeople for Africa in the outside world, I don't think that's how we're perceived by our friends there.
Presenter: Do you ever worry that, whilst you go into this, I know, with the very best of intentions, that you're actually making the people into curiosities, almost into museum exhibits?
Bob: We don't see our work in that light. We don't go in thinking: 'Now, what will they make of this back home?' or 'How does this tie in with what's been seen elsewhere?'

Our project is all about explaining, in a very sympathetic and comprehensive way, extremely important traditions that have real meaning for the people involved. And because we know that 20% of what's in our book no longer exists, we're also aware that, at the same time, we're making a record for future generations of young Africans. Although I should stress that we've no wish to influence their view of these events.

But the fact remains that the twenty-first century is encroaching with such speed and aggressiveness that many people feel these traditions may not exist in another fifty years, so it's important that they don't go unrecorded.

Presenter: Well, let's hope that's not the case. Bob and Hilary, thank you.

Part 4

You will hear two well-known singer-songwriters, Cathy and Paul, talking about their approach to writing songs. For questions 23–28, decide whether the opinions are expressed by only one of the speakers, or whether the speakers agree. Write C for Cathy, P for Paul, or B for Both, when they agree.

Interviewer: It's not often that I get the opportunity to have, not just one, but *two* celebrity musicians in the studio with me! But here we are: Cathy McTavern and Paul Martin, who really need no introduction from me. Now, you've each been on the popular music circuit for over fifteen years and I think we can easily say that your talents as songwriters have stood the test of time, when, of course, others haven't. I suppose what everyone really wants to know is: how you do it? How do you write one hit after another?

Cathy: Well, yes, of course, that's the public perception, but there are *just a few* other songs in between that don't make it on to an album. Well, there has to be.

Paul: You can say that again! Some get as far as a rehearsal session, but most bite the dust long before that. Yes, well, how do we do it? I may differ from Cathy here, 'cos I think she's a nicer person than I am, but in my view, if you're in the music industry, then you can only look at the profession in the same way as you might … I don't know … teaching a class of kids.

Cathy: The thing is that there are people who dabble, you know, write the odd song which takes forever and then they think, goodness, how does anyone do this for a living?

Paul: But of course, the only way you actually manage it is by churning it out.

Cathy: Well, I might still have written some great songs, but I certainly wouldn't be here today if I wasn't productive.

Paul: Although having said that, there has been the odd occasion in my career when I've just felt jaded and the creativity has just slackened off as a result.

Cathy: I can't believe you're saying that. I'd love to have that scale of problem. I can be prolific for six months, nine months, and then, bang, nothing; I'm into a creative void.

Paul: It always comes back, though.

Cathy: Miraculously, but there's always that slight nagging worry each time that I'll lose it completely.

Paul: But having come this far, you probably never would, of course.

Cathy: No.

Paul: When I was writing that blues number, 'Ain't my style', I was playing around with several different endings.

Cathy: But isn't it a case of, this is going to be one of those tough ones, but it'll be a winner in the end? Now that's tricky, if it doesn't just fall into place.

Paul: Yeah, I've got pages of half-written lyrics that could be chart toppers.

Cathy: So how long do you give it?

Paul: A couple of hours. After that I can't see the point.

Cathy: I know what you mean, and when you've got an album to do by *yesterday*, then you have to go for it. But, well, 'Love like this' and 'Soul mate' wouldn't exist if I'd stuck by that principle.

Paul: But there's a difference, isn't there, between the two songs you've just mentioned and things like 'Hug me', which has such a straightforward melody. I mean how long did that take you?

Cathy: About twenty minutes! And it was in the charts for seventeen weeks!

Paul: It's just like 'Catch me falling', which I wrote sitting in the back of a taxi to kill time – and nearly left there!

Cathy: I'd always wanted to ask you where you got the idea for that song.

Paul: That's an interesting question. And I've talked to quite a few people about this, 'cos I used to think that you had to have some kind of stimulus …

Cathy: …like a dream or something. Or a shattered heart!

Paul: And it came as a complete surprise really that I could just pick up a guitar and do it.

Cathy: What, they just roll off the tongue?

Paul: Well, don't yours?

Cathy: I'll have to try that. There might be a whole new world of songs out there waiting to be written.

Paul: Well, that's the thing about song writing. No matter how many songs people come up with, there's always another one.

Test 4

Part 1

You will hear four different extracts. For questions 1–8, choose the answer (A, B or C) which fits best according to what you hear. There are two questions for each extract.

Extract One

Achieving moderate renown is hardly the stuff rock and roll dreams are made of, so it wasn't surprising when the American band *Fluxx* came stuttering to an end just over a year ago. They were one of those groups to which the prefix 'influential' was usually attached rather than 'successful', although they'd released five fine albums in seven years, gaining an enthusiastic niche audience in the process. They started out as standard bearers of underground rock in the USA, their songs a sly blend of fuzzy guitar experimentalism, elliptical rhythms, esoteric lyrics and melodies that grew progressively sweeter as the band evolved.

Their farewell concert took place in a suitably middling-sized venue at the end of last year. A pair of handcuffs dangled from the microphone stand – symbol, claimed singer MM, of what it was like to be in a band. He was the principal engineer behind the group's shut-down and now he resurfaces with his first solo album. Our reporter Gayle Tilney caught up with him in New York.

Extract Two

Man: The biggest problems come from unsupported software. There are so many different types of software application, and kinds of PC set up for them to work with.
Woman: Yeah, that's right. Then add inexperienced users to the mix and you've got a sure-fire recipe for trouble. You know, dad installs a new game for little Jimmy, but it goes wrong and Jimmy gets upset; then Dad's straight on to us in a ripe old state blaming us for supposedly spoiling his son's birthday – we get it all the time.
Man: Once or twice, when things have really got awkward, I get rid of them by telling them to look something up in the manual and then get back to me. With any luck, if we're busy, they'll get put through to someone else when they do!
Woman: Yeah. Probably me!

Extract Three

Presenter: A British manual on running a sweet shop, published as long ago as 1939 says, and I quote: 'There are few better shoppers than children, who are always on the lookout for something new, and want good value for money.' To today's reader, there is something both quaint and sinister about this advice: in the great respect that it seems to accord young shoppers, anxious to make the most of their pocket money, and in that untroubled assumption that children's enthusiasm for the 'new' is a mark of their sophistication rather than their vulnerability. For me, this really says a lot about just how far consumer culture has come, a topic we'll be investigating with my guest today, Amanda Burley, who came across that quote as she was scouring the archives for material for her new book on marketing history. Amanda, welcome.
Amanda: Hello.
Presenter: Now, one of the things ...

Extract Four

This is my favourite because it reminds me of my brilliant tutor. It was done in the last session before Christmas. The model was lit from below with candles reflected in bowls of water. The studio was in total darkness so I couldn't see what I was doing as I drew. I worked quickly, afraid that the candle would burn down before I'd finished. When the lights were turned on, the result took my breath away.

It was soon after that, though, that I found myself outgrowing formal teaching. I was starting to question what I was being taught – a sure sign that it was time to move on. I was beginning to have confidence in my own ideas, so I started to have a model at home. I mean, this is really tough; they're so expensive and the pressure is on to make the most of them, but one of the things I've learnt is that when I am brave, I get the best results. So I persevere.

Part 2

You will hear a radio report about a wildlife holiday in the Yellowstone National Park in the USA. For questions 9–17, complete the sentences with a word or short phrase.

Announcer: And our next report is from Michela Jenson, who's been wolf watching in the Yellowstone National Park in the USA.
Michela: It all started some years ago on a trip to Canada. In a place called Dawson City, I met a man who had just had his first sighting of a wild wolf. His eyes positively lit up every time he spoke of it and I could see that he had been deeply moved by the experience. Ever since then, I had been looking forward to the day when I might share that feeling.
Wolves once roamed freely across North America, but after 200 years of being regarded as a pest and persecuted mercilessly, few remain, and they now feature on the official list of endangered species. I was told that the best chance of seeing one was to head for the Yellowstone National Park in the US state of Wyoming. The US National Parks Service reintroduced wolves into the Yellowstone some years ago in an attempt to recreate the balanced ecosystem lost to hunting over the centuries. Yellowstone has more than three million visitors a year, 140,000 of whom visit, as I did, in the winter, the best time for wolf spotting. And an estimated 20,000 of those are thought to have been lucky enough to get a sighting since the wolf reintroduction programme began.

There are no direct flights from London to Yellowstone, so I flew to Salt Lake City via Phoenix, Arizona, and then on into Wyoming by road. It was a seven-day organised wolf-watching trip offered by the company known as Wildlife Windows, and so my visit began with an evening lecture given by a park warden. He explained that the wolves are now one of the park's biggest winter attractions, for the animals are easier to see in the snow. For people travelling alone through the park there was, he explained, little chance of seeing a wolf although many people mistake the much commoner coyote for one. The coyote is smaller, with longer ears and a paler coat. Wolves, which vary in colour from grey to jet black, have longer legs.

Fortunately, my own personal guide was already booked as part of the package tour I had bought, and for the next six days he led me around the park. His name was Ken and he'd studied to be a biologist before retraining as a professional guide.

There is only one road open through the park in the winter, and it was fairly packed with wolf watchers, environmentalists and photographers, and so Ken's advice was invaluable. He explained that about 50 per cent of the wolves have been fitted with devices known as tracking collars, which send out a signal, so it was possible to know whereabouts to start our search. Nonetheless, the animals tended to keep away from the road unless they wanted to cross it, and large numbers of cars parked along one stretch of road was an indication that there'd been a sighting, but the wolves wouldn't be hanging around.

Ken told me that wolf packs tend to operate over fairly large territories, but he was fairly sure he knew where we'd spot some. He told me not to bother scouring the forested verges and nearby hillsides, but to keep my binoculars trained on the distant slopes, where I should keep my eyes peeled for grey rocks sticking up out of the snow. When I saw one move, we'd stop and take a closer look.

When it came, my one wolf sighting was over very quickly. My heart leapt into my mouth when I spotted one, just a few hundred metres away on the side of a hill. A young male, he had a flecked grey coat and surprisingly piercing yellow eyes, clearly visible through the excellent telescope Ken thrust into my hand. I might have been in the relative safety of the car, but I could still feel myself struggling to breathe with the excitement. My friend in Canada had been right; this was a unique experience, well worth waiting for.

Announcer: Michela Jenson there, reporting from the USA.

Part 3

You will hear an interview with a woman called Tansy Burton, who runs a company which makes beauty products. For questions 18–22, choose the answer (A, B, C or D) which fits best according to what you hear.

Presenter: My guest today, Tansy Burton, has an enviable nose. She and her husband have built up a multi-million pound fragrance and skin care business that now threatens to overtake some of the big names in the industry. Tansy, welcome. So is it a nose for fragrances or a nose for business that has got you where you are?

Tansy: Hi. Well, I love creating things, sure, but I also love the idea of making someone want to buy them. I guess I'm a merchant at heart, although that was hardly my background. I mean, my mother was a beautician, and I just followed in her footsteps. I used to watch her as a child, and she used to make her own face masks and things out of sandalwood and rosewater, you know, the standard stuff, and I was fascinated.

Presenter: So is that how it all began?

Tansy: Well, I started out as a beautician working from home, and when people came round for a facial or whatever, I'd give them a bottle of my home-made bath oil. One day, a customer asked for one hundred bottles to put by each place-setting at a dinner party as gifts. When eighty-six of those people came back for more,

I thought, 'Um … There could be a future in this.' And the production company followed on from that.

Presenter: So you knew how to set up a business like that?

Tansy: Well, I'm blessed with the gift of the gab, you know, I can talk people into things and that was my approach. I've never written a business plan in my life, and I've no intention of starting, but I'm good at coming up with the ideas and convincing people of the potential in them. Once I'd found the right backers, I would tend to move on to the promotional side and leave the bookkeeping to my husband, Colin. He trained as a builder, but he's really found his niche on the business side, so I'm happy to leave him to it.

Presenter: So what makes your products so appealing? Are you able to analyse it?

Tansy: Well, it's partly seeing the way the market's going and responding to that. If your idea of a fragrance is some wondrous liquid that smells divine, comes in a beautiful crystal glass bottle and costs a bomb, then you're seriously out of date. Of course, there are still some perfumes whose sole function is just to smell nice – and some of these sell on their reassuring retro imagery – but on the whole, they are being pushed to the back of the shelves by much more active fragrances.

Presenter: Active?

Tansy: Yes, fragrances these days are usually required to do a whole lot more than just smell nice; they need, so to speak, to sing and dance for their supper. They have to energise and tranquillise, deal with depression and jealousy; they need to uplift and to inspire. Fragrance is permeating more aspects of our lives than ever before and the full capacity of fragrance to enhance and improve our lives has yet to be fully exploited.

Presenter: So that's the way the business is going?

Tansy: If you like. It's all about pushing boundaries. People are already talking about air conditioning units that will fragrance rooms. People these days want versatile fragrances, which in practice means that instead of sticking to one grand perfume which they just use on their person, many people now have a wardrobe of perfumes for different purposes.

Presenter: So, the market's up for grabs is it?

Tansy: Well, the more of a relationship you can build between customer and product, the more multi-sensorial you can make it, the more it converts the customer. Meanwhile, every fashion house that relies on fragrances to bolster its profits is putting more and more energy into providing ways to add extra layers of fragrance to our lives.

Presenter: So you won't be resting on your laurels?

Tansy: Indeed not.

Presenter: Well, Tansy, thank you for joining us today.

Tansy: Thank you.

Part 4

You will hear two media critics, Mathew and Daniella, talking about a recently released film. For questions 23–28, decide whether the opinions are expressed by only one of the speakers, or whether the speakers agree. Write M for Matthew, D for Daniella or B for Both, when they agree.

Presenter: Anyone who has seen the film 'The Island', is likely to have something to say about it afterwards but not everyone, it seems, subscribes to the view that it merits the fanfare it has received. It is, nevertheless, a box office hit. Critics Mathew Walters and Daniella McCarthy discuss why they think this is so.

Mathew: It's the perennial search for paradise and the desire to escape the social constraints imposed by so-called civilised society – nothing unusual there. But the treatment is far less run-of-the-mill and I think we have to give the director some credit for this. It's basically about a group of young travellers who've found an unspoilt tropical island and have decided to eke out an alternative existence there.

Daniella: We've only to think of a couple of famous children's novels to recognise what's going on. They create their own moral code and attempt to live by it and of course, as we all know, that's not possible when human beings are involved!

Mathew: I do think Guy Johnson, the actor who plays the central character, works pretty hard for his reputed $20 million fee.

Daniella: Indeed. He's really very good as the smart backpacker who seeks the island out.

Mathew: I think part of the 'force' of the film is created by the technique the director uses of having the central character basically talk the audience through the plot as the story evolves.

Daniella: He plays the role of narrator, doesn't he?

Mathew: Yes, and I found it quite eerie at times and that sort of added atmosphere to the story, though I'm at a loss to pinpoint exactly why.

Daniella: I think it depends on how it strikes you when you first hear it. I was engrossed pretty quickly in the opening scene when he meets up with Ericson and finds out where the island is. But then Johnson's faceless running commentary struck me as rather odd. In the end, it interfered for me, became almost tedious.

Mathew: It's an unusual device.

Daniella: Also, it makes it 'his' story.

Mathew: And in a way, the film *is* about him.

Daniella: Mm. There's barely a scene that doesn't have him in it but I felt that the focus should really have been on the island community. It's the group, living in paradise, getting on and then not getting on that, well, that makes the story.

Mathew: Looking at the group or community – there are all the typical personalities for this genre of film. But, apart from Johnson, I found that they didn't really jump out of the screen in any way; no-one stood out.

Daniella: Well, interestingly, the leader of the group's female, but yes, then there are all the classic stereotypes, and with them come all the tensions, the jealousies and rivalries and then, of course, there's Johnson, the newcomer to the group who adds fuel to these.

Mathew: Because he brings the threat of encroachment from the outside world. The group senses that the little haven that they've established might soon be exposed and, thus, destroyed.

Daniella: It's a potentially explosive situation and I think that's what does it, makes it work, even though that situation never really detonates with the power that you'd hope for.

Mathew: I think the individual relationships are well sketched. It promises a great deal but, to be honest, it never quite delivers in the end.

Daniella: But I think we can live with that.

Mathew: I think I'd defy anyone who's seen the film to say that they weren't gripped by it. You can't help but sit there and contemplate the nature of things – human life and the world we live in.

Daniella: Although it's clearly the gap year student who's supposed to identify most with it – the characters are all hippie, soul-searching types – the script transcends that.

Mathew: It presents a powerful polemic on the shaky politics of paradise.

Daniella: And though you find yourself thinking 'not this idea again', as you say, Matthew, it does draw you in.

Presenter: And for anyone who hasn't seen it yet …

Test 5

Part 1

You will hear four different extracts. For questions 1–8, choose the answer (A, B or C) which fits best according to what you hear. There are two questions for each extract.

Extract One

This is a novel with a message by a writer with a mission. Barbara Kingsolver is passionate about conservation, especially in that part of the Appalachian Mountains where she was brought up, and where she has placed her three heroines. The book's full of lyrical elegies for extinct species, loving descriptions of creatures still extant and persuasive arguments for maintaining the balance of nature. This American pastoral is not a book that an urbanite like myself would normally choose, while anyone allergic to mawkish acknowledgements might get no further than the opening three pages of gushing authorial gratitude. Skip them, but do read this interesting novel. Kingsolver's exquisite style is the spoonful of sugar that makes the green medicine go down.

Extract Two

A journalist friend of mine is passionate about transport issues. He thinks more should be done to encourage cycling in London. He dislikes the popular image of cyclists as mad keen environmentalists and says there should be a publicity campaign to get the message across that there is no such thing as a typical cyclist.

Fair enough, you may say, but I'm afraid when it comes to the message, I beg to differ. One of my pet hates when driving around London are those people for whom the bicycle represents as much of a political statement as it does a practical means of transport.

No doubt they're not the majority, but these people often have scant regard for anyone else's rights and so tend to give cyclists a bad name.

They're to be seen ignoring red lights, for example, and cycling at night without lights and occasionally even kicking your car if they think you're too close to the kerb. As for hand signals, these they seem to regard as optional, unless obscene. And what really infuriates drivers is that these cyclists always appear to get away with it all.

Extract Three

If you're like me, you'll have at least one dilapidated pair of shoes in your wardrobe that you just can't bring yourself to throw away. Unlike some things, shoes seem to grow on us, become friendlier with the years, as we wear them in, so that discarding them is rather like a ceremony. Of course, there was a time when repair was a time-honoured custom. People respected the past of damaged things, restored them as though healing a child and looked on their handiwork with satisfaction. Once repaired, the object was made anew and was able to occupy the social position of the 'broken' one. So worn out shoes went to the anvil, holed socks went on the darning list and books and toys were stuck back together again. But now we live in a throw-away culture; although quality hand-made shoes are widely available, it's the cheap and shoddy ones that sell, and it's no longer economical to repair *them*, so we just trot off to the nearest shoe store for the latest …

Extract Four

Woman: What does 'handrailing' mean?
Man: Sorry?
Woman: Here in your report. It says: 'In an attempt to promote the handrailing strategy of …'
Man: Oh right, um … Well, it's what Bill said in the meeting.
Woman: Oh, I see. When people like Bill start wittering on in business meetings in this kind of impenetrable jargon, it's usually because they've got nothing particular to contribute but urgently need to sound important. What did Oscar Wilde say? 'He had nothing to say and said it at length.' Something like that.
Man: OK. Well, you can take it out if you don't like it. But, you know, if you're trying to convince investors to pour money into your next e-commerce venture or whatever, then all this impressive-sounding vocab can really help your cause.
Woman: Yes, and you know why? It's because whatever rubbish you spout, you can be sure that your words will meet with a lot of sage nodding because nobody in that sector would dare admit they weren't up to date with the latest buzzwords. You could make them up and nobody would ever know the difference.
Man: Do you think Bill made up 'handrailing'?
Woman: Hardly, though he'd go up in my estimation if he had!

Part 2

You will hear the beginning of a radio programme about the use of fingerprints in criminal investigations. For questions 9–17, complete the sentences with a word or short phrase.

Well, if you're a fan of crime novels or television detective series, you'll certainly be aware of the role played in criminal investigations by fingerprints, those seemingly invisible marks left by people on everything they touch.

Research into fingerprints began as long ago as the 1790s, but it was only in 1901 that police in London began to make use of them, the idea really taking off nationally after 1905 when they provided the crucial evidence in a notorious case known as the Deptford murders. A couple living above a shop had been murdered and some fingerprints were found on a cash box within the premises. Two suspects were arrested on the strength of descriptions given by witnesses who'd seen them making their escape. But because these suspects had been wearing masks, the evidence was inconclusive until their fingerprints were taken and the prints found in the shop were matched to those of one of the men. A conviction followed.

Today, roughly ten thousand fingerprint identifications are made every year in England and Wales, and over six million sets of prints are held on file. Although they still play a role in high profile cases such as murder and blackmail, it is in the solving of cases such as burglary and car crime that they are particularly effective.

There are, of course, still surfaces that are very difficult to get fingerprints from. But techniques are developing all the time and the police now have a powerful device based on ultra-violet light which allows them to find marks on, for instance, surfaces which have been highly polished and light switches, two places which it is in general very difficult to retrieve fingerprints from.

The process of collecting fingerprints from the scene of a crime has changed very little over the years. Police officers still dust with a brush, but they've progressed from the simple black powders of years ago to aluminium powders and gels. These react with the chemicals in sweat and reveal the print. Once the prints are taken, however, a very sophisticated system kicks into action.

If the quality's good enough, the prints are immediately scanned on to a database known as the National Automated Finger Identification System, or NAFIS for short. This powerful system will highlight possible matches for the fingerprint experts to sift through and see whether any of the marks collected at a scene-of-crime do actually match any of the prints on file.

So, despite the high-tech input, the actual matching is still done by real people, though they *are* sitting in front of computer screens. The job itself is rather like the children's game called 'spot the difference', you know, the one where you have two almost identical pictures and you have to find the few details which do not match. And this is because most people's fingerprints conform to one of three basic patterns: they are either arched, arranged in spirals or they have a series of loops. And although within these groups, all fingerprints have the same pattern and the same shape, there are subtle differences about them. And it's these little tiny characteristics that make each and every one of your fingers unique to you. So, every one of your fingers will be different, and every one of your fingers will be different from mine or anyone else's. Even identical twins have different fingerprints. You're born with specific fingerprints and they remain with you, unchanged, throughout your entire lifetime.

And it is this constancy which makes them such an effective means of identification. Because even if you damage your fingers, and in the past some criminals have gone to great and painful lengths in an attempt to obscure or change their fingerprints, in the vast majority of cases the prints will grow back in exactly the same position.

I went along to the headquarters of the …

Part 3

You will hear a interview with Harry Newland, a young film actor. For questions 18–22, choose the answer (A, B, C or D) which fits best according to what you hear.

Presenter: My next guest was the darling of Hollywood by the age of ten, playing child parts in many top films. By the time he was fifteen, he'd been nominated for an Oscar. Now nineteen, and at college, Harry Newland is taking time out from his career to study. I asked him when he'd first felt the urge to perform.

Harry: Although technically it wasn't acting, I remember when I was a kid of two or three, having a collection of plastic masks and I'd run around the backyard pretending to be different characters, you know, everything from Donald Duck to my own superheroes. And, of course, my father, he's an actor, and I *was* raised in Hollywood after all. But I think it was more than that with me. There's no getting round the fact that I was born with the bug, had the right instincts from the start, and that's what my Dad spotted and developed. One of the most important things he taught me was that acting is believing. That's at the heart of every performance I give.

Presenter: So when did it come, that first performance?

Harry: I guess I was about five. Like a lot of young actors, it began with television advertising, but I quickly moved up to playing, sort of, cute-as-a-button grandsons in various run-of-the-mill TV dramas, you know the sort of thing? It's easy to run them down, but I try to avoid that because, you know, that's how you cut your teeth in the business, learn the ropes. You can't just go in as a child movie star and hope to steal the show; that just doesn't happen without the right background. In the end, I got a role in a film that made it quite big at the box office, not thanks to me I should add, but I had a bit part and that's what got me noticed.

Presenter: Since when you've worked with some pretty big names. How did they take to you? Didn't they worry about being upstaged by a cute kid?

Harry: Well, if that worried them, they wouldn't be accepting these roles in the first place. No, I never had any trouble being accepted. Basically, if they respect your work and providing you're mature enough to cope with the situation, then actors treat one another like equals and that's mostly what I've experienced. I never felt patronised in any way and I wouldn't have accepted colleagues coming on as sort of authority figures, and I guess they recognised that. It was like having friends on the set most of the time.

Presenter: But you worked on some pretty big projects.

Harry: It never strikes me to be intimidated by making big movies. I try to do my best with every performance. I concentrate on the job and not the size of the production. It's up to the director to worry about the big picture, and mostly they're great. It must be tough keeping so many things in your head at once, knowing every single detail. I rely on them to indicate what the character should be feeling, to suggest different ways I could play it. Not all actors like that, but I listened and did my best to follow and tried not to worry about what other people on the set were up to.

Presenter: And the result of all this was a nomination for Best Supporting Actor. I mean, how did you cope with all that? It must have gone to your head a bit.

Harry: That was a really big surprise. I never thought it would happen to me, let alone so early. But, getting back to your question, I was lucky in that my parents really had their heads screwed on. All the attention you get in that situation is certainly flattering, but if you don't keep your feet firmly on the ground, you can lose yourself to it really easily. Seeing that, my parents hit a pretty subtle balance, actually. I had their support, practical and emotional, but I wasn't pushed beyond what I was capable of, and they managed to keep me pretty much on track as far as friends, schoolwork and all that was concerned.

Presenter: As for the future?

Harry: I'm keeping an open mind until I've finished college, but I haven't given up acting altogether. Although I guess your movies should get better as you get older, shouldn't they? So I might find that a bit of a challenge!

Part 4

You will hear two friends, Adam and Kayleigh, talking about people's attitudes to technological change in consumer goods. For questions 23–28, decide whether the opinions are expressed by only one of the speakers, or whether the speakers agree. Write A for Adam, K for Kayleigh or B for Both, when they agree.

Adam: You hardly need a brain these days, there are so many gadgets to do things for you. Did you hear about the online doctor who can give you a medical once over without you ever having to set foot in a surgery?

Kayleigh: Well Adam, that's not a gadget exactly.

Adam: Oh it is, Kayleigh, because you need the right type of mobile phone apparently to access it, but not many people have them yet, unfortunately.

Kayleigh: Well you say 'yet' but actually some of these new gadgets and gizmos are just not taking off in the way that people expected them to. And let's face it, with so much new technology coming through these days, is it any wonder we're suffering from innovation fatigue?

Adam: Well, most of us take it in our stride, actually, especially the young. There'll always be some who don't, though.

Kayleigh: Well, the majority don't, if you ask me. Take mobile phones. We've had analogue, digital, WAP, Internet-linked, all hot on the heels of one another and it's bewildering for the average person.

Adam: Well, did you hear that the Government's offering free digital TV, Internet and e-mail access to whole neighbourhoods in some parts of the country in an effort to get more people switched on?

Kayleigh: Yeah, though they're not doing it round here, I notice, which is typical. But I'm not convinced it's the answer anyway. If people don't want or need things, they won't use them, even if they're given away.

Adam: Oh, I wouldn't be so sure about that. I guess they're targeting people who otherwise couldn't afford it, rather than those who're not interested.

Kayleigh: Maybe. But it seems we *are* less interested in some of these latest gadgets and so we pay them less attention. I remember a time when new technology in the home really meant something to people.

Adam: Like if somebody got a new car or washing machine it was something to shout about, to make the neighbours envious?

Kayleigh: It was an event. Okay, now, the washing machine's commonplace. But it transformed people's lives at the time. Now they're all much of a muchness; no longer at the cutting edge. Cars, on the other hand, I do still see as status symbols, actually.

Adam: Well, they've got more and more similar and, to be honest, if you see a new model, you hardly notice because they all look much the same. And if somebody gets a new computer now, it may be that they don't even mention it to their friends, even if it does all sorts of wonderful new things, because it's no big deal any more.

Kayleigh: More likely they haven't got their heads around exactly what it *can* do, and don't want to advertise the fact. I mean, that's the real problem, I'm afraid.

Adam: Well Kayleigh, no doubt there *is* something in that. It's down to all the pressure on manufacturers to get their latest developments out before they become obsolete, or before the competition beats them to it.

Kayleigh: But it's not only that. On my mobile, for example, you can preview a movie to help you decide if you want to go and see it. But do I want to? I've managed to live without this thing until now. I think, frankly, they're trying to persuade us that they've found answers to questions we haven't asked. The voice of the end user's being neglected.

Adam: But the customer's opinion's not always that helpful, is it? I mean, before they introduced their walkman, Sony gave it to market researchers, only to be told that people didn't like the idea of pocket-sized tape players with headphones. Sony ignored all this, recognising that the public didn't yet know what it wanted.

Kayleigh: Well it was a brilliant idea. But today everything's technology-led. All I'm saying is that it should be more market-led. Because in the end, Adam, people won't buy what they don't like.

Adam: Exactly.

Test 6

You will hear four different extracts. For questions 1–8, choose the answer (A, B or C) which fits best according to what you hear. There are two questions for each extract.

Extract One

Presenter: It is no wonder that the appeal of mirrors is so enduring. While scientists reckon to achieve near perfect images of other worlds through the most accurate reflections possible, most of us mere mortals are bent on finding a mirror that somehow deceives us by creating a benevolent illusion. It is this 'somehow' that fascinates makers and collectors of decorative mirrors. I went to visit Wendy Reid, an artist who has evolved delightful mirror-framing techniques.

Wendy: Oh, I have a house full of mirrors. My favourite is this slightly damaged, antique Venetian piece. I call it my 'princess mirror' because it flatters everyone who looks in it. In my own work, I produce frames with rather intricate mosaic-like squares in greens, pinks and blues. People are attracted to patterns in the frame, because these draw the eye away from the mirror glass at the centre, so they become less obsessed with flaws in their own image. They also tend, subconsciously I guess, to choose frames in the colours they think suit them, so they see a more harmonious image when they look at themselves.

Extract Two

Presenter: If sailing is a minority sport, somebody should tell that to the 12,000 sailors racing round the Isle of Wight off the south coast of England this weekend. The Round the Island race has become one of the biggest and best-supported events in international yacht racing with an eclectic carnival feel, despite some needle-sharp tactical racing around a challenging 50-mile course. I asked top sailor, Bob Hollison what the appeal of the race was.

Bob: It reminds me of a big city marathon actually, because there are many parallels with that kind of event. Most of the yachts taking part are cruising boats, just here for a wonderful day out. They take it seriously enough, but it might be the only racing they do all year, because most events hike up the fees to keep out amateurs. But here leisure sailors are encouraged to take part alongside Olympic and America Cup celebrities. And although the glamour belongs to the big, powerful yachts, it's often the little chaps who walk off with the trophies, thanks to the handicap system, and that's a great incentive too.

Extract Three

Imagine, just for a moment, that traditional men's evening dress, 'black tie' or 'penguin suit' as it's commonly known, didn't exist and that some hot new designer was trying to launch it as a brand new apparel category. To begin with, he'd have to persuade male customers to pay a huge amount of money, probably more than they'd spend on any other item in their wardrobe, for an outfit that will only be worn once or twice a year, to events where every other man will be dressed almost identically.

Only minor adjustments to the design would be available and accessories, which also cost a bomb, will be fiddly and arcane; the black tie itself, almost preposterously flamboyant. The designer could then hype up the new style by warning that any major tweaking or fooling around with the stipulated design will be greeted with derision by one's peers, whilst failure to invest sufficient funds and a certain amount of sartorial elegance in the garment will result in your being mistaken for a waiter. Or even worse, a snooker player!

Extract Four

Woman: Arguing over possessions and territory are among the most common causes of sibling rivalry, but it's also about who they think is getting more attention.
Man: That's right. In a domestic situation, you can actually reduce the number of conflicts by treating each child as an individual and by being scrupulously fair in your dealings with them. Older children, in particular, may get resentful if they feel you are 'softer' on younger ones in some way.
Woman: I'd go along with that up to a point, but I'd add that it's usually best to leave them to sort conflicts out for themselves, because once you enter the fray yourself, it'll certainly become a battle for gaining favour. Then problems build up with whichever one hasn't managed to convince you or your partner that they're the wronged party.
Man: Yes, if you *can* stay out of the way, fine, then do. But remember that it'll be in their own way when they do sort things out, and that may be nothing like what you would've wanted. So, in that case, you've got to keep your views to yourself, or you'll be back to square one.

Part 2

You will hear part of a talk by a woman who runs a wildlife reserve in Africa, which is devoted to saving the rhinoceros. For questions 9–17, complete the sentences with a word or short phrase.

Good evening. I've come to talk to you this evening about the wildlife sanctuary that I founded and now help run in Africa, originally for the benefit of one highly endangered animal that lives there – the rhinoceros, or rhino, as we call it. The area now covered by the sanctuary extends over thousands of square kilometres of plains and thorn bush with deep valleys. It's actually a working ranch, where cattle are reared, but which also supports an astonishing range of wild creatures, from small birds and insects to elephants and rhinos.

Now I'm a farmer, not a trained naturalist, and when I first became interested in doing something to protect these wonderful creatures, I read up all about rhino eating habits and digestive processes, but could find little about their social habits, apart from the commonly held view that they were short-sighted, bad-tempered and stupid. Compared to the elephant, which can perform amusing tricks with its trunk and which seems to have a recognisable character, the rhino appears rather dull. Because we live largely through our eyes, and have a huge vocabulary to deal with what we can see, whilst the rhino understands the world around it through smells and sounds, it's harder for us to relate to this creature than it is to those which interpret the world as we do.

And unlike the elephant, the rhino is also rather solitary, favouring small groups rather than large herds. When a female rhino has a calf, she keeps it with her for up to four years and, as the experts tell us, the longer the period of mother-child interdependence, the more intelligent the animal and the more it depends on learned rather than instinctive behaviour. So I don't go along with the idea that they are stupid. Indeed, through my own observations, I've seen that the rhino is also able to use its lips and horn to a surprising extent. I have seen these used to open gates, even car doors, when food was on the other side.

The rhino is more closely related to the horse than to any other domestic animal, and much of the body language it uses is similar. Ears sharply pricked mean great interest, tail up or curled means it's alarmed; whereas if the nose is wrinkled, the lips drawn back, then a fight or charge is imminent.

The focus of my work, however, is the protection of the animal's natural environment, rather than the study of its behaviour. And, in order to ensure its long-term survival, it's essential that the sanctuary should benefit those who live on its periphery, not just the animals. The installation of an electric boundary fence two metres high has helped local people a great deal. Before this, a single elephant could, in just one night, wreck an entire crop on any of the adjacent smallholdings. Now, this danger has been removed – a great step forward in public goodwill towards our project.

Encouraging people to visit the area – and the rhinos *are* a great attraction – is also providing a potential market for locally produced handicrafts. And part of our project has always been helping to build primary schools and health care centres in communities on our boundary. Local children already come to see our wildlife, and their visits could be extended, if we could provide overnight facilities.
Children cannot appreciate the beauty of their heritage if they never see it.

Our aim is to become financially independent within five years and no longer have to depend on donations for the huge expenditure needed to keep our rhinos safe. We want to prove that domestic stock can share land with wildlife without suffering and that wildlife can benefit local people; that these lands can prosper if properly managed. To achieve this, we have to raise the capital to build a small tourist lodge. The sanctuary came about because of the development of a very important idea: that this generation is responsible for holding land in trust for future generations. We hope our guests will leave not only with good photos, but with compassion for these great creatures and with a determination to ensure that all endangered wildlife has a future.

Part 3

You will hear an interview with Simon Hemmings, who works as a fight director in the theatre. For questions 18–22, choose the answer (A, B, C or D) which fits best according to what you hear.

Presenter: For the forthcoming holiday season, one London theatre has decided to stage a version of the French classic 'The Three Musketeers'. Now anyone who's seen the film or read the book will know that fighting, or to be more precise, sword fighting, plays a pretty central part in the action. So perhaps it's not surprising that unusually high on the list of credits is the name of the fight director, Simon Hemmings, who joins me today in the studio. Simon, welcome.

Simon: Hi.

Presenter: So what exactly does the job of fight director involve?

Simon: Well, you need a range of qualifications including First Aid, of course. Without wanting to get too precious about it, every time you do a fight you deal with people's lives because we use real swords. They're not sharp, but they are real. Even if there are rubber tips on the end, you can still get hurt if there are accidents. The fighting has to look dangerous but be safe. If it looks tame, it's pointless. But it's also about inspiring confidence and suspending disbelief. What you want to do is to make the audience relax about the actors and feel terribly worried about the characters.

Presenter: So if you are going to have a fight that looks real, you've got to have skilled fighters?

Simon: Exactly. When they did the casting for 'The Three Musketeers', the theatre held fight auditions before it held acting auditions. Only actors already trained in sword fighting were invited, even if they'd not used those skills on stage. But those selected nonetheless spent much of the five-week rehearsal period working on their existing duelling skills. This was partly because of the nature of the set. Far from being safely confined behind a proscenium arch, the show is played in the round and on narrow catwalks that run across the auditorium. Fight scenes in this context were new to us all.

Presenter: Perilously close to the audience.

Simon: That's right. In a rehearsal room, you only have bits of tape on the floor, but these actors had to get used to an audience, because an audience makes the place seem very small and suddenly you have people sitting right alongside the stage. If you forget your lines on stage, you can make them up and nobody gets hurt. But if you forget your fight, the best thing to do is to get off as quickly as possible.

Presenter: So, no room for inspired moments of improvisation?

Simon: Indeed. Every move is tightly choreographed.

Every movement is notated, as in a dance, so there are two texts for the show – the written one and the fight one. There are lots of different types of notation, each move has a name. You read the text left to right, and down and across. So if, half way down, a third character comes in, the text gets a little wider, and so on. If you've got nine people on stage you've got a very wide fight text.

Presenter: So is safety the key issue?

Simon: Well it is important, but choreographing a fight is not only about avoiding accidents, it also has to convince, which is tricky in a circular auditorium because you can't hide anything, and it has to be creative. There's a lot of fighting in this play, so to avoid it getting tedious, you have to find as many variations on two men fighting as you can. Fortunately it's a comedy, which gives you more scope. At one point, one character even does a cartwheel on one hand, sword in the other, and comes up fighting. It's unrealistic, of course, but it gets a laugh, so we keep it in.

Presenter: Does it ever worry you, people laughing at violence?

Simon: Well, different shows call for different approaches. It's not glorifying violence, there's a lot of sword fighting, but there's no blood. It has to be believable. It really is the context in which the violence is set that determines whether we laugh at it or whether we're horrified by it. It depends on the play which of those is appropriate, but ultimately it has to be truthful. It mustn't become slick. It has to look spontaneous every night.

Presenter: Simon, thank you for joining me today, and best of luck with the show.

Simon: My pleasure.

Part 4

You will hear part of a discussion programme in which two people, Andrew and Clarissa, are talking about airports. For questions 23–28, decide whether the opinions are expressed by only one of the speakers, or whether the speakers agree. Write A for Andrew, C for Clarissa or B for Both, when they agree.

Andrew: They're curious places airports, aren't they Clarissa? Sort of on the cusp between coming and going. They're transient places because you're always moving forward, aren't you, in an airport.

Clarissa: Well, Andrew, it always makes me think of a factory, it's like some great mechanised production line, only what's being produced in the airport is quite simply flow of people as everyone gets expedited on their way.

Andrew: Well, I'm less than wholly convinced by the industrial analogy, but actually 'flow' is a good word to describe how you feel, because there is this notion of throughput, isn't there? Of it all being somehow beyond your control.

Clarissa: And that's all something to do with the set process involved because, you know, you hand over your papers together with your treasured items, in full expectation of getting them back intact. I mean, you put blind faith in the system, don't you? It's a wonder really that people are willing to meekly go along with it all.

Andrew: Well, that's because the routine's actually rather reassuring, you know; the fact that you do exactly what everyone else does means that you'll be okay, that nothing untoward will happen to you. Anyway, it's such a relief to get that bit over and done with. You know, when you put yourself in someone else's hands. It's liberating, isn't it?

Clarissa: Hardly. I mean you're directed by people in uniform, you're told to follow arrows, and all the time you're being pushed further and further along a blind alley.

I mean, the only thing you're free to do is spend money in all those dreadful shops, and even then, you can bet they've got the close-circuit video trained on you.

Andrew: OK, trust you to see the drama in it, Clarissa. To my mind all that waiting is just boring. I'm afraid the sinister aspects of it all are lost on me.

Clarissa: Really? Well, I mean, compare it to a railway station. The trains are perfectly evident as you arrive at the station, and the whole place is full of people going about their normal business. In the airport, however, it's only at the last minute, long after you've left the real world, that you see the aircraft itself, when you're in the final departure lounge.

Andrew: Well, you might have a point there. It's as if they want to protect you for as long as possible from the fact that you're about to go up in a little tube of metal, in case you lose your nerve.

Clarissa: And there's no turning back. No, it may be thrilling the first time you fly from a big airport, but for me there's a sort of futuristic side to them, like something out of a science fiction novel.

Andrew: So are you suggesting that if we look at an airport now, we're seeing how cities might appear in, say, ten years' time?

Clarissa: Not just cities, the whole of society. I think there are um, if you consider how many people use airports these days and, you know, trends that start there spread out into the whole of society and become part and parcel of our everyday existence.

Andrew: I find that a bit far-fetched. For me, the more worrying aspect of airports in the future is the possible environmental damage.

Clarissa: Well, I think you can take *that* as read, but it's actually on a par with a lot of other things going on around us these days. I mean look at the motorcar.

Andrew: Maybe, but I think there's an even greater potential for harm in the case of airports. You're not going to start defending them suddenly, are you?

Clarissa: No way.

Andrew: I thought not!